Get Me Out of Here

Get Me Out of Here

My Recovery from Borderline Personality Disorder

RACHEL REILAND

Hazelden
Publishing

Hazelden Publishing
Center City, Minnesota 55012-0176
hazelden.org/bookstore

First published by Eggshells Press, 2002
(Original edition titled *I'm Not Supposed to Be Here*)
First published by Hazelden, 2004. All rights reserved
Printed in the United States of America

Library of Congress Cataloging-in-Publication Data
Reiland, Rachel.
  [I'm not supposed to be here]
  Get me out of here : my recovery from borderline personality disorder /
Rachel Reiland.
     p. cm.
  Previously published: I'm not supposed to be here. Minnesota : Eggshells
Press, 2002.
  ISBN 978-1-59285-099-0
  1. Reiland, Rachel—Mental health. 2. Borderline personality disorder—
Patients—United States—Biography. 3. Borderline personality disorder—
Treatment. I. Title.

RC569.5.B67R45 2004
616.85'852'0092—dc22
[B]   2004047373

Editor's note
This publication is designed to provide accurate information in regard to
the subject matter covered. It is sold with the understanding that the pub-
lisher and author are not engaged in rendering psychological, financial,
legal, or other professional services. If expert counseling is needed, the
services of a competent professional should be sought.

   To protect the anonymity of the author, her family, her friends, and the
many professionals who helped the author through the therapeutic
process, pseudonymous names have been used to represent all people,
locations, and institutions described in this book.

20   12 13 14

Cover design by David Spohn
Typesetting by Tursso Companies

Note from Original Publisher

Dear Readers:

Seven years ago, I met Rachel Reiland on my Welcome to Oz Internet Listserv support group for people with borderline partners.

The members of my group were living in the midst of a capricious tornado: alternately confused, terrorized, and hopeless. Then Rachel stepped in.

Recovered from her illness—an incredible accomplishment—she explained to members what probably lay behind their partners' illogical behavior. She revealed the inner terror she experienced as a borderline, enabling them to see beyond their partners' controlling and abusive behavior.

And because she was recovered, she gave them hope.

When she showed me her first draft of this book, I was awed by her courageous escape from the prison of her own mind. And as an author and writer, I was taken away by the raw power of her writing style. She survived; then she wrote about it with a profundity that made her story unforgettable.

Though I was working on my own publications, I made it my mission to ensure that Rachel's story be heard by the entire community of individuals and clinicians interested in borderline personality disorder (BPD). I knew that the book would take readers on a journey of understanding of what it's like to have BPD, give new hope to the borderline community, and help erase the myth that borderlines never get better.

With the support of others eager to tell Rachel's story to the world, I published this book with my own imprint, Eggshells Press. Hazelden Publishing and Educational Services then bought the publishing rights to bring this book to a larger audience.

Whether your life has been touched by borderline personality disorder or not, Rachel's journey through mental illness is fascinating and cathartic. It shows that fundamental change is possible if we have the courage to face our own demons, look them in the eye, and banish them from our self-perception. It doesn't matter what we have to overcome: BPD, anorexia, or some other mental illness. The point is that with help and a commitment to recovery and healing, we can overcome it and heal our emotional and spiritual wounds.

In a way, this book is a love story: a mother's love for her children, her husband, her psychiatrist, and, ultimately, for herself. My hope for you, the reader, is that this book impacts your emotions, gives you the experience of what it's like to have BPD, and shows you that if a person is committed to recovery, recovery is possible.

I hope you find it as richly rewarding and life changing as I have. And may it give you a better understanding of how it feels to not just be symptom-free, but to live with contentment, self-love, and true joy.

—Randi Kreger
Coauthor, *Stop Walking on Eggshells* and *The Stop Walking on Eggshells Workbook*; Owner, www.bpdcentral.com and the Welcome to Oz family of thirty-five Listserv support groups for family members of people with a borderline in their lives

Foreword

Rachel Reiland's courageous struggle with borderline personality disorder (BPD) is a tale that is both harrowing and reassuring, disturbing but sustaining. Her battle is typical yet unique. These paradoxes are like the illness itself. BPD is a disorder characterized by contradictions. Its cure is derived by navigating through the straits of emotional extremes into the tranquil waters of compromise and consolidation.

Get Me Out of Here details Reiland's recovery. Her triumph results from the collaboration with her talented and unconditionally accepting psychiatrist. In the doctor, she found compromise between her desperate childhood fears of abandonment and her adult-derived defenses of self-destructiveness, attacking rage, and nihilism. From the remnants of her frightened, vulnerable childhood (which she labeled "Vulno") and her "Tough Chick" personae, Reiland fashioned her individual humanity.

Some of this story is typical: early family conflicts, abusive relationships, feelings of insecurity contributing to destructive behaviors such as rage attacks, promiscuity, and anorexia. The extreme behaviors of BPD constitute the high drama in the stories of those who endure its ravages. But Reiland does not focus only on the flamboyance of the symptoms. She also describes the small, intimate nicks and cuts that bleed slowly and painfully, day to day.

Reiland's recovery is, in many ways, atypical. It is attained through an intensive, four-year course of traditional, psychoanalytically oriented psychotherapy, punctuated by several hospitalizations, some lasting for several weeks. Unfortunately, such a treatment program would be unavailable to most patients today. Most hospital psychiatric units are not geared for extended stays of more than a few days, and most insurance will not support this intensive treatment regimen.

Fortunately, Reiland possessed financial support to pay for her care. She also maintained a supportive, loving relationship with her husband and children. And she developed a trusting relationship with an experienced, knowledgeable psychiatrist. Although many sufferers may not share all of these blessings, they can, nevertheless, still achieve the victories she accomplished through the same persistence and courage she demonstrated.

BPD is the monstrous, metastatic malignancy of psychiatry. Most professionals shun patients with this diagnosis, convinced that they are exhausting, hopeless, and often terminal. The sickest, most severely psychotic schizophrenic patient is preferred over one with BPD, because at least there is some feeling of control over the treatment process. Hospitalization and medication can easily and quickly subdue the schizophrenia monster. But BPD symptoms can rage unpredictably, are difficult to control, require months or years to detect improvement, and can overwhelm the vulnerable therapist.

Until recently, a diagnosis of BPD was a label of hopelessness for both the patient and the doctor. With a suicide rate of almost 10 percent and no consistent treatment approaches offered, the prognosis was considered to be poor. However, with developments over the last ten years, such pessimism is no longer warranted.

Refined treatment approaches, such as dialectical behavioral therapy and adapted psychoanalytic techniques, have demonstrated significant effectiveness. Long-term follow-up studies, just now becoming available, illustrate that individuals with BPD can survive and thrive. Recent studies confirm that many borderline symptoms resolve over the years.

Although continuous treatment significantly augments the recovery rate, many patients achieve remission even without therapy. Over time spans ranging from six to fifteen years, as many as three-fourths of all patients with BPD will have resolved symptoms such that they no longer qualify for the BPD diagnosis. These patients would then, within the medical lexicon, be considered cured. Few other chronic medical conditions (e.g., diabetes, emphysema, hypertension, and schizophrenia) can achieve this ultimate level.

Reiland's *Get Me Out of Here* is here to declare that raging mental illness can be cured. Like Reiland, we must recognize that despite disappointments even from those whom we count on—family, friends, health care providers, insurers—survival ultimately depends on the individual's courage to explore his or her own unique humanity. Then we can embrace the support and caring available to all of us. As

Dr. Padgett insists to Reiland, "Love is infinitely more powerful than hate."

—Jerold J. Kreisman, M.D.
Coauthor, *I Hate You, Don't Leave Me: Understanding the Borderline Personality* and *Sometimes I Act Crazy: Living with Borderline Personality Disorder*

Acknowledgments

My recovery was not an individual effort but was only possible with the help of more great people than I could ever list here—many of whom probably have no idea just how much of a difference they made in my life.

In particular, I'd like to thank Dr. Padgett and Father Rick, who led the way on my journey to healing; Randi Kreger, whose persistence and encouragement has enabled my story to make it to print; my loving children and my husband, Tim, who refused to give up on me even in the darkest of times. His love, loyalty, and laughter have made ours the best marriage I could ever be blessed to have.

Prologue

How could my mother have done this to me? She told me that kindergarten would be such fun. She lied. She wanted me out of the house and out of her hair—the same as always.

Mrs. Schwarzheuser knelt beside Cindy, heaping praise on her perfect yellow-green trees. Cindy's mother would be so proud. My orange, purple, and brown paint had run together, and my picture looked like a putrid blob.

Golden-haired Cindy was Mrs. Schwarzheuser's favorite. I hated her—those perfect little ringlets tied up in colorful ribbon, that perky little nose, the blue cotton dress with the frilly lace around the collar. Ribbons, lace, dresses—sickening. Mrs. Schwarzheuser hated me, but that suited me just fine. I hated her too.

I seethed with jealousy as Mrs. Schwarzheuser showered Cindy with compliments. Suddenly, rage overwhelmed me. I seized a cup of brown paint and dumped half of it over my picture. Glaring at Cindy, I leaned across the table and dumped the other half over her drawing. I felt a surge of relief. Now Cindy's picture looked as awful as mine.

"Rachel!" Mrs. Schwarzheuser yelled. "You've completely destroyed Cindy's beautiful trees. Shame on you. You are a *horrible* little girl. The paint is everywhere—look at your jeans."

My blue jeans were soaked with brown paint. They looked ugly. I looked ugly. Mrs. Schwarzheuser frantically wiped up paint to keep it from dripping onto the floor. Everyone was watching.

I felt my body go numb. My legs, arms, and head were weightless. Floating. It was the same way I felt when Daddy pulled off his belt and snapped it. Anticipation of worse things to come—things I had brought on myself because I was different.

"In all my years, I've never seen a child like you. You are the *worst* little girl I've ever taught. Go sit in the corner, immediately!"

Shame on Rachel. That language I understood. And deserved. I wasn't like the other little girls. I hated dolls and other "girly," pink toys. I hated being a girl more than anything. I wasn't any good at it. If I had been a boy, things would have been different. But somehow God put me into a girl's body by mistake. I wondered if I would go to hell for daring to think God made a mistake.

Mrs. Schwarzheuser was right. I was horrible.

∞

The concealed amusement of my twelve-year-old classmates sustained me as I swaggered out of Sister Mary's homeroom. My defiance faded the moment the door closed behind me.

Although I'd never admit it, the hallway was a lonely, frightening place. Without the admiring glances of my classmates, I was totally alone, praying fervently that the principal wouldn't see me without a hall pass. A futile prayer to a God who loved everyone but me.

Sister Luisa's tall, thin frame emerged from her office. She sauntered a few steps past me then deliberately turned and stared—a piercing gaze that made me wish I could dissolve into the wall.

"Miss Marsten," Sister Luisa said disapprovingly. "I see you have managed to get yourself thrown out of the classroom again. What was it this time? A smart remark? Or just your usual disrespect?"

Sister Luisa's questions were not intended to be answered: they *were* the answers. She waved me toward her stark office, a place even more frightening than the empty school corridor. The office felt bare and cold despite the charts and religious poems taped to the cinder-block wall. A lone, large wooden crucifix hung behind the worn metal desk. The face of Jesus stared at me with disgust.

"Miss Marsten," she said, "I am not going to tolerate this type of behavior in my school. The notes we send to your parents don't seem to have much effect. But rest assured, young lady, I will end this nonsense with or without the cooperation of your parents."

The notes. My parents had no reason to believe the notes. Smarting off in class was one thing; smart remarks at home were unthinkable. Authority reigned there. Control. Express an inappropriate emotion, expect a slap. The same expressionless stoicism Sister Luisa witnessed in her office was the norm at home. I stayed out of the way in the house. My grades and test scores were excellent, so my parents ignored the scathing notes from frustrated teachers.

"You have twisted the brilliance God has given you." Sister Luisa's ruddy face, pinched by the white headband of her veil, framed a scowling intensity. "It is a sinful waste."

"Sinful." "Shameful." Words so familiar they were a part of me now. *So what, Sister Luisa? Tell me something I don't know.*

"So smug. So smart. You think you're a hero among your friends, don't you? Don't fool yourself. You're their entertainment. They're not your friends. They aren't laughing with you, they are laughing at you."

My stomach churned, bile rising in my throat. Weightless. Dizzy. The brave demeanor crumbling. Sister Luisa continued, and her face grew harsher. She had penetrated my core and wasn't about to waste the opportunity to humble me. I began sobbing like a little girl. Her thin lips turned upward slightly as she tasted victory. I wanted to disappear.

"We both know that God blessed you with a great talent for words. Words can be used to accomplish something worthy. But words can also destroy. And, young lady, your tongue can slice like a knife. If you don't control it, you won't have a friend to your name. Your classmates will fear both you and the destruction your words can cause."

Fear me. Like a wild animal. Out of control. Crazy. Once again, Sister Luisa didn't tell me anything new. No one feared me more than myself.

∞

"You're going to eat this bacon—even if I have to shove it down your goddamned throat!" My father thrust the plate inches from my face, his eyes wide and threatening.

I knew better than to defy him. Yet, as much as I feared him, the food on the plate was more terrifying. Fat. Dripping, greasy, bloating fat. I could not disobey him, but I couldn't give in. I could not be derailed from The Diet. Everyone wanted to sabotage The Diet. Friends, teachers, coaches. Now the same man who called my oldest sister "fat ass" when she neared the freezer was determined to make me the same way. Fat. Disgusting. Humiliated. I'd rather he kill me.

"Dad," my sister pleaded, "she needs help. She needs a doctor."

Bold of her. And stupid. She never learned.

"What your sister needs is a good kick in the ass."

"She's starving, Dad. What does she weigh now? Seventy?"

"Your father is right," my mother interjected, her voice cracking with emotion. She used this tone so frequently that no one paid attention. "She's fifteen years old. She's a bright girl. She's just going through a phase."

"It's not a phase. She's sick. She's anorexic. If she doesn't get help, she's going to die," said Nancy.

"What do you mean—help?" My father's focus shifted to her and away from me. The question needed no answer. It was a dare.

"I mean a psychiatrist," she answered.

"A *psychiatrist?*" he roared. My mother tried to calm him down.

"Nancy, honey, you know we can't do that," my mother said. "What would people say? Your sister is an intelligent girl. She's just stubborn. She'll come to her senses."

My father leaned toward Nancy and shouted, "She needs a kick in the ass, not a shrink!" Nancy cowered in retreat.

Another fight between the three of them, talking about me as if I had left the room. I shoveled the two strips of bacon into my mouth. Peace broker once again.

"See! You can't coddle this kind of bullshit. You have to put your foot down."

As the battle continued, I quietly left the kitchen and tiptoed into the bathroom. The bacon, which had been tucked tightly in my cheeks, flew directly into the toilet. The perfect solution. He thought he won. Let him.

∞

Sitting in the living room waiting on a jar of piss. What a way to spend the weekend. According to instructions, it took two hours for three little drops of urine squeezed into the jar to render judgment. A quarter after ten. Fifteen minutes to go.

Tim read the sports section, occasionally looking up and giving me that reassuring smile that melted me so often. Unbelievably steady. Calm. What a welcome change from the neurotic and narcissistic types I'd been hooking up with for years. In the four months I had known Tim, I still couldn't fathom why this attractive man with sparkling eyes was still faithful—and still around.

He worked in a factory as a line foreman. I had been high school valedictorian—a National Merit Scholar, the varsity field hockey captain, on the dean's list at Saint Robert's. I had worked as a cocktail waitress. Hustled trays of imported beers to arrogant Yuppies, smiling at the measly tips and hating almost every one of them. Hating myself. Smoking joints in the closed bar as the sun rose while my former classmates hit the showers and commuted to the kinds of jobs I should have. I was twenty-four years old.

I'd been through this pregnancy scare before. But Tim was the first man to sit through the grueling ordeal with me. At least this time I could be certain of who the other party to the scare was. At least this time I was nearly convinced that, if anyone could love me, this man might.

It was 10:30 A.M. Tim put his arm around me as we went to check on the jar. My Ouija board to the future. I couldn't bear to look. Tim did the honors, peering into it. He asked for the instruction pamphlet. Clutching it in his hand, he looked into the jar again.

"What is it?" I asked.

He embraced me. "Positive, Rachel. It's positive."

"Are you sure?"

"Go ahead and look for yourself," he said gently.

A brown ring, thick and clear, not subtle at all. A bang-you-over-the-head ring. One that says, "You're pregnant, stupid! Now what are you going to do?"

Abortion had always been the fallback position— mercifully, one I'd never had to consider. Being virtually convinced of God's nonexistence, the prospect shouldn't have bothered me. Yet it did.

Now it was time for Tim to leave. Now was the time for the relationship I considered too good to be true to prove that it was. With the abortion option, there was no excuse to be trapped by a situation like this. Yet I felt as if the world were closing in on me, my life catching up with me, as if justice had been rendered. I'd played roulette with an empty box of Trojans and lost.

"Marry me," Tim said.

What? Didn't he know he didn't need to be trapped? Didn't he know how easy it would be for him to walk right now, that I would understand?

"If you want an abortion, I'll support you. But I'm not talking about a shotgun wedding. I've never met anyone like you, Rachel. I want to spend the rest of my life with you. Trust me on this one. I wouldn't lie to you. Will you marry me?"

I'd taken so many chances in my life. Sex. Drugs. Life had been a series of impulsive gambles. Dangerous moves. Foolish choices. Why not take a chance on this one? Why not marry a man who loved me so obviously even I had begun to believe it?

"Yes."

∞

Our child passed away in a miscarriage long before its birth. A frenzy of crunching pain, a sea of blood, a small life expelled into the toilet, and sorrow for the life we had already begun to love. Yet the child had created a bond. The wedding went on as planned. The tiny life had fulfilled its purpose. The product of our impulsive recklessness had brought us together in permanence, allowing us to marry for love alone.

Within months I was pregnant again. Jeffrey Aaron Reiland was born in June shortly after we signed the closing papers on our first home. Savoring the newfound joy of nurturing and nursing an infant, I devoted myself to full-time motherhood. Melissa Anne Reiland was born two years later.

It was a period of unparalleled contentedness. A family. A home. A future. The American Dream. Perhaps, I thought, I might just be normal after all.

Alas, no. . . .

Chapter 1

The house was a disaster.

The kids had strewn toys all over the floor; disposable diapers overflowed the trash can. Crackers lay smashed on the milk-stained hardwood floor. Overloaded ash trays on every tabletop. Fast-food wrappers littered the house.

God, I should get to this. I'm home for chrissakes. What kind of a mother am I? How in the hell can we afford all this fast food—much less what it must be doing to us? *What in the hell am I doing here?*

Picking up an armful of clothes, I headed for the steps. Damned drafty old house. Two years after closing, it was still half done with no money to finish it. Gaping holes in the staircase waited for someone to put up the quarter round—or couldn't we afford that either? Eyeing the antique oak ball we'd put on the stair rail, visions of Jimmy Stewart rushed through my mind. I wished I could slam it down. I had news for Jimmy: it was anything but "a wonderful life." It was a trap.

Finally, the injustice of it all was catching up with me. I was supposed to be someone. Instead, I was broke. Disheveled. A three-year-old and an infant were nursing the life right out of me. They were napping. I was lonely and restless. I headed for the telephone.

"Umm, is Tim there?"

"Please hold, and I'll see if he's still here, *Rachel*."

God, how I hated that secretary—the way she spit out my name, the way she'd always keep me on hold forever and toy with me as if Tim might not be there, even though she knew very well that he was. She was a goddamned secretary, no less, who thought she was a CEO. And I envied her. *Bitch*.

"This is Tim."

"Hi, Tim. . . ."

Dead silence. What in the hell had I called to say anyway? God, I was pathetic. "Rachel? Are you there?"

"Yes, I'm here."

"Well, what do you want, hon? I'm kind of busy here. I've got an appointment in a half hour."

"Oh."

"Is something wrong?"

"I hate this house, Tim. I just hate it. It's a fucking mess. The kids are napping, but I just don't feel like cleaning it."

"Then don't clean it. Take a nap yourself. I can help you clean when I get home."

"When are you coming home?"

"I dunno. I have a whole-life insurance presentation in a half hour, and then I have a call-in on my annuities ad. I thought I'd go over there at about five."

"Then you won't be home until six or seven."

"I know, but I haven't gotten a lot done lately."

"And it's my fault, isn't it?" I interrupted.

"I didn't say it's your fault, honey. It's just that . . . well, I've got to get some stuff done." I began to twist the phone cord around my finger, tempted to wrap it around my neck.

"I'm a real pain in the ass, aren't I? You're pissed, aren't you?" Tim tried to keep his patience, but I could still hear him sigh.

"Please, Rachel. I've got to make a living."

"Like I don't do anything around here? Is that it? Like I'm some kind of stupid housewife who doesn't do a god-damned thing? Is that what you're getting at?" Another sigh.

"Okay. Look, sweetheart. I've got to do this presentation this afternoon because it's too late to cancel. But I'll see if I can reschedule the annuity guy for tomorrow. I'll be home by four o'clock, and I'll help you clean up the house."

"No, no, no!"

I was beginning to cry.

"What now?"

"God, Tim. I'm such an idiot. Such a baby. I don't do a thing around this house, and here I am, wanting you to help me clean. I must make you sick."

"You don't make me sick, sweetheart. Okay? You don't. Look, I'm really sorry, but I've got to go."

The tears reached full strength. The cry became a moan that turned to piercing screams. *Why in the hell can't I control myself? The man has to make a living. He's such a good guy; he doesn't deserve me—no one should have to put up with me!*

"Rachel? Rachel? Please calm down. Please! Come on. You're gonna wake up the kids; the neighbors are gonna wonder what in the hell is going on. Rachel?"

"Fuck you! Is that all you care about, what the *neighbors* think? Fuck you, then. I don't need you home. I don't want you home. Let this fucking house rot; let the fucking

11

kids starve. I don't give a shit. And I don't need your shit!"

"Rachel, listen to me. I'm canceling the whole-life appointment, and I'll be home in a few minutes. Okay?"

"You must really hate me," I sobbed. "You really hate me, don't you?"

"No, sweetheart," he sighed audibly. "I don't hate you."

After hanging up the phone, I sat there, frozen, staring at it. Why did I do this kind of shit? Tim was trying hard to build his own insurance business. I knew how much it took to build a business. After all, my father had worked seventy to eighty hours a week running his business. And my mother wouldn't have dared pull him away from it the way I just yanked Tim home.

My mother. My dependent mother who never did a damned thing with her life. My mother, who spent half her days at the shopping mall and the other half in front of the television set. My mother, who was unable to make the simplest decision without my father. She had been wholly dependent on him. She'd made me sick. And as I sat in the kitchen, the stench of dirty dishes and the overflowing garbage reminded me that even she had been more worthy than me. My God, I thought, I'm ending up to be a dependent little piece of shit. Worse than my mother.

Tim wasn't able to reschedule the whole-life appointment.

The prospect had gone to a competitor. The annuity prospect fell through as well. He'd been in the business now for over six months and was barely able to meet the business expenses, much less the household ones. This meant having to take handouts from my parents—handouts with many strings attached. Strings of I-told-you-so's.

I didn't grow up in poverty. Thanks to my parents, I

wasn't destined to know what that was like. I did, however, know the bitter taste of failure. It became increasingly hard not to place that same label on Tim. Why, oh why, with all the men I knew and dated—all the men with degrees—had I chosen a college dropout whose only means of making anything significant of himself was selling insurance? Why couldn't he be more of a man, like my father: practical, steady, and successful?

Then again, what was wrong with me? I had lots of credentials but was sitting at home not doing anything.

I began to press Tim to go out and get a regular salaried job with the same insistence I used to get him to come home and be with me. He was beginning to feel like a failure too. His initial zest for the insurance business, his carefully projected income goals, his dreams of huge college funds and a totally renovated house—all of this waned. And so did his ability to close the sale.

Doubting his own ability to succeed in insurance, he began to search the want ads, send out résumés, go on interviews, and get rejection letters. There wasn't much work that paid the kind of money equaling the handouts. He was getting dejected, as was I.

I didn't make it any easier for him. Somehow he was still patient with my constant phone calls. But he was clearly more irritable. If I couldn't handle his absence when he worked at a place where he set his own hours, how would I handle it with a boss who would force him to be there from nine to five? It was a wretched situation, a catch-22, and I hated myself because so much of it was my fault. Yet I couldn't stop making it worse.

If only I could just disappear. Run away. Far away. If only Tim wasn't in the picture, I could have. Indeed, in past relationships I would have been long gone at the first signs of my own dependency. Then I could appear to be independent, not needing a soul.

But it wasn't just Tim anymore. I loved my kids. Perhaps they tied me down. But I loved them. I loved Tim too, of course. But he could make it without me—in fact, do much better without me. Jeffrey and Melissa, however, needed me more than anyone in my life ever had. No, I was just plain stuck in a life that seemed to spiral further downward at every turn.

∞

It was nearly midnight when we got home from Tim's softball game. It had been a late game followed by some bad directions that led us to drive aimlessly through the West Side for over an hour, doors locked, streets dark, totally lost. We'd blamed each other. The kids were asleep in their car seats. We bickered in hushed tones as we passed block after block of boarded-up brownstones. Juggling irritated toddlers, diaper bags, bat, ball, and glove, we put them to bed and fell asleep ourselves—angry with each other but too exhausted to fight.

I was still in bed when Tim was heading out the door to work. I heard him swearing and complaining that he couldn't find his wallet. I joined him in a search that led us to every room of the house, under every sofa cushion, and through piles of dirty laundry. It had vanished.

"What did you do with it?" he demanded impatiently. "I had *two hundred dollars* in there."

"What do you mean, what did *I* do with it?"

"I handed it to you, damnit. Don't you remember? I

14

took in all the softball stuff and Jeffrey; you took Melissa, the diaper bag, and the wallet."

He was right.

"Well, what the fuck did you expect?" I yelled defensively. "You dragged us to that stupid game way too late and got us lost on the goddamned West Side. Then you expect me to bring all this shit in."

"Give me a break, Rachel. There was *two hundred fucking dollars* in there. I can't believe, as much as you bitch about money, that you act like it's nothing."

The tears came back. Then the moan. Then the screaming wail. I'd really blown it. But Tim, on this early summer morning, would have none of it. He slammed down his fist, picked up his briefcase, and headed out the front door. He'd never walked out on me when I was crying. I'd crossed the line and driven him out the door. I'd lost him. Forever.

∞

As it turns out, I didn't "lose" Tim. He returned at dinnertime as usual—still a little irritated but feeling slightly guilty that he had walked out on me. Shortly after dinner, a neighbor returned the wallet. The two hundred dollars, credit cards, and pictures were still there. The Good Samaritan even apologized for taking so long. Although he'd seen the wallet on top of our car that morning, he had been running late for work and had to wait until evening to return it.

Tim was relieved. I should have been relieved. But now that the missing money was no longer an issue, I started to seethe about how he had walked out on me.

"Well," Tim said with a smile as he took a long drag on his cigarette, "I guess there's still some honest people around.

15

Imagine, going to the trouble to return it and apologizing for not giving it to us sooner."

"Yeah," I sniffed. "At least *he* apologized."

"What do you mean?"

"I mean, you walked out on me this morning, you sonofabitch! You blamed me for everything even though it was mostly your fault."

"*My* fault?" Tim looked stunned.

"Yes, *your* fault. You dragged us out to that game, didn't you? We didn't want to go."

"You wanted to go to that game." His patience was fading again.

Twice in a day, I thought, panicked. He's pissed again. I'm going to drive him away. Why was I so dependent on him? Why can't I walk out on him?

The moan began again. This time, I didn't make it to the screaming part.

"No, not again, Rachel. Don't do this again. I can't take anymore of it!"

That cinched it. He hated me. He'd leave me, broke, with these two little kids and the piece of shit house. *No, no! He couldn't leave me. I wouldn't give the sonofabitch the satisfaction.*

The tears halted immediately, and I felt a rush of energy. Barefoot, in gym shorts, without so much as grabbing the car keys, I ran out the door and down the alley. I could hear Tim pleading with me to come back and frantically apologizing for losing his patience. I felt power rising within me. I didn't look back and kept on going.

I didn't have a destination in mind, but as I kept jogging down the streets of the city, I realized I was heading to the West Side. If I were lucky, I'd make it to the projects. If I were even luckier, the God I didn't really believe existed would have mercy on me and let me become just another crime statistic. Suicide roulette. I ran for miles, barefoot and westward through the glass-strewn sidewalks of declining neighborhoods.

I called Tim. Twice. He answered the phone, relieved to hear from me. He pled with me to come home, apologizing for anything he could think of. He begged me to tell him where I was so he could come and pick me up. Instead I told him I was going to die and that he would be better off without me. I hung up without giving him a clue as to where I was.

I didn't quite make it to the projects. I'd run about five miles, which burned off some of my excess energy and a lot of my anger. It was dusk—about two hours since I'd left the house—and I started to feel afraid. But I wasn't about to call and tell him where I was. That would mean admitting my stupidity. I sat on a park bench and suddenly spied our red Dodge. Tim pulled up, the kids looking out the windows from their car seats.

I climbed in, and he drove home without one word of admonishment. He was too tired and scared, afraid, I guessed, that I'd go running out the door again and the next time I wouldn't be so lucky.

∞

For the next few weeks I was a tornado, raging out of control, fury swelling, destroying everything in my path. The run became a nightly routine. Tim was concerned about my safety in the darkness of the neighborhood, but he didn't try to stop me from the ritual. Perhaps he was afraid that if he

17

were to resist me, I wouldn't stay within our neighborhood but would instead begin heading westward again. The moans were more frequent now, and Tim stopped making night appointments for fear of what could happen in his absence.

I don't know why, but up to this point, I had not taken out my fears, frustrations, and anger on my children. As wildly erratic as I could be with Tim and others, a calm came over me when dealing with Jeffrey and Melissa. The demons within me were at peace for a while, and I was much more patient with them than a lot of other mothers are with their children. Seldom, if ever, had I become impatient or lost my temper with the kids.

But in the spinning fury of my loss of control, even this bond began to fray. Jeffrey was talking like a boy twice his age. Unfortunately, he was capable of understanding the words I had begun to hurl at him. I saw a stunned look of betrayal in his eyes; he'd never seen anything like this before. He was frightened. And I was frightening myself.

One Friday in late June, about three weeks after my "West Side Run," I woke up shaky, irritable, and more out of control than usual. I restlessly tried to read a book and lose myself in it in an attempt to kill time.

Jeffrey, however, kept trying to crawl onto my lap. Irritated, I shoved him away, not wanting to touch him. At first Jeffrey thought it was some kind of game. But finally something snapped, and I slapped him so hard he went reeling to the floor.

I looked at him lying there, crying in earnest as the thoughts began to spin in my head. *Jesus Christ, Rachel, you aren't even a good mother anymore. You have nothing. You are hateful, crazy, awful.*

Jeffrey didn't take his eyes off me, nor would he stop

18

crying. He lay there on the floor, wailing, and the sight and sound reminded me of what a wretched human being I was.

"Goddamnit, Jeffrey. Stop it!" I screamed.

Jeffrey didn't stop.

"Goddamnit, you little pain in the ass. Shut the fuck up!"

He didn't.

Overwhelmed with rage, I grabbed him hard by the shoulder and began to vigorously spank him until my hand was red and stinging. I couldn't stop—until I got another look at his eyes.

He had stopped crying, his fright overcoming his need to express his emotions. But his eyes were wide open, as big as I'd ever seen them. And absolutely, unequivocally horrified. That look stopped me.

The familiar feeling of weightlessness overtook me again. I knew Jeffrey's look. I knew that feeling.

It had been a common part of my childhood—enduring rages that began and ended just as unpredictably. The reality slowly sunk in. I had beaten my child. Just as my father had beaten his. Just as I swore I never ever would. A wave of nausea rose within me. *I was just like my father.* Even my children would be better off without me. There was no longer any reason to stay alive.

Suddenly I felt a great sense of calm. I knew what I needed to do. I was going to die. Yet somewhere within me a shred of self-preservation insisted I give myself one more chance. Fully "floating" by now, I calmly gathered the children as if I were someone else, asking them to play in the yard. I had a phone call to make. I was a death-row prisoner awaiting execution at my own hands, making one final attempt for a reprieve—one I was not altogether sure I wanted.

I didn't call Tim. Lord knows I'd done enough to Tim. Instead, I called a church-sponsored family crisis hotline. I stayed on the phone for over an hour and a half. I spilled out a wild flood of self-hatred, punctuated by moments when I would interrupt the conversation to check on the children.

I'm horrible, I told the man on the other end of the phone. I hate myself. I'm crazy. It would really surprise him that once upon a time I used to be somebody. I used to accomplish things. People who knew me, I told him, wouldn't believe that all of this was going on. It was probably hard to believe, but they think I'm a nice person. *They don't know me.*

The man, however, was not about to let me off the line. Again and again he tried to get my name and phone number. But I refused. I didn't want him to stop me from my destiny.

But finally, thoroughly exhausted, I relented and gave him my name and number. As I suspected, he said he was going to call an ambulance to come get me. I couldn't imagine it—the sirens going and everyone on the block coming to see what was going on with their crazy neighbor. An ambulance simply wasn't an option.

What followed was a negotiation as the man sold me on the importance of not being alone right then. He insisted that if I couldn't come up with a better plan, he was going to call 9-1-1 within the next five minutes. I ultimately agreed to call a teenager to watch the kids, and I agreed to see the pastor of my church. He was vigilant; if I hung up the phone, or if my pastor reported I had not arrived, he would call the police and an ambulance.

By then, however, it didn't make a difference. I was resigned to go ahead with the meeting as promised, to give life one more chance—albeit a temporary one.

I mechanically picked up my Walkman, kissed the children good-bye, and walked to the church rectory—stopping for a Big Gulp and a carton of cigarettes along the way. Why a carton and not a pack? Perhaps I knew where I was destined to go.

Without much effort, the pastor persuaded me to let him take me to the emergency room. Numb by then, I acquiesced.

Never once in this whole surreal episode did I call Tim, nor would I allow anyone else to do so on my behalf.

I'd agreed to their terms. They'd agree to mine.

Chapter 2

It was all too surreal. Me. A psychiatric inpatient.

Sitting back in a generously padded chair, drawing hard on a cigarette, I tried to make sense of it all. Tim, whom I'd finally contacted once I was settled in my room, hadn't been as disgusted or angry as I'd anticipated. Indeed, he'd been relieved. Perhaps tonight he'd sleep well. He needed it; he looked like hell. A number of other patients were socializing in the smoking lounge. Most wore blue jeans and sweatshirts. A group of them sat on the sofas, bantering, laughing, and acting as if this were some sort of party. No one wore the dowdy, overlaundered hospital robes or paper slippers I'd expected. I stayed in a corner, alone. These people were *mental* patients. I wondered how these laughing women, who appeared more like carefree coeds, had ended up in this place.

Of course, I was also a mental patient, although I'd had no idea that a trip to the emergency room would lead to this.

I wasn't sure I belonged here. I mean, I'd been upset and all, but this—*this* was extreme. As bursts of laughter echoed through the lounge, I couldn't help but feel they were laughing at me, speculating on what had brought me here.

Panic hit me. I didn't want to be here. I didn't ask to be here. I didn't need to be here. I would leave first thing in the morning.

At ten o'clock I heard the squeaking wheels of a cart as it was pulled into the lounge. A nurse, the "Good Humor man," was dispensing a kaleidoscope of medications. The laughing "coeds" gravitated to the cart, almost greedy for their pills. It was straight out of *One Flew over the Cuckoo's Nest*. Mind control. It frightened me.

At first I refused the tiny, white anti-anxiety pill and the black, round sleeping pill he tried to give me. I needed my wits about me in this place where I didn't belong. Ultimately, I relented. It wasn't like I was a novice at drugs. How could a few pills hurt? I'd be leaving in the morning anyway.

At midnight a new shift came on duty, and a heavyset nurse with a jet-black pageboy haircut, excessive makeup, and an attitude of authority came into the lounge, grabbed the TV remote, shut it off, and announced that it was bedtime. Bedtime? What gave her the right to tell me when I can or can't watch TV or go to bed?

I made a few snippy remarks that she obviously didn't appreciate—a fact that placated me. But the pills I had taken dulled my ability to stand up for myself. I reminded myself that I was going to bed because I wanted to, not because some drill sergeant in white had ordered me to do so.

∞

My stark room had two single beds, institutional carpet, a built-in desk with a Formica top, and nearly empty walls. The place lacked the antiseptic tile floors of a typical hospital wing, but it wasn't quite like a dorm room. And it wasn't like a hospital either.

What was this place? Why was I here? Panic filled me, despite the numbing effects of the pills. They were beginning to wear off anyway. I was wide awake. Alone. It was two o'clock in the morning. I was convinced that I couldn't stay in this place, with the drug cart and the nurses who ordered patients around as if they were children. No, I couldn't stay another minute.

Tim, in his haste and worry, had forgotten to bring me clothes. So I had been forced to wear one of the hospital-issue gowns I so hated. The drill sergeant got some sort of strange satisfaction out of that. She wanted me to look like a mental patient. She wanted me to go crazy. Forget it. Cheap gown or not, I was getting out of this place. Right now.

As I crept down the hallway, I saw her sitting there at the nurse's station, reading *Vogue* and sipping coffee. Sitting on her fat ass. No wonder she was so insistent that I go to bed: she was lazy.

It was laughably simple to get past her, her eyes riveted to the magazine. Quietly I tiptoed toward the double entry doors to the ward and slowly, silently opened them. The fresh, cooler air of the hallway and the cold tile floor were proof that I had successfully escaped. When I left the building and inhaled the brisk outdoor air, reality set in.

Where the hell did I intend to go?

I didn't have a car. I hadn't brought my purse. Tim had gone home and was probably getting the good night's sleep he'd seemed to anticipate with a little too much relish.

I thought about Tim's visit. He'd been relieved. I was in the psych ward with all of these mental patients, forced into a fog of complacency. And the sonofabitch was relieved! I'd called myself crazy in front of him before, and he'd always gently answer, "No, sweetheart, you aren't crazy." Fucking liar, he did think I was crazy. He'd kept looking at his watch the whole time he visited me—couldn't wait to get out of there and leave his wife a prisoner in the loony bin.

Screw him, I thought. He doesn't want me around. *Well, I don't want to be with him anyway!*

There was only one place to go. West. Only the most dangerous neighborhoods of the West Side were much closer from here than they had been from home. And it was night-time. Perfect. This time, I would make it all the way to the projects. And this time, I wouldn't make it out alive.

I was on the sidewalk of a major thoroughfare, moving as quickly as my drug-numbed body would let me. I shuddered and sobbed uncontrollably as I headed west in my bare feet. I knew damn well I was the perfect victim—which is precisely what I wanted to be.

I didn't get very far when a uniformed security guard approached me, a logo of the hospital on his pocket. Resistance? I hadn't planned on resistance. I didn't have the energy for it.

"Ma'am, do you realize it's two in the morning? I don't know where you think you're going, but the streets aren't very safe around here at night."

His words were music to my ears.

"I'm going west," I sobbed. "These streets are too safe, goddamnit. I gotta get outta here."

He put his hand on my shoulder. I wanted to push it off and start running in earnest, but the damned medications dulled my reactions. The guard soon realized I was from the psych ward and escorted me back to the unit. I didn't fight him. I just wanted to go to sleep.

The night nurse/drill sergeant had set down her coffee and magazine and was standing by the double entry doors to the unit, arms folded, awaiting my return. She was clearly angry and wasn't going to let me go to sleep until she'd had her say.

"Where have you been?" she demanded, her brown eyes burning into me. "You don't leave this unit at this time of night. You don't leave this unit without a signed pass from a doctor. What on earth is wrong with you?"

Don't you know, you idiot? I'm in the goddamned psych ward. I'm crazy. And I'm doing what crazy people do!

"I want to go home," I mumbled through my tears. "I just want to go home. I'm not supposed to be here. I don't belong here."

"Humph," she sniffed. "We'll let the doctor be the judge of that. If he decides to release you or gives you a pass, fine. But you do not leave this place without one, and you surely don't do it at two in the morning. As long as I'm the charge nurse responsible for you, you aren't going anywhere. Look at you—you're a mess. You're in a hospital gown for God's sake. You've taken some pretty large doses of drugs. It was downright dangerous."

It was my turn to be angry. "Hey! This is a free country, and I can go any goddamned place I please. You made it easy actually—just sitting up there on your big fat ass reading. You just don't want to have to stop reading and get up from your little throne behind the desk. You don't care about me. You're only pissed because you screwed up, and you're scared you'll lose your fucking job!"

"Look," she practically spit the word at me, her eyes narrowed, "you obviously don't like me. Well, I don't much like you either. I don't have to like you. But I'll tell you one thing. I'm not going to lose my job over someone like you. I've worked here for ten years. I don't know what your problem is, but let me tell you one thing. Don't mess with me because you'll be in lockup so fast your head will spin. You don't scare me, you don't move me, you don't intimidate me. And if you want to make this all into some sort of a game, I guarantee you that I'll win it. So don't even think about trying it again. Do you understand?"

I nodded. I was numb, way too tired to fight.

Glaring at her, I shuffled back into my room and then fell asleep, defeated, hating the night and its mind-deafening silence.

∞

Morning brought a new atmosphere to the ward. Different nurses appeared, and the bantering patients filled the smoking lounge once again. The ward smelled of hospital food, and I could hear the clattering of tray carts, the whir of the housekeeping vacuums, and cartoons on TV. The place was not nearly as frightening as it had been the night before, although I was still convinced I didn't belong there.

As I pushed aside my half-eaten tray of cold pancakes, powdered eggs, and soggy bacon, the day nurse tapped me on the shoulder.

"Rachel, Dr. Padgett is here to see you. He's the on-call psychiatrist assigned to your case."

Psychiatrist. My case. Reality slapped me again. I was a mental patient. It was all a mistake. I felt fine. A little upset yesterday, but today I was okay.

I turned around to see Dr. Padgett. He was smiling broadly in almost a goofy sort of way, a slightly built man of average height. He was dressed not in a lab coat, but in a short-sleeved plaid shirt and a pair of tan Dockers. His fine, black hair was slicked straight back, and a pair of thick wire-rim glasses magnified the brown eyes behind them. He appeared neat except for an unruly mustache in dire need of a trim. He didn't look like a psychiatrist. He looked like a geek. I sized him up. He wouldn't pose a problem. A few minutes with him and I would talk my way out of this place by afternoon.

∞

"Small conference room" was a misnomer. It was a cubicle with barely enough room for a small, round table and two chairs. White walls. No windows. No pictures. I sat in my chair, and Dr. Padgett sat across from me. I fidgeted, deciphered the pattern of the carpet, counted the acoustic ceiling tiles. Silent. I had nothing to say to this man. He was supposed to be the psychiatrist; let him ask the questions.

I was waiting for a barrage of open-ended inquiries. Why did I think I was there? What did I think of my mother, my father, my childhood? When I looked into the ink splotch, what did I see? I waited for him to try to get into my head, something I was convinced he would never be able to do. I wanted out. Today.

Yet he sat there, as silently as I did, not saying a word, and seemingly content not to do so. At first I was determined to outlast him; after all, he couldn't stay there all day, could he? Soon, however, the silence became oppressive. My emotions were spinning, nearly overwhelming me. I looked up into his eyes, which were intensely focused on me. Not a stare, exactly. Nor was it a look of clinical dissection, of trying to categorize me. It was a look of genuine concern. As much as I had been determined to distance myself from the man—to control the meeting—I found myself drawn to those eyes.

Finally, I couldn't contain my emotions.

"I'm not supposed to be here, Dr. Padgett," I finally told him. "I went a little overboard yesterday, maybe, but I can handle it. I just kind of went along with what the pastor at my church suggested, but I didn't realize I'd end up here. I don't need to be here. And I don't need a psychiatrist."

"Then why do you think you're here?"

The words spoken in a different tone could have been authoritative, admonishing, or sarcastic. But something in the way he said them made me believe he was honestly interested in my answer.

"I got upset yesterday. Very upset. I thought I wanted to die; I called a hotline. But I wasn't really going to do anything. I wish I had the guts, but I don't. I'm a fraud. I've never actually tried to kill myself, and I never will. The old 'cry for help' thing.

"But I really don't need any help. I've got a great husband, two beautiful kids, parents who love me, lots of friends, a good education, and a good mind. I've got the world going for me, doctor. Everybody says so. I just need to keep reminding myself of what I have. That's all."

Dr. Padgett remained silent.

"I'm tough, do you know that? I've been through my fair share of shit in life, but I don't need to go running to some shrink to cry about it. I've always gotten by. I don't need anyone at all. You're not going to sit here and pick my brain and come up with your conclusions, because I know what guys like you are all about. You start playing with someone's head, and before they know it, you've got them convinced that they are so screwed up they can't get by without you. You make them dependent, blame everything on their parents, their dog, anyone but themselves. Absolve them of everything—for a fee—even though they are probably just plain lousy people.

"Well, if you think you're gonna do that to me, then fuck you. Because you aren't. If I've learned anything in this shitty life, it's that you can't count on anyone else to deal with your shit. They've got their own shit to deal with. Life sucks. Period. People lie and cheat and steal and murder and fight wars, and it's always been that way and it always will. I'm the sanest one in the bunch. I'm *not* crazy, just smart enough to realize that you don't get through this life by playing little touchy-feely fantasy games, believing in gods that are just a big hoax, sucking up to shrinks who kiss your ass and try to convince you life isn't the piece of shit that it is. You get it by being tougher than the next guy. Survival of the fittest. And I'm very fit to survive. I can handle whatever comes my way, and I don't need anyone else to do it. Period."

If Dr. Padgett disagreed with my philosophies, he didn't show it. He sat there and listened. Just listened. My feelings began to flood the room. I began to tell him about my semi-shotgun marriage. All the forays into drugs. The dozens of men I slept with, not hearing from many of them the next day. The near-rape in college. The times I had come close to suicide but never had the guts to go through with it. The hypocrisy I felt because I had so many friends who seemed to like me, when I just knew that if they really knew me they'd all disappear and run like hell. As they should.

I told him I couldn't understand how everyone was so nice to me when I clearly didn't deserve it. I shared the tales of some of the horribly vindictive things I'd done in my life, the awful thoughts I'd had, and my secret desire to just be lobotomized. Simple. Stupid. Because I was sure that I simply thought too much and brought a lot of my pain onto myself. I was too self-absorbed and just too smart for my own good. My mind should have been given to someone good and decent, not me.

I continued on with this diatribe, the emotions, thoughts, and words forcing their way out of me with the vehemence of a hurricane. Until, finally, I felt spent. And incredibly foolish, embarrassed, and ashamed. As Sister Luisa had told me, words are powerful. Once you speak them, you can't take them back. I slumped back in my chair, remorseful for all that I had said. Maybe I'd said too much, and he would lock me up for life.

Finally Dr. Padgett spoke in a gentle, rather squeaky, but soothing voice.

"You've been through a lot of pain. And it's hard to trust anyone, hard to believe that anyone could care because you've always hated yourself. On one level, you've wanted people to believe your tough facade. But on a deeper level, you've wished that someone would be able to get past it, to get inside you and listen to your heart. But you've been afraid that no one in the world would understand—or worse, that you would drive them away.

"Life is really hard for you because you wish you could have been born male. You see males as tough and strong. And you put on a great facade of a male. You walk the walk and talk the talk. But deepest within you, you know that you aren't male. You are female, which you see as weak, manipulative, and worthless. No matter how hard you try to mask it, you cannot change the reality of your gender. So you stay in this trap of putting forth a charade, feeling hypocritical, while inside you secretly seethe in anger and bask in shame because you are unequivocally female. Deeply vulnerable and hurting within as you act tough outside. You do need people; you need them so much so that it scares you to death. You drive them away so they don't get too close; yet you regret it every time you do.

"You claim you don't want anyone to understand you. But you do. You want it very much. It's just that you don't believe that it is possible for anyone to understand, and you cannot bear to be let down again."

My eyes glazed with tears, and I felt an incredible warmth inside. I was lured to this man. How did he know I hated being a woman? I never told him that. How did he know about the tough facade, how I would brush people aside, attacking them as if they didn't matter—meanwhile wishing that they cared?

Dr. Padgett had put my thoughts, even unconscious ones, into words. As soon as he gave them a voice, I knew they were undeniably true. In just a single meeting, he had touched a place within me that no one had ever touched before. It was more than a matter of him understanding me. His understanding was couched in empathy and concern. He wanted to help.

I was drawn to him in that very first visit more than I had ever been drawn to anyone in my life. I'd gone in intending to pierce his facade, and instead he had gently unveiled mine. I had been wrong.

This was no ordinary man.

∞

I was in a fog of these emotions when I went back to my room. Visiting hours had begun, and Tim was waiting there for me. Tim hugged me, handed me a bouquet of flowers, and we began to talk about what it was like in the hospital and how the kids were doing. But my mind wasn't really in it. I was still trying to absorb all that had transpired with Dr. Padgett. I couldn't get him off my mind.

As if the doctor sensed that, there was a knock on my open door, and Dr. Padgett walked in and introduced himself to Tim. They shook hands, and Dr. Padgett handed me a thin packet of written material.

"I've thought this over and have decided that I'd like to work with you in therapy. You've got some very serious problems, Rachel, and I think the kind of treatment I offer can help you. In fact, in your case, I think this type of therapy is the only kind that will work. This pamphlet outlines the therapy I'm talking about and should answer a lot of your questions.

"Why don't you take a look at it and see what you think? If you have any more concerns, you can call my office."

With that, he walked out of the room. Tim and I immediately began to read the pamphlet entitled *Psychoanalytic Psychotherapy*. Much of it reiterated terminology that I vaguely recalled from an introductory psychology course I'd taken years earlier. The origins of neurosis and emotional pain developed in early childhood. The therapist would work with the patient to reveal painful, buried emotions. The patient's natural desire was to keep them buried through defense mechanisms, but the fears would become manageable in the light of adult, rational understanding, along with free association and uncensored thoughts.

The therapist would align himself with the patient to cut through her defenses and allow the frozen feelings to surface. As a "blank screen," he would reveal little of his personal life or his feelings to facilitate transference, the phenomenon whereby patients direct emotions intended for someone else in their lives, most likely from childhood, onto the therapist. This transference often reveals more of a patient's buried feelings and subconscious motivations.

It was interesting stuff, but nothing I hadn't seen before. It was the Freud and Jung I had at one time memorized and regurgitated back on tests.

The final part of the pamphlet stirred the most discussion. The therapy was conducted on a regular schedule—once, twice, or three times a week. A few patients found "relief" from their symptoms within a year, but most took at least one to three years to complete the therapy, and sometimes five or more years. The pamphlet stressed that such therapy meant a lot of time and money for the patient and required a great degree of commitment from the therapist as well. There were no guarantees, it said, but many people who had been through it had found it to be worth the time and money spent.

Both of us sat there on the bed dumbfounded. One hundred twenty dollars an hour three times a week. Who on earth could afford that? We began to joke about what kind of "psychos" would need or warrant therapy for half a decade, but the unspoken issue was financial.

We decided that I'd go ahead and look into it but not commit to anything yet. Perhaps, being fairly intelligent and driven, I could get by with once-a-week sessions and "lick the thing" in six months or less. After all, it wasn't as if I had that big of a problem anyway. Actually, we both agreed, I didn't even belong in the hospital. But on that issue, too, we decided to wait it out and see where things led.

By midafternoon, the psych floor was nearly deserted. Most of the patients, it seemed, were out on weekend passes. I was informed that newly arrived patients didn't get passes. *Newly arrived?* I thought. *Just how long do these people expect me to be here?*

Tim had left for an afternoon appointment, and I was restless and bored. Weekend meetings, group therapy, and other activities were few because most of the patients were gone. I had absolutely nothing to do. Tim had brought me a few library books, but I couldn't concentrate on reading. I wasn't up for watching television, no one was around to talk to, and the few patients who stayed seemed either so out of it or so despondent I didn't want to be near them.

Anxiety flooded in and took the form of energy. I wanted to run in the most desperate way, but I couldn't leave the floor, much less the hospital building. So I did the next best thing: I power walked.

With the sounds of Supertramp blaring in my ear through my Walkman, I began to walk in a circular path through the corridors of the unit, pumping my arms and legs. Adrenaline flowed, and I found myself walking faster and faster until I finally broke into a jog, then a run. As I turned the corner, a familiar figure was standing there, a scowl on her face, arms folded. It was *her*. The drill sergeant from hell, working a different shift.

"This is a hospital ward," she informed me, with the terse authority of a grade school nun, "not a gymnasium. You can't run laps in here. It's disturbing me and the other nurses, and it's upsetting the other patients too."

"There's nothing to do here," I retorted. "Absolutely

nothing. What am I supposed to do?"

"I'd suggest you find something. Something other than running."

I walked past her, restraining the urge to tell her off, and put my Walkman back on. Certainly she couldn't object if I just walked, if I didn't actually run. I indulged myself in a few more laps of vigorous power walking. Again, she appeared.

"I told you this isn't a gymnasium. It's not a health club. It's a hospital. Now put the Walkman away and go do something else."

"You told me not to run," I said indignantly. "I wasn't running. I was walking. Just plain walking. I have the right to do that, you know. Don't I?"

"I don't know what you call whatever it was you were just doing, but I certainly wouldn't call it 'just plain walking.' Obviously you can't control yourself. Hand over the Walkman now."

"You can't do this to me!" I cried hysterically. "You can't trap me in this nut ward with nothing to do, no one to talk to but these—these—*psychos!* You can't take away my Walkman. You can't!"

"I am authorized to do anything I need to do to keep this ward safe and comfortable for everyone here. And I want the Walkman. Now!"

This was an absolute nightmare. I wanted to scream, to spit, to flail at her with my fists. Instead I walked away, pretending to ignore her. As I resumed my power walking, I heard her tirade of admonishment despite the high volume of Supertramp. I turned around and looked at her. I absolutely loathed her. I took off my headphones, grabbed the Walkman in my right hand, and hurled it at her, aiming for her head. It missed by a few inches, the cassette door breaking off as it fell with a thud to the carpeted floor.

"*Are you happy now?*" I screamed hysterically. "It's all fucked up. I can't use it anymore. I hope you're happy, you fucking bitch!"

"You are absolutely out of control. I'm calling Dr. Padgett."

"I don't give a fuck what you do. Call him. What? Do you think I'm scared of the bastard? Give me a fucking break."

Truth be told, I was glad she was calling Dr. Padgett. Dr. Padgett didn't hate me the way she did. He would understand how unfair the nurse was being. I'd let him know just what had happened, just what horrible things the nurse had said about not liking me, about not having to like me. He was the doctor. He was in charge. The bitch wasn't going to have a leg to stand on by the time I was finished.

Having connected to Dr. Padgett, the nurse directed me to pick up one of the patient phones. Ha! She was too intimidated to let me take the phone at the nurses' station because of what I might do. Good. She should be scared. She deserved to be.

"Rachel." I was calmed by the sound of his voice. "What just went on?"

I told my side of the story, not sparing a detail. Like a defendant on *The People's Court*, I was a polished advocate for myself. I waited for him to concur with my conclusions, to get the nurse back on the line, and to give her a word or two about compassion for patients.

It didn't happen.

"You can't do that, Rachel," he said, still with the underlying gentleness but with an added element of firmness. "What you did was wrong. It was inexcusable and out of control. You can't get any better if you just let your

38

emotions explode anytime the mood strikes. If you can't control yourself, I'm going to have no choice but to put you in restraints in the lockup ward."

Betrayal sliced through me like a knife. Dr. Padgett was on her side. He was one of them.

"Dr. Padgett," I sobbed my hurt and sense of betrayal into the phone, "how can you do that to me?"

"I'm not doing anything to you, Rachel, and you know that. If you feel compelled to act out, then you are going to have to face the consequences. I'm not going to sit here and listen to you try to justify what you did because it isn't defensible. It's destructive. Now please go let the nurse know I want her to pick up the line. I will tell her exactly what I told you. If you continue to act out of control, you will be placed in a more controlled environment. I'll see you on Monday morning rounds."

I informed the nurse and hung up the phone, numbed. Dr. Padgett had seemed so sympathetic and understanding in our consultation. Now he was as angry as the nurse. I'd pissed him off. I'd blown it. He hated me. And I wouldn't be seeing him again until Monday.

Monday seemed like an eternity.

∞

I got through the rest of Saturday and Sunday by acting docile, moping in my room most of the time. I did mingle a bit with a few of the other patients but still preferred solitude. When I was with the others, I did my best to appear in control. It was only holed up in my room, away from scrutiny, that I let the depression that was swallowing me show.

Every time the drug cart pulled up, I was first in line. I

wanted to be numb so I could forget where I was. Most of all, I wanted to forget the faces of my two children. They had been so happy, but confused, to visit me. The sadness in their eyes when they realized I would not be going home overwhelmed me with guilt and made me ashamed of all the responsibilities that I had thrust on Tim. I felt mortified when I thought about all of the money my hospital stay was going to cost, knowing that I was virtually abandoning my children. Whatever they gave me to wash down with the water from the paper cup could never be enough. The drugs only blunted the edge, whereas I wanted to be completely wasted. Oblivious.

I went to bed early on Sunday night, not wanting to be awake for the change of shift, lest I be forced to see the drill sergeant again. I had drifted to sleep fairly easily, but I found myself awake, sitting bolt upright, at two in the morning. What was it about two o'clock?

I couldn't stand the darkness that enveloped me with a fear so choking I could barely breathe. I tried to will myself back to sleep, but I couldn't. My mind turned in on itself, as it had so often in the past. Swelling, sweeping emotions, building to a crescendo, virtually screamed in my ear. My heart was pounding. I stood up. I had to stand up. I had to run.

I started again on the power walk/run, this time discreet enough to do it up and down a small segment of the hall, out of sight and earshot of the nurses' station. The adrenaline rushed through me again, the pumping arms became punches, the pumping legs karate kicks. The more I let loose, the more I wanted to run. I smacked into the plaster, literally bouncing off the walls with a thud, energized by the pain to my hips and arms. Running faster, bouncing harder. It wasn't enough pain. I wanted to shatter myself into pieces just like the Walkman and smash the feelings right out of me.

The shadowy figures that approached me from the end of the hall had other ideas. They were big, bouncerlike men, the military police of the hospital scene. The drill sergeant was behind them, scowling as always, directing the two men to take me by force if necessary. I struggled with them with everything I had left, but I was no match for these two uniformed thugs who bound my arms in restraints and carried me down the hall. I was screaming profanity about civil rights and patient dignity, but it didn't faze them. I got the impression they were used to doing this sort of thing.

I heard the buzz of a secure door with a tiny grilled window and found myself in another unit.

I was flooded with both shock and nausea. Weightlessness. This was lockup. The real thing. Instantly filled with remorse, I tried in every conceivable way to talk myself out of there. But it wasn't going to happen. I felt ashamed and violated as they made me remove the shoelaces from my shoes, and then I watched them go through the contents of my purse they had taken from my room and catalog every item.

"*No!*" I shrieked when they took my cigarettes and lighter. They informed me that in the intensive care unit, the pleasant euphemism for lockup, patients weren't allowed to keep entire packs of cigarettes, lest they smoke them all day. Nor were they allowed to have lighters or matches for the destructive acts that could be performed with them. I went straight to bed in the same room as a grotesquely obese woman who was tied to her bed with restraints. She screamed out in her sleep every few minutes. Mercifully, I was given a large and very potent sleeping pill. It was strong enough to drown out the screams and my fear of being cooped up in a room with a woman big enough to take on three security guards and apparently violent enough to require restraints.

∞

I awoke in the morning to see Dr. Padgett standing at my bedside. Smiling, damn him. Like nothing had happened. Like I was still supposed to be stupid enough to believe that he cared about me when he had incarcerated me in this prison of the insane.

"Heard you took a little shadowboxing run last night," he said.

"I wasn't shadowboxing. I was power walking. Whatever that nurse told you is a lie. She's a complete bitch. She hates my guts. She got these big animals to throw me in this hellhole."

"She did that, Rachel," the smile faded from his face, "because it was what I directed her to do."

"You rotten sonofabitch. How could you do this to me?"

"You were out of control. You knew the consequences. You needed to be here."

The gentleness was barely audible in his voice. The firmness, however, was loud and clear. How dare this man, whom I barely even knew, take it upon himself to control my life, to decide what I needed and what I didn't?

"I demand that you release me from this unit right now. I mean, *right now*."

"You were out of control, Rachel. Admit it."

"I know my rights, you asshole. I had all weekend in this fucking place. I have the right to leave with six hours advance notice. You can't incarcerate me, you prick. I'll go against medical advice. I don't give a shit. I want out, now!"

"You have the right to be released AMA [against medical advice] with written notice," he said calmly. "But I have the right to commit you for ninety-six hours if I can show a court that you represent a threat to yourself or to anyone else."

"Fuck you, asshole. I'll have your fucking license. My godfather is one of the best trial attorneys in this city, and he'll have your ass on a platter."

"All of it is legal. And there isn't a shred of doubt in my mind that I could easily convince a judge that you are a threat to yourself."

"What did I do?" I sobbed. "What did I do?'"

"You went walking out in the middle of the night, half naked and on very potent medications, admitting to the guard that you were trying to get yourself killed. And you're very lucky you didn't. You went running around the halls of the unit and threw a radio at a nurse's head. You're very lucky it didn't hit her. Then, last night, you started slamming yourself into walls and kicking them. Just look at the bruises all over your body. Convincing a judge that you are a clear threat to yourself would be a cakewalk under these circumstances."

His eyes drilled into me with the same determined intensity with which I was glaring at him. If I were tough, he was tougher. It didn't happen often, but I had met my match. Slight of build, perhaps. A geek, perhaps. But he wasn't afraid to draw a line in the sand. He had drawn it clearly. I wasn't going to win this battle. I also wasn't going to let him know I knew that.

"I'll be seeing you tomorrow morning during my rounds. Take care of yourself, Rachel. We'll talk more tomorrow."

"What? You're just going to come in and threaten me like that and then just walk? Coward! Asshole! I'll fucking have your license, you bastard—"

"Listen carefully, Rachel, I'm only going to say this once. I'm not threatening you. You are a clear danger to yourself, and it is my right and duty as your psychiatrist to do whatever is necessary to protect you from yourself. What you choose to do when you're released from the hospital is your business; you can go ahead with therapy, or you can forget the whole thing. I care about you, I want to help you, and I think I can help you. But whatever you do is your decision. So long as you are a patient here, however, I am your psychiatrist. None of this is a threat.

"You, however, have threatened me, and I'm not going to stand here and listen to it all day because it isn't what you most deeply feel, and it isn't going to benefit anybody. As a matter of fact, letting you rant on is only going to let you spin further out of control. So I'm leaving now. I'll be back tomorrow. And when you can show me clear evidence that you have regained control of yourself, I will let you out of lockup.

"You can blame all of this on anyone you want, Rachel, but it isn't going to change the reality that I do care, that what I'm doing is in your best interest, and that you have the ability to control yourself—if you so choose."

With that he left, paying no heed to the final barrage of insults I raged at him as he walked out the door. Part of me wondered if I would ever see him again—if I had overstepped the bounds and made him have second thoughts about his offer to treat me.

∞

The lockup ward, although adjacent to the regular psych floor, was a vastly different world. Here there was no confusion as to whether or not this was a mental ward; it was painfully obvious. There was only one sitting area, and all the patients were there. An elderly man with a pasted-on grin and vacuous look mumbled unintelligibly and shuffled up and down the hall in pajamas that were too big for him. A wild-eyed woman with overpermed, bleached hair sat at the table telling anyone who would listen how she had been sent by Jesus to let all people know that the world was ending and we were just moments away from a fiery eternity. A young teenage girl with slice marks all over her arms and the gaunt dark-circled ashen look of the near-dead slumped in a chair. She had just been released from surgery to thwart the effects of her latest suicide attempt—her tenth in a year. It made me feel positively sane. I hovered by the nurses, engaging them in conversation, trying to cling to my sanity in the face of those who had clearly lost theirs.

There were four nurses working the unit, all African American (as opposed to the regular psych floor where all of the nurses were white). They were energetic, witty, and unbelievably patient as they dealt with a ward full of people who needed constant assistance. Behavior that the drill sergeant would never tolerate was nothing to these nurses on the front line of the mentally ill. How they could so easily placate the erratic patients and still keep smiles on their faces absolutely amazed me.

"Girl," one of them said to me, "what on God's green earth happened this mornin'? You know, honey, you really blew it. Dr. Padgett came in here all set to release you back to the other ward until you let him have it."

"He was really going to release me?"

"Yes, ma'am. He had the papers all ready, just wanted to talk to you first before he signed 'em. Shit, girl. What in the world were you sayin' in there? I could hear the cussin' all the way back in the nurses' station."

I winced at the thought. Everybody knew I'd lost control.

"I dunno. I guess I was just pissed to be here. I still don't know why I'm *here*, especially. These people are hardcore. I don't belong here."

"Well, you sure didn't do much of a job convincing the good doctor of that. I don't see Dr. Padgett lose his cool like that very often, so you managed to really piss 'im off, honey. I wouldn't mess with him. He's in charge of the whole psychiatric division of this hospital. He may not act like it, but he's a powerful man, that Dr. Padgett. Big brass around here. I mean *big*. Also happens to be one of the best docs around. How'd you end up with him, anyway?"

"He was the guy on call."

"Well, honey, you're a very lucky lady. You got the best. Don't blow it. Next time you're feelin' pissed off, bite a pillow or something. Because if you're trying to convince this guy you don't need to be here, you're goin' about it the wrong way. I can tell you're a smart lady, Rachel. Next time, why don't you use some of those brains God gave you? You can say and do a lot of things on the outside and no one pays it any mind, but in here you're under a microscope. If you wanna get out of this unit, honey, you gotta watch your p's and q's. You're way too young and smart to be stuck in this scene for too long. Don't waste the gifts God gave you, honey."

I waited to be released all day, well-behaved, helping the nurses and keeping them company. I had called my husband and calmly explained where I was and my version of the unjust circumstances that had led to my confinement in lockup. Tim, believing every word I said, vowed to help me be released. He called Dr. Padgett's office and spoke to him and heard an entirely different version of the story.

"But she always goes running late at night, Dr. Padgett. She's been doing it for a long time. She has a lot of nervous energy. The running helps her."

"At two o'clock in the morning?" Dr. Padgett had replied. "It may be something she always does, but do you really think it's normal?"

Truth be told, Tim didn't find it normal. He had merely coped with it, the same as he had with so many other erratic emotions and behaviors. He was torn between the wishes of his wife and the common sense of her doctor. Ultimately, he decided to continue to support me but to leave the decisions up to the doctor whose judgment he trusted a lot more than his own.

That day I gave the nurses the six-hour AMA written request, complete with witness signatures. It was an eloquently worded contract of sorts in which I agreed not to exit the hospital if I were released back into the regular psych ward before the six hours were up. Dr. Padgett waited until the last minute of the last hour before he signed the order to let me out of lockup, return my personal items, and move me back to my previous room.

Several months later he told me he had received the written notice within fifteen minutes of my handing it to the nurses. He knew he would ultimately sign it and release me, but he had me wait for the rest of the day for him to do so. It was in my best interest, he said.

Chapter 3

As it turned out, many of my fellow patients in the "regular" psych ward (otherwise known as the stress unit) viewed my short stay in the lockup unit as a rite of initiation, a badge of courage. They simply had to meet the woman who'd gained grapevine infamy for hurling a radio at the charge nurse's head and being thrown in lockup for kickboxing. My weightless, frightening lockup experience became, in retrospect, a tale of brave antiauthoritarianism and defiance. I told my story with the same tough, false bravado I'd displayed in grade school when I got into trouble. James Dean with lipstick. Never let 'em see you sweat.

It became a fraternity of sorts, a half-dozen of us masking our pain by trading war stories of lockup and nurse oppression, mocking the instructors, giving them all nicknames, and basically turning the whole experience of psychiatric hospitalization into a running joke.

There was "Yoko Ono," the Asian American psychodrama

specialist. She led us through bizarre, emotionally venting psychodramas complete with pillow bats to beat the object of inner anger. "Peppy" was a young, blonde, perpetually smiling and energetic activities therapist. "Weebles" was our code name for the group therapy leader whose sessions we always disrupted, thus named for her disproportionately bottom-heavy physique (as in "Weebles wobble, but they don't fall down").

By the end of the first week, I had become quite comfortable in the hospital environment. As patients were released and new ones admitted, I emerged as a ringleader of sorts. A veteran. It was a replay of the sixth grade as I led the laughter, making a mockery of scheduled activities with little of the fear of consequences I had at twelve. What could they do? I was an adult. And a mental patient. I relished my daily visits with Dr. Padgett when he did rounds, the soothing tonic quality of his voice. Tim and the kids visited most evenings, and after that I settled into the ritual of dorm-style, late-night bull sessions. I was beginning to enjoy having my every need taken care of—no cooking, cleaning, or giving the kids a bath. My "frat" buddies spoke of the place as if it were a prison, counting the days until they would be "sprung," and I would chime right in with them. The truth was, however, I was getting too comfortable and beginning to secretly wish I might never be released—a covert desire I'd damn well never share with the others.

Dr. Padgett, alas, did know. He sensed my attachment and felt that the hospital environment was making me "lose touch with reality" and "regressing me to childhood." With both fear and profound disappointment, I received the news he had ordered my release for the next day. If I were still amenable, I was to be in his office at 3:00 P.M. the day after to start psychoanalytic therapy in earnest. Being ordered to return home was like being sent back out into the hall as a kid. To a scary place. Alone. Without my cohorts to keep my mind off a reality I couldn't bear to face.

In a little over three weeks, my inpatient stay had only served to place me on the proper anti-anxiety and anti-depressant medications and monitor their effects.

The rest, it seemed, had been a very expensive game indeed. Wasted time. Wasted money.

∞

I could hardly wait for my first official, full-length therapy session with Dr. Padgett. With the exception of our first consultation meeting, his visits in the hospital had been disappointingly short—typically ten minutes or less. I relished the thought of a full hour with the man, hoping that the magical moments of the initial meeting would be replayed and that the hunger to be understood that he'd awakened in me would once again be satiated. Unlike my childhood teachers, whose attention increased proportionately to my level of disruption, Dr. Padgett seemed to have grown more distant to me in the hospital as my psych ward antics increased. Now that I was released, I was ready to be serious again—and even more ready to receive his kind words and affection. I was determined to win him back.

Although it was located on the first floor of the hospital wing, very little was institutional about Dr. Padgett's office. The waiting room walls were a muted eggshell-white, adorned with inoffensive nature scenes—higher quality than their counterparts in the unit upstairs. The furniture was comfortable, but unlike that of the ward smoking lounge, it was contemporary and expensive.

With the bronze plaque on the door identifying him as "Medical Director of Psychiatry," the geek with plaid shirts and squeaky voice gave way to a new image of a very powerful man indeed. I was intimidated to be waiting in this room for Dr. Padgett to emerge, hoping no one I knew would walk in and see me here in this strange place.

After a few moments, Dr. Padgett appeared from around the corner with the same broad smile I was beginning to realize was his trademark. I followed him into his office.

If the waiting room had been an exercise of subtle high quality, Dr. Padgett's private office was even more so. Portraits hung on the wall, some appearing to be originals. Cherry wood bookcases were built into the wall, filled with leather-bound books on a host of psychiatric topics. The desk was carved of cherry as well, the surface immaculate. The subdued lighting and luxurious furniture softly—and expensively—whispered professionalism.

The only indications of the Freudian purpose of the office were the full-length couch and the presence of designer tissue boxes at several places throughout the room. Two contemporary armchairs faced each other with a small mahogany table in between. I quickly sank into one of the chairs as Dr. Padgett sat comfortably in the other.

While the office made a strong impression on me, the first session itself was a disappointment—much more like a professor outlining a course than the riveting emotional catharsis of our initial consultation. It was dry, unemotional fare as he listed his session fees, elaborated upon the terms and methodologies mentioned in the pamphlet, described schedules and billing procedures, and checked up on my medications.

Finally, he laid down the ground rules of therapy. There were plenty of them. Therapy was conducted with heavy reliance on free association—uncensored thoughts in a controlled setting bounded by a daunting number of rules. An "hour" was only fifty minutes, whereupon sessions would end regardless of the point we'd reached. Questions about his academic credentials would be answered at any time, but none whatsoever about his personal life. I was, at all times, to be candid. If he sensed that I wasn't, or was hiding behind defenses, he would interrupt and redirect the conversation. It was not his policy to take phone calls from patients while in session with another patient, nor was it his policy to allow after-hours calls to turn into therapy by phone. I had fifty minutes of his undivided attention and focus to explore my feelings in session, and I would need to learn to make good use of that time rather than act out the emotions elsewhere.

Free association? Somehow the context seemed anything but free.

In the final minutes of the session, as he glanced at a digital clock on the table that only he could see, he handed me a three-page report to review before our next session. It was the result of a multiple choice, fill-in-the-dot psychological profile test I'd taken and barely recalled from my first full day as a hospital inpatient. As I read the first paragraph, I was gripped by nausea. I could tell that I had flunked it.

Before I could read further, Dr. Padgett smiled, nodded his head, and said, "That's all for today."

It was a phrase I would learn to despise with all of my being.

∞

After finding a chair in a relatively private corner of the hospital lobby, I proceeded to read the entire report. I couldn't say what I had expected, but it wasn't the stinging barrage of labels I read in that report. I could have handled words such as "tough," "misunderstood," "erratic," or "unruly." Instead this bitingly clinical text literally ripped my character to shreds. *Manipulative. Seductive and promiscuous. Over-dramatic. Demanding to be the center of attention. Overdependent. Histrionic—at times, hysterical. Severe mood swings. Clear suicidal tendencies, as well as sociopathological ones.*

It took all the self-control I could muster not to vomit on the floor. I was shaking. I was in shock. I checked the cover page again to make sure that this report was about me and I hadn't somehow been handed someone else's. I noticed that the report had been compiled by the same psychologist who had conducted group therapy. Weebles. My hurt and shock transformed to righteous indignation. Weebles had framed me because her group sessions were ineffective whinefests. Because she was really just a pushy bitch who didn't want to hear from those who wanted to talk and stomped on the privacy of those who didn't. Just because I wasn't going to play along with her group orgy of touchy-feely talk. Because of all that, she'd decided to get even and nail me with the test results. She'd made me look like shit. Cheap, dirty, low shots. Fuck her!

And Padgett, it dawned on me, went right along with her. The sonofabitch. He'd lied to me, led me on, betrayed me. How could I have trusted him? How could I have been so stupid to think that he cared?

Still shaking, now with rage instead of shock, I headed for the nearest pay phone in the lobby foyer. While fumbling angrily for Dr. Padgett's card and a quarter, my purse strap broke and the leather bag fell to the floor. With the coin and card in hand, I kicked my purse, catapulting it against the other wall, its contents spilling out on the rug. Finally, I put the coin in the phone and dialed.

"Dr. Padgett's office."

"I need to talk to Dr. Padgett. Now!"

"I'm sorry. He's in with a patient now. Can I take a message?"

Another goddamned patient. How much was he toying with that one's mind? Jealousy washed over me at the thought that he could be in with anybody besides me.

"Listen, I need to talk to him now! No, no, wait a minute—fuck it. Go ahead; leave him a message. You tell that bastard he can take his therapy and shove it up his ass. You can cancel my appointments now. I'm finished with that lying sonofabitch, and you can tell him that too."

"Excuse me, ma'am. . . . Ma'am? Please hold for just a minute."

The phone clicked, and Dr. Padgett came on the line. My Pavlovian wilting response to his voice made me even angrier.

"You sonofabitch!" I was screaming in tears, and the woman at the information desk in the lobby was staring at me through the glass double doors. "What is this bullshit? Huh? These fucking lies. Why didn't you just have her write 'asshole' and be done with it?"

"Rachel," he replied calmly, seemingly having ignored the outburst, "it's a report compiled from questions you answered. It doesn't fully define you."

"Then you admit it's a pack of lies? Huh? Will you admit it?"

"I didn't say it was inaccurate. I said it was incomplete."

"Did you read it?" I was whining now, pleading for sympathy. "Did you? My God—the words. 'Manipulative.' 'Psychotic.' 'Dependent.' Goddamnit, Dr. Padgett, do you really hate me that much?"

"You know I don't hate you, Rachel. You have serious problems, but I don't hate you, and you aren't an asshole. We'll work on it together. Obviously we're going to need to discuss this report in much further detail."

His voice was a soothing tonic again, almost hypnotic, entrancing. I needed him. Right then. I needed him to bump his other patient and talk to me, soothe me with his healing words for hours as he had the first day we'd met.

"Could we meet right now?" I begged him.

"I have appointments the rest of today and a full day tomorrow. Maybe Regina could set something up for you on Thursday."

"Not Thursday," I demanded, my hysterical tears peaked to crescendo. "Now, goddamnit. Now! I've gotta see you *now!*"

"I'm sorry. That just isn't possible. We can discuss this at our next session."

"I've got news for you, asshole. There's not gonna be a next session. How dare you hand me a piece of shit report like that and then just turn your back on me? You knew it would kill me. Well, fuck you and your Freudian bullshit. I quit!"

In a firm tone of finality, he simply replied, "What you do is up to you. I hope you stay. I think I can help you, but it's your choice to decide if you can trust me or not. I really can't discuss this now. We can explore it more in our next session. Good-bye, Rachel."

The phone clicked back to the receptionist, and I promptly slammed down the receiver, and the sound echoed through the foyer. He may as well have just plunged a knife through my heart. My head was spinning. Had I been too out of line, or had I not told him off nearly enough? Did I hate his guts and not care if he dropped off the face of the earth, or did I need him more than anyone I had ever known?

Dropping down to my hands and knees, I slowly gathered the contents of my purse, remaining frozen there for a while in uncontrollable tears, shrieking and shaking wildly like a rabid animal. The information desk clerk, clearly disturbed by this sight, got up and approached the double doors to further investigate. Humiliated, I pulled myself together and somehow, miraculously, managed to start driving myself home.

The hysterics and profane epithets of betrayal, the alternating pains of righteous indignation and acute embarrassment and shame nearly drove me over the edge. Goddamnit. I was crazy. Totally crazy. The hospital and Dr. Padgett had made me worse, cut me loose. I'd snapped.

At home Tim was on my side, listening to my account of the story. He, too, thought Weebles had engaged in outrageous character assassination. Yet that was small consolation. Dr. Padgett sided with her. Dr. Padgett was the one who counted. Already I was addicted to the man, and I hated myself for it.

Early the next morning, I called his office and sheepishly asked Regina to go ahead and schedule me the Thursday appointment, if it were still available. It was. Dr. Padgett had left it open.

Chapter 4

The two days between Tuesday's turbulent phone call and Thursday's session seemed like an eternity. I was despondent at the contents of the report, whose labels were beginning to ring with an undeniable truth. Disgusted with myself for having reacted so vehemently, for having made a complete ass out of myself, I was ashamed. Yet I was overwhelmed by the aching need to see him again. I could barely tolerate the time until our next session, all the while despising myself for my growing dependency.

In the waiting room I buried my face behind *Newsweek* so the receptionist who had witnessed my raging lunacy wouldn't see me. On my very first day of therapy, I'd managed to shatter every rule and erupt with vicious emotion at a time and place that were out of bounds. I braced myself for the coming lecture, admonishment, terse retribution, or—the worst conceivable possibility—that Dr. Padgett would decide he no longer wanted me as a patient.

"You can come on in now."

It was The Voice again. The soothing-tonic voice. Frozen for a moment, cowering behind *Newsweek* in burning shame, I finally looked up to see him. The trademark smile was there again, as if the telephone incident had never occurred.

Once seated in his office, my eyes cast downward to the floor, afraid and unwilling to meet his, I began to stammer through profuse apologies. In a darkened confessional of the soul, he was God and I was the sinner. The remorse and penance began.

"I'm sorry, oh my God, I'm *so* sorry. I lost control. So out of line. I don't know what to say. I'm such a horrible patient. The report—it's true. Every word of it. I showed it. I proved it. You must hate me. I'm disgusting. I understand if you don't want to go through with this anymore after all the shit I've pulled, all the horrible things I said."

I continued with my tearful apology for a while longer before realizing that Dr. Padgett had no intention of scolding or criticizing me or of concurring with my scathing self-assessment.

"I'm not here to judge your behavior," he said gently, as my eyes remained fixed on the floor. "I've committed to therapy with you, I want to help you, and I will honor that commitment. Maybe people have left you before or turned their backs when things got too rough. I won't do that. So long as you keep coming here, no matter what might happen, what you might say or do, it isn't going to drive me away. I'll be here. You can count on that. The only person that will leave this therapy is you; you will make that decision, not me. I'll be here for as long as it takes."

Clearly this wasn't what I had anticipated. Looking up to see his face, I saw it filled with genuine concern, with sincerity. But how could he say such things without knowing what I might do? As much as I wanted his words to be true, I found them impossible to believe. It wasn't that I thought he was dishonest, just that he didn't know how crazy and awful I was inside.

"You probably find this hard to accept," he continued, reading my thoughts once again. "But it's the truth. It's genuine. It's called unconditional acceptance, the kind of unconditional acceptance and love that every child deserves, that every child needs to make her whole. The kind you never got from your own parents."

How does he know anything about my parents? I've never said anything about them. Why do they have to be an issue here? This isn't about them. I'm the screwup, not them. Dad was right; these guys all blame everything on the parents.

"This makes it hard to trust. Trust is very, very hard for you. I know that. I don't expect you to believe me or trust me right now. And I don't expect you to take me on my word. Talk is cheap. I'm sure you've heard plenty of talk. No, trust can't be proven by anything I say, but by what I do. You should be skeptical—questioning me at every turn. That's part of the process."

I was numb. It was almost too much to fathom, to absorb. I didn't want to be skeptical, didn't want to doubt him. How could I dare doubt him after he was kind enough to say these things, considering the horrible things I'd said to him? Yet I doubted him nonetheless. And he was telling me, much to my astonishment, that it was okay. I wasn't sure if he was a liar, a fool, or a masochist.

We then discussed my psychological profile and its revelations about the darkest side of my character. They were truths of which I was mortally ashamed, but truths nonetheless.

The darkness of my soul revealed in all its ugly nakedness. Dr. Padgett surprised me once again.

"I don't place much stock in psychological profiles," he said. He explained they served a limited purpose, perhaps, but they were just a series of oversimplified labels that could not come close to encompassing the complexities of an individual's character, including mine. By design, such profile tests sought to uncover the most unhealthy aspects of a person's nature, seeking to identify pathologies. He had wanted me to see it so that I would know just how serious the situation was, to know what we—the two of us—would be facing together. Still, the report had not touched on the many good qualities within me, the ones he saw in that very first meeting. The ones that prompted him to "choose" me as a patient.

Choose me. A part of me was slightly stuck by the arguably arrogant implications of such a statement. After all, I was paying *him*—$120 a session to be exact. *I* was the one doing the choosing. Yet the notion of being chosen because of what he saw in me was too comforting a thought to dismiss. Why did everything have to be so confusing?

"You are like a diamond," he said to me. "A rough diamond. Only covered in dirt so you can't see it for yourself. And I am like the one who discovered you. My role is to help you slowly scrape away the caked-on dirt until we get to the diamond itself. If you know anything about diamonds, though, you know that they don't have much value in rough form. Diamonds gain their value according to how skillfully they're cut.

"Your parents never recognized the possible value. You were never finely cut, and you never got the chance to see the value and the beauty you possessed. So you covered yourself in mud and buried and hid yourself there because that is what you thought you were. Dirt.

"Well, once we remove the soil, we will work together to cut that diamond and give it more value, beauty, and shining brilliance than you ever could have believed. You don't see the potential yet. You don't see the inherent value and beauty you have. But I do. And that's why I chose you. Someday you'll see it too, and believe it, just as much as I do."

There he goes again, the "choosing me" thing. He's bringing my parents into it again. What is this obsession with my parents? What do they have to do with anything? He doesn't even know them. And yet . . . a diamond, not just any stone, but a diamond.

Once again Dr. Padgett had somehow burrowed through my massive fortress of walls and gently touched me. There was an inherent poetry in the man, words and feelings that lured and lulled me. Only he could find a way to turn "dirt" into poetry. Only he could find a way, for however brief a moment, to make me feel good about myself.

∞

Soon we'd agreed to increase the frequency of sessions to three times a week, which still did not seem like enough. Much of our discussion focused on the issues of trust, my fear of abandonment, and the therapy relationship. I would delve into some of the painful events of my life, nearly all of them from adolescence and early adulthood.

Dr. Padgett tried to bring the focus to my early childhood. I would respond with vehement resistance and terse reminders to Dr. Padgett that *I* was the one who screwed up. These were *my* problems, *my* character flaws. My parents had been good ones and should be left out of it. Discussing my early childhood was an invasion of my family's privacy. It was tantamount to a betrayal that I felt, in all of their generosity, my parents did not deserve.

Often the mere mention of this issue would provoke me into a tirade of profanity as vehement as any I'd displayed in the hospital. It would prove to be a contentious issue for the next several months. I thought my vehemence was justified; Dr. Padgett saw it as a sign that there was, indeed, something disturbing enough to elicit such reactions. It was an interpretation we argued over nearly every single session— or, more aptly, over which *I* argued. It was difficult to arouse much passion in Dr. Padgett, yet another phenomenon of therapy that gave me fits.

Another contentious issue was the severity of my illness and the extent of my need for therapy. At $120 per hour, I felt at times that therapy was an indulgence. The fact that financial support from my parents—who simply pretended my problems weren't happening—made such a luxury possible simply increased my guilt over being there at all. Yet I couldn't bring myself to stop going, which at times made me feel both like an addict and an emotional hypochondriac.

Dr. Padgett, however, saw it differently. To him, it was a grave situation. I was a time bomb of sorts, he thought, and as such, intensive therapy was not a matter of luxury, but life or death. I couldn't decide whether his assessment was correct or just his attempt to soothe my guilt over the time and expense and keep collecting his fees. I was reluctant to bring this up, but when I did, Dr. Padgett would calmly say that I needed to sort out this skepticism myself and reach my own conclusions. The proverbial ball, as always, was back on my side of the court.

∞

Life at home was unpredictable. Occasionally I felt periods of numbed calm, as if everything was back to normal and I didn't need therapy. But more frequently, particularly after intense sessions marked by one-sided combat, I could lose control completely. Screaming. Swearing. Crying. Impulsively bursting out of the house for midnight runs. I had never experienced such acute anxiety. For the first time, I began to have hyperventilating panic attacks and episodes of agoraphobia, a paralyzing fear of being in public places.

One day I'd broken into hysterical tears and hyperventilated as the four of us drove to McDonald's. I pled with Tim to take me home and go by himself with the kids. I then called Dr. Padgett, asking him if I could take a stronger anti-anxiety medication. As it was late Friday afternoon, he prescribed one over the phone. I remember him telling me that Mellaril had a 1-in-100,000 chance of causing seizurelike convulsions. But I didn't think much of it. Besides, with as many illegal drugs as I'd used in my day, I wasn't too concerned about one that was actually legal, pharmaceutical, and prescribed.

∞

"Come on, Rachel. *Count!* Ten, nine, eight, seven . . . Please, please, do this. *Please!* Ten, nine, eight . . ."

I was lying on the bed, Tim's face just inches above mine. He was frantic. I wished he'd quit bothering me and just let me sleep. I closed my eyes. "No. No." Tim was now shaking me vigorously. "Don't sleep! Come on, let's count. Ten, nine, eight . . ."

"Okay, okay," I relented, anything to appease him so

he'd leave me alone. "Ten, nine, eight, seven, six, five, four, three, two, one. I did it, all right? Now will you let me sleep?"

"Rachel," he said, noticeably relieved I had responded. "You have to stay awake. You had a seizure. Dr. Padgett told me to keep you awake for at least an hour or two."

That woke me up in a hurry. A seizure? The last thing I remembered was watching TV with Tim. But how did I get from there into the bedroom? A blackout. Scary. But it wasn't nearly as scary as it must have been to Tim who'd witnessed the entire incident.

I listened in amazement as he told me what had happened. I'd been lying on the couch. We'd talked a bit during the commercials. Then I'd begun to stare at the ceiling, a far-away look in my eyes. Then suddenly I'd started shaking uncontrollably, rocking back and forth, eyeballs rolling. Drooling. Tim had stayed by my side, scared beyond belief, afraid I'd swallow my tongue and asphyxiate. The episode stopped as suddenly as it had come on, and I'd passed out.

He'd called Dr. Padgett's emergency number immediately, and the doctor said it sounded like a grand mal seizure and told Tim to take me to the emergency room right away. When Tim mentioned the late hour and the fact that Jeffrey and Melissa were soundly sleeping, Dr. Padgett instructed him to wake me up, get me to count, keep me awake, call him back, and go the hospital the absolute first thing in the morning.

The next morning I sat in the hospital while someone pasted electrodes to my scalp for an EEG. A few days later I was injected with a dye and had a CT scan. A neurologist put me on Tegretol, an antiseizure and antidepression medication. Because Tegretol is known, in some cases, to reduce the white platelet count in the bloodstream and inhibit the body's natural immune system, I had to go to the hospital outpatient center twice a week to monitor my white cell levels.

I was probed, pricked, zapped, injected, placed in strange claustrophobic devices, referred to a number of physicians, and had various test procedures in Dr. Padgett's thorough quest to make sure that I had no underlying physiological illness or condition that had prompted the seizure. Overkill, I had thought at the time. But his concern for me was obvious—at least some consolation for my newfound status as a human guinea pig.

There were a wide number of possibilities, the most likely being an adverse reaction to Mellaril. But I was still tested to exclude every other potential problem.

After a month on Tegretol, my white platelet count was steadily plummeting and approaching the danger zone. In the meantime, I was losing control of my emotions and was out of touch with reality. I exploded into hysterical tirades with increasing frequency at home and in sessions. Finally, in late August, Dr. Padgett and I agreed that I needed to be hospitalized again. This time I would start in the intensive care unit—lockup. Ostensibly the placement was because the facility was better equipped to monitor physical conditions. I wondered, however, if I wasn't being sent there because I'd simply spun so far out of control that I was crazy to the point of no return.

∞

If the first hospitalization could be summarized as a three-week frat party, the second was like a three-week stint as a laboratory test animal.

My blood was taken twice daily. I had an EEG. I had an MRI, gaining the distinction of being the first adult in the lab's history to somehow wiggle my way back out of the claustrophobic tunnel after the test had begun. Now I was pricked and probed, injected, and scanned on a daily basis. After a week in intensive care, Dr. Padgett gave up on the Tegretol, switched my antidepressant, and transferred me to the stress unit.

It was a series of human experiments, described in dressed-up clinical terms as "medication adjustments." I adjusted to the new antidepressant and different anti-anxiety pills by throwing up, passing out, shaking uncontrollably, and hallucinating my way through a host of medications to find the right combination. It reached the point where I manifested nearly every possible side effect of every medication I tried.

Finally I demanded to be taken off all of them. Dr. Padgett wasn't sure if I was really physiologically averse to the drugs or if some of the reactions were a self-fulfilling prophecy. I was growing impatient with both him and his infuriatingly calm insistence that this was the trial-and-error nature of determining the correct psychiatric pharmaceuticals for an individual's chemistry. Easy enough for him to say, I thought.

The demographics of the general psych ward patients this time were considerably older and disproportionately female in comparison to my first stay. Most were veterans of previous stays, as well as psychiatric drug "adjustment" scenarios.

Because I had gained little benefit from classes and group sessions during my first hospital stay—and indeed had distracted from the benefits others may have gained—I did not go to group therapy or psychodrama sessions.

This stay was far lonelier than the first one. I spent most of it questioning whether embarking on therapy with Dr. Padgett had been a wise decision. Could I ever trust him again? And—as much as I hated to ponder it—I wondered if I were destined to spend the rest of my life in and out of the psych ward, like some of the patients I'd met who were in for the third, fourth, and even tenth time. Was I a lifer? Had I snapped irrevocably—the crazy old aunt in the attic?

Still, as depressing as the hospital ward was, I feared the life that awaited me on the outside even more. It was one I wasn't sure I was equipped to handle now or maybe ever. The news of my release order was, once again, a disappointment, although I was careful not to let Dr. Padgett know.

∞

After my release, I proceeded to act more out of control than ever. I carried around a renewed skepticism and resentment of Dr. Padgett and a heightened fear that I had been rendered irrevocably insane—something I also blamed on the doctor. Therapy sessions followed a consistent pattern. I was either belligerent, defensive, and hostile, attacking everything that Dr. Padgett said. Or I was numb, without emotion. I'd cross my arms and state flatly that therapy was a waste of time and money, and I had nothing to talk about. Dr. Padgett was pressing even harder to get to the early childhood issues, and I resisted him with all the fury I could muster. I not only threatened my own life but also threatened to tell both the American Medical Association and the media that he was an incompetent fraud, something I sincerely believed.

"My father was right about you shrinks," I told him. "You are nothing more than a bunch of greedy quacks, screwing with people's heads and trying to get people hooked on you."

It was hard to remember that there had ever been soothing moments and harder yet to figure out why, despite all the hatred I felt toward him, I was still paying $120 a session, three days a week, to see him. I couldn't imagine life without him. It was too late to walk away now, I thought. I was already hooked and convinced that the only way out of this downwardly spiraling trap was to die.

Clearly the therapy had lost its stride. We were rehashing the same issues, and I was throwing up explosive roadblocks to the exploration of anything new. I was quickly losing confidence, not only in the process, but also in myself.

Thus Dr. Padgett suggested a more intensive form of therapy: use of the couch. The couch, the therapist in a chair vaguely nodding, the patient on her back, staring at the ceiling. It was the epitome of the psychotherapy stereotype. Vienna-style. At the beginning of the next session, I headed straight for the couch.

"Umm, this is weird," I said, staring at the ceiling to spot its imperfections and distract myself from a surprising jolt of anxiety. "Dr. Padgett? Are you there?"

"Yes," I heard his voice, the gentle tonic. "I'm here, right here."

I was surprised by how much his words reassured me. Without the eye contact, I felt strangely isolated. This, indeed, was more intense than I'd thought it would be.

"Dr. Padgett?"

"Yes."

"What do I do here? I mean, what am I supposed to say?" Anxiety was beginning to overwhelm me.

"Say anything that comes to your mind. Just relax. I'm

here. Just say what's on your mind."

After a short period of silence, a vision flashed in my mind. I began to whimper. I wanted to stop, but I couldn't.

"It's okay," he said in a hypnotic voice. "What's happening right now?"

"I'm in my room." I was breathing heavily, my heart pounding. I began to sweat. "Looking out my window. It's black out there. Total darkness. Scary. And I'm thinking about what happens when I die, about where I was before I was born, and it's really scaring me. What was I before I was born?"

"How old are you?"

"I'm little. Maybe six." I could feel myself starting to hyperventilate.

"It's okay. I'm here. Why don't you go tell someone? Why don't you go get your parents?"

"I can't! They'll get so mad at me. I'm a baby—afraid of the dark. I think about such stupid things anyway. They hate that. They're already mad at me. I can't bother them anymore. It's late, they'd . . . they'd . . ."

I was visibly shaking by now.

"It's okay. I'm here. What would they do?"

"I have to go to the bathroom. Really bad."

"So why don't you?"

"Because I can't leave my room. I'm afraid. He's in his underwear; he's mad; he told me he didn't want to see my goddamned face anymore tonight if I know what's good for me. He'll see me; he'll . . . he'll . . ."

"What will he do?"

"He'll take out the belt. He told me to shut up and go to bed. I *have* to stay here. I'm too scared."

"Too scared to go to the bathroom when you need to?"

"He told me to shut up and go to bed. I can't leave here.

I'm scared! I kind of wish I could be dead, but I can't because I don't know what happens to dead people. I don't know where I came from."

"Haven't you talked to them about death? About how much it scares you?"

"I can't! Grandpa just died. They don't wanna talk about it. She cries all the time; he never cries at all. No one talks about it. They tell me I think too much, and that's bad. Very bad. I just think I'm too smart for my own good, but I'm not that smart. I just want to be the center of attention. I can't tell them! I can't go to the bathroom! I can't even die. I'm too scared. Please help me!"

"It's okay. You're here in my office, and I'm with you. These are feelings, that's all. The feelings can't hurt you. You aren't there anymore; you're here. And you're safe with me."

My breathing slowed a bit.

"So you're feeling very frightened. You want to die, but you're afraid of it because you aren't sure what happens. You need to go to the bathroom, but you're afraid to do that too. So what happens? What do you do with these feelings?"

"I . . . I . . . I can't tell you that."

"Why can't you tell me that?"

"Because it's a dirty, horrible, filthy, disgusting sin, and I'll burn in hell for it."

"There's nothing a six-year-old can do to make her burn in hell, but if you don't want to tell me, it's okay."

As if I didn't hear him, I continued. "Daddy caught me once, started snapping the belt. Told me how dirty and shameful I was. Told me if he ever caught me doing something that shameful again, he'd use it on me."

"The belt?"

I nodded in tears.

"Did you feel ashamed?"

"Yes! It was really bad. I . . . I . . . I was playing with myself. I was masturbating. I'm gonna die and go to hell! Grandma's looking down on me, saying how nasty and shameful I am. She was a saint, and I'm horrible, and she hates me!"

"Does it feel pleasurable to masturbate?"

"Yes! That's what's so bad about it. I know it's nasty and sinful. It's shameful. But I like doing it. I can't stop. I do it every night, really quiet. Sneaky. I'm really bad."

"No, you weren't bad. You were very afraid, so you were doing something to mix some pleasurable feelings to drown out the terrible ones so you could stand it. There's nothing wrong with that. Nothing shameful or bad. You were only six, doing what you needed to do in a very scary place."

I was crying in a nearly piercing wail by then, flooded with feelings of the scene, almost trapped in it.

"We only have ten minutes left in the session," said Dr. Padgett. "Why don't you go ahead and sit up. That's good."

Looking in his eyes, finally, I was transfixed by them. He wasn't crying, like me, nor visibly anguished as I was. But even through the blank screen of his face, I could see the sadness in his eyes and felt a rebirth of connection. We'd been through something together, something intense and shameful to me, and he'd stood by me, guiding me through it. He hadn't laughed, judged, scolded—or left me.

"You need to remember," he said, "that what you just experienced are memories. Of the past. They feel very shameful to you, but they weren't shameful at all. The only people who deserve to feel some shame are your parents for making you feel that way. You're an adult now; they can't hurt you like that anymore. You aren't so dependent on them as you were then. This is the present. And you're with me

73

now. It's safe here. It took a lot of courage to endure what you just did now and what you did then. You survived it. You made it. You grew to be an adult. You should be proud."

I was completely drained and numb from the entire ordeal. Words couldn't find their way out of my mouth, but I could have listened to him forever. When the time was up, I tried to burst out of the room, still crying, but Dr. Padgett stopped me. He bent the rules. The session went on for over an hour, delaying the next patient. As I was still visibly shaken, he offered to let me collect myself in an adjacent conference room while he saw his waiting patient. But I declined. The scene was still all too real for me, and I had trouble negotiating the blurry line between past and present. I just wanted to get out of there, as far from that couch and those memories as possible.

Choking in a heavy fog of emotion, I headed to the hospital parking lot, which was cluttered with a dizzying array of detours, barricades, and yellow caution lights to facilitate a major expansion. After starting my car, I proceeded to crash into every wooden barricade, smashing them to pieces—energized and accelerating at the sickening sound of scraping metal and splintering wood.

It was the only time we ever tried the couch. I was neither emotionally ready nor stable enough to handle the intensity. Still, the lid had been taken off the desperately guarded Pandora's box of my early childhood. And I was about to face a past I had denied for years, a reality I had feared so much that even death had seemed preferable. Indeed, the notion of death was comforting in comparison.

∞

74

The shattered barricades were only the beginning of a rapid descent out of reality and into loss of control.

I was more caustic, sarcastic, and belligerent than ever in sessions as I tried desperately to slam the lid down on the past. I was barely functioning at home, shrieking obscenities, hurling objects at the wall, sometimes writhing on the floor in howling agony, as a stunned and frightened pair of children looked on and a helpless Tim feared what might happen next. About the only stability the kids had was at the babysitter's.

I was more convinced than ever that I had snapped and insanity had taken over permanently. And I was just as convinced that it was Dr. Padgett's fault. I hated him—at least, I fervently wanted to hate him—and yet, the angrier and more erratic I became, the more I felt I couldn't survive without him. Not even between sessions.

It was becoming a nightly ritual. I'd go off like a detonated explosive, and in the aftermath of the tirades and vicious acts of self-destruction, I would immediately call Dr. Padgett. I wanted him to see me this way, to know how crazy and despicable I was, to know how crazy he'd made me by toying with the past.

Secretly, more than anything, I wanted him to put me back in the stress unit. I was safe there.

It was a shameful, embarrassing feeling, one I did not dare share with Dr. Padgett or anyone else. Who could possibly want to be on the psych floor instead of at home with family? What kind of a sick, twisted, and pathetic individual would want to be stripped of the adult freedoms of coming and going as she pleased?

Horrified by these secret desires, but nonetheless compelled by them, I expressed them in an indirect fashion. If I was destructive enough—could clearly display my utter insanity—Dr. Padgett would have to put me there.

Chapter 5

I'd been outside the house raking leaves when Tim called out to me from the front porch.

"Rachel! Telephone!"

Damnit, I thought. I'll never get these stupid leaves raked up.

"It's Dr. Padgett."

I dropped the rake as my heart raced with excitement. Imagine, Dr. Padgett calling *me!* Maybe he wanted to tell me how worried sick he was about me. Maybe I'd convinced him to admit me on the psych floor again. I ran as quickly as I could and breathlessly picked up the phone.

But he spoke neither of worry nor of hospital wards. He was calling to say he wanted Tim to accompany me to my next session. I was confused and disappointed. Why did he want Tim there? As it was, I only had the doctor to myself for three painfully short fifty-minute "hours" a week—not nearly enough. The last thing I wanted was to be forced to share my time with Dr. Padgett with Tim. I was overwhelmed with jealousy until a possibility came to mind. Maybe he wanted Tim there to drive the car home if he chose to admit me as an inpatient.

I wished Tuesday was now so I could find out.

∞

Tim pretended to focus on a pamphlet about depression as he fidgeted in the waiting room. I stared at him with burning resentment. This wasn't a trip to the obstetrician. He didn't belong here. It was *my* place. Tim knew this, as I'd been griping about it since Dr. Padgett's call.

The doctor appeared with his customary broad smile and gave Tim a firm handshake. *He shook Tim's hand!* I seethed with envy. Dr. Padgett had never ever so much as touched my hand. He strictly prohibited any physical contact whatsoever (another of his many rules), and here he was shaking Tim's hand.

The doctor invited both of us into his office. By then I was ready to explode. Dr. Padgett sat behind his immaculate desk instead of his usual chair.

Then he began speaking to both of us. "As you both know, Rachel has been completely out of control these past few weeks. Losing contact with reality. Losing awareness of her responsibilities. Every act of self-destruction just seems to fuel this; to make it worse . . ."

My ears perked up. This had all the earmarks of a preadmission announcement.

". . . I just can't be available all the time, and neither can you, Tim. This is becoming a dangerous situation . . ."

I crossed my fingers. This was music to my ears. Please

put me back in the ward, Dr. Padgett, please!

". . . which is completely unacceptable. Rachel, you have it within yourself to regain and maintain control. But you aren't doing that. I can't conduct psychoanalysis with a child in tantrum. You have to participate too. You have to be able to find some insights. And you can't do that when you've lost all control. I'm going to have to draw the line here. If you can't get it together, therapy just can't have any benefit. It's accomplishing nothing and costing a lot of money. If you can't bring yourself to at least some degree of rational reality, I see no other choice but to temporarily suspend our therapy."

Numb weightlessness and shock consumed me, a knot of nausea balling in my stomach. A stinging sensation as if I had been slapped in the face. Hard. I had really blown it. I'd pushed too far, and now Dr. Padgett was bailing out. How could he? *I ought to kill myself,* I fumed. *It would serve the sonofabitch right for leading me on and then dumping me.*

Tim, meanwhile, was open-jawed in near panic, probably wondering how he could possibly manage my uncontrollable outbursts on his own. He, too, in a short time, had come to rely on Dr. Padgett.

As if sensing this, Dr. Padgett continued firmly, "I told you, Rachel, that I will not abandon therapy, and I won't. This is a temporary break I'm talking about, just until you can show me you're ready to be an active part of therapy. If you can't manage that and your behavior becomes a threat to your own life or your family, I will commit you. But not to this hospital. If you can't afford another stay and your insurance limit is up, it may have to be the state hospital."

State hospital! I gulped hard. The government-funded state hospital was a chilling nightmare. I'd be trapped with felons, junkies, and psychotics. Those scary people with rusty grocery carts filled with crumpled newspapers, mumbling to themselves. I shuddered at the thought of being locked up in the closest thing to a prison not run by a warden.

Dr. Padgett continued to lob bombshells. If I were placed in the state or any other hospital, therapy would come to a temporary halt until I was released. He would refer me to another competent psychiatrist to make rounds visits and monitor medications. Dr. Padgett would continue to consult and closely follow my progress, but we would have no direct contact until I was released and my self-control had significantly improved—as long as that might take. At the state hospital, there would be no insurance company demands to release me.

In the interim, my constant after-hours emergency calls to him had been a privilege I had grossly abused. Taking pains to preface that this was not based on any inconvenience to him, he explained that the constant calls were undermining my ability to control my own behavior. Until further notice, he limited me to one call per week. Period.

I was stunned, as was Tim, at the hard-line stance taken by this gentle man. Clearly Dr. Padgett meant business. There was no doubt in either of our minds that the doctor would follow through on everything he said if he felt it were necessary. White-faced and shaking, I tried to open my mouth and say something, to cry, to protest—anything. But nothing came out.

"This isn't cruelty, Rachel," Dr. Padgett said, maintaining his firm edge. "You might think that it is. But it isn't a punishment, and I'm not abandoning you. The more you lose control, the worse it gets. You're playing with fire here. Therapy isn't a luxury for you. It is a matter of life or death."

His voice softened a bit. "I care about you very much," he said. "I think I've shown you that. I'll do whatever I have to do, no matter how harsh it might seem to you right now, to act in your best interests, to protect you and your family from your biggest threat—yourself. I'm not going to sugarcoat or play games with this. This is your life we're talking about here. I made a promise to stay with you through the worst of times. And I'm keeping it."

Dr. Padgett made his points compellingly and transformed the course of our therapy in a single consultation that lasted less than thirty minutes. It would be years until I fully comprehended the courage that his stand had entailed. It had been a tremendous risk on his part, given my erratic state of mind at the time. I could have chosen that abbreviated but shocking session as the catalyst for suicide or as a reason to terminate therapy completely—dumping him before he dumped me first (which I was convinced was inevitable).

However, it worked. Many more moments of suicidal ideation would come, many more angry rages. Through all of them, however, I would somehow manage to maintain at least some contact with reality, albeit with only a precarious link at times.

That single abbreviated session, nearly four months after our first meeting, was when the real work of psychoanalysis began in earnest.

∞

Inherent in our work together was delving into the issues of childhood. Still, it was difficult for me to look past the airbrushed portrait of my childhood. I clung to it in desperation to avoid the hell it had really been. I had invented my own version and repeated it so frequently that it had become my truth. I had been the favored child, the precious baby of the family. Daddy's little girl, the highest achiever, the one my parents were most proud of.

Mine had been a fortunate childhood, wanting for nothing. I'd had the advantage of the best private schools. Dad took care of everything for us kids. I'd always perceived myself as lucky. I'd been convinced that any internal anguish I might have felt was because I was somehow born defective. It was the only way I could explain living amid all this richness and love yet being unable to fully appreciate it.

Okay, so maybe Dad had pulled out the belt here and there. He'd raised his voice, said some things, lost his temper. But he'd been an important man, providing well for us and dealing with the daily stresses of a successful business. I'd been proud of him. He'd been strict, maybe sometimes a little too strict, but he'd done so with the best of intentions, not wanting us to grow to be "too big for our britches." He hadn't hit me as much as he did the others. I was Daddy's little girl.

And yes, Mom had gotten upset a lot too. Her strikes hadn't been as powerful as Dad's, so she'd thrown things. Sometimes she had hysterical tirades and tearful fits that didn't seem to make sense. But once again, these had been directed more frequently at my older siblings than me. There had been lots of feigned illnesses. Lots of times she'd enlisted Dad to take over and mete out the punishment. I hadn't thought too much of this. That was just the way Mom had been. She was weak, perhaps, but harmless. And often I'd been in the position, as the youngest child, for her to confide in me about the great pain caused to her by my older brothers and sisters. This role that had made me feel special and strong. She'd needed me.

Case closed, Dr. Padgett. My childhood wasn't perfect, but whose was?

Dr. Padgett, however, knew that there was much more to my childhood than I would dare recall. He also knew that if I didn't face the truth, I would never be free.

It was a difficult task indeed, as my loyalties, by then, were divided. I'd grown to depend on Dr. Padgett as much as I had depended on my parents. I felt as if, somehow, I was being forced to choose. It was a painful dilemma.

"I love them, Dr. Padgett," I told him, "and I know they love me. How could I feel that way still if it had been so horrible back then?"

Whereupon, he told me the duck-test story.

"Some scientists were conducting an experiment," he said, "trying to gauge the impact of abuse on children. Ducks, like people, develop bonds between mother and young. They call it imprinting. So the scientists set out to test how that imprint bond would be affected by abuse.

"The control group was a real mother duck and her ducklings. For the experimental group, the scientist used a mechanical duck they had created—feathers, sound, and all—which would, at timed intervals, peck the ducklings with its mechanical beak. A painful peck, one a real duck would not give. They varied these groups. Each group was pecked with a different level of frequency. And then they watched the ducklings grow and imprint bond with their mother.

"Over time," he went on, "the ducklings in the control group would waddle along behind their mother. But as they grew, there would be more distance between them. They'd wander and explore.

"The ducklings with the pecking mechanical mother, though, followed much more closely. Even the scientists were stunned to discover that the group that bonded and followed most closely was the one that had been pecked repeatedly with the greatest frequency. *The more the ducklings were pecked and abused, the more closely they followed.* The scientists repeated the experiment and got the same results."

It was a compelling story that resonated within me. Even I had to admit the possibility that my fierce loyalty to my parents may not have been because I wasn't abused, but because I *had been*. It was frightening. My airbrushed memories of the past hid a reality I'd spent a lifetime avoiding, a truth so painful that I had considered death to be a preferable option to facing it. My father hadn't spared me because I was Daddy's little girl. It was because he worked such long hours and because I had witnessed so much I had become adept at avoiding him. Often his explosive violence had been irrational and triggered by the slightest provocation: a facial expression he found disrespectful, tears he didn't want to see, any expression of emotion he didn't have patience for. And the rules changed all the time. Something that could bring him to smile or laugh one day could provoke him to angrily pull off his belt a few days or hours later.

In truth I'd been unable to completely avoid his explosive temper either. I had just become a master of concealing emotion, making myself virtually invisible when I thought I saw an explosion coming. I blamed my own inadequacies when I failed to escape.

Dad had been far harsher on his daughters than his sons, particularly verbally. To a man who coveted control and saw any emotion, particularly tears, as weakness, his daughters could provoke the worst in him. In his mind women were weak, manipulative, overemotional, and inferior. The special bond I'd felt with him was not as Daddy's little girl, but as my best attempt at being Daddy's little boy. This realization helped explain why I had always hated being female.

Adopting the hatred of femininity from my father, I'd viewed my mother this way as well. Granted, she could be nurturing at times, and sometimes I could feel great love for her. But I could not recall having ever respected her. I'd seen her as everything negative Dad claimed was inherent in being female. And I'd vowed to be nothing at all like her.

It was hardest of all to admit that my mother had a great impact on my life, which continued to affect me years after I'd left home. She'd given the appearance that Dad was in control when all the while she'd been a matriarch in her own right, a more powerful figure than I'd cared to admit. Highly dependent upon my father for many of the simplest tasks or crises, she didn't want to share him with any of us. So she took the role of gatekeeper, a medium of sorts, listening to the things we wanted to tell him, the feelings we wanted to share, and responded by telling us her own rendition of "how Dad felt," as if Dad could not speak for himself. She'd created distorted or fictitious stories, twisting our words to Dad so that he would come home and discipline us upon her command. She'd helped plant the seeds for my airbrushed portrait of life as it had been, repeating the mantras so often I believed them to be true.

It had been critical to her to get as much of Dad's time as was possible with his workaholic lifestyle. Thus she had feigned illnesses and twisted events that had occurred before his arrival home to become terrible things "we had done to her." Then she quietly left the room as Daddy pulled off the belt—the knight in shining armor rushing to the aid of the damsel in distress. She'd done the same thing with me and my siblings, pitting one against the other, endlessly comparing and contrasting and playing upon the natural rivalries until we were a family of brothers and sisters who seldom associated with each other. She'd made herself the center of it all. She, too, had shared Dad's view of the inherent inferiority of females and thus had openly favored her sons; she viewed her daughters as competition for Dad's affection.

Dreams and fantasies smashed to pieces. Violent and angry defenses turned to seemingly inconsolable sorrow. Why had Dr. Padgett insisted upon opening this box? So what if it was the truth? What purpose had it served? Why couldn't he have left well enough alone?

Now I was not just filled with self-loathing and anger, but also despair. The bubble had been irrevocably burst, and I feared my vulnerability. I began to wonder if any feelings or beliefs I had were genuine or if everything was an illusion.

∞

One day during this period I was lying in bed and began to examine my thighs. They appeared huge, dimpled, and growing. Fat. Soft. Weak. Like Mom. How had I lost track of this? When had I lost self-control? Filled with disgust, I vowed that this, at least, was one thing about myself I could change. Dad had despised fat daughters, and I knew that Dr. Padgett must secretly harbor the same disgust. Thus a little before the Thanksgiving holiday, my diet began.

At five feet, six inches, and 140 pounds, I knew I needed to lose at least ten of them. Perhaps fifteen or twenty. I'd been cautious about diets ever since the adolescent episode when my weight had plunged to a skeletal 75 pounds. I had managed to lose the "baby fat" after childbirth successfully without going to extremes. I was convinced that this time I would be able to manage as well.

Chapter 6

Early winter was a time of hard work. To help dig our way out of the financial hole, I did as much freelance accounting work as I could. I stepped up my volunteer activities in the church. For once the house was immaculate. I purchased several of the latest exercise videos and faithfully worked out to them each day, often doing two or more workouts in succession.

This same fierce motivation and drive became a part of therapy. Determined to make the most effective use of every session, I'd stopped arguing with Dr. Padgett. I worked hard to reveal my thoughts and fears, explore the past, and understand the insights offered by the doctor and myself.

The work of therapy was not confined to sessions. Nearly each day I would write for hours, reflecting and analyzing even further. I would often stay up until one or two in the morning preparing for therapy by reading psychoanalytic books and becoming well-versed in its terminology.

On the diet front, the scale was moving in the right

direction. I was losing weight and was filled with drive, energy, and a sense of control. Everything was coming together. I could feel the "old me" returning, the "can-do" me. Transformed and confident, I was determined I would overcome my problems. I had the will.

∞

In sessions Dr. Padgett began to rehash old terms, introduce new ones, and point out examples each time one occurred. Old academic terminology started making sense.

"Transference" was happening when I made Dr. Padgett a substitute for someone else in my life—an important person from my early years when I'd been afraid to respond. By uncovering these buried feelings, we could explore them more closely.

The "blank screen" explained why Dr. Padgett maintained relative anonymity and lacked emotional reactions. The less he revealed about himself, the more transference was fostered.

"Black-and-white thinking" was based on absolute extremes—natural in very young children but unsettling in adult relationships. I saw people as either good or evil. When they were "good," I vaulted them to the top of a pedestal. They could do no wrong, and I loved them with all of my being. When they were "bad," they became objects of scorn and revenge.

In relationships with those closest to me, the "good" and "bad" assessments could alternate wildly, sometimes from one hour to the next. The unrealistic expectations of perfection that came with the good-guy pedestal were destined to be unfulfilled, which led to disappointment and a sense of betrayal.

"All-or-nothing thinking" and "splitting" came in tandem with black-and-white thinking. Every strong feeling was not only absolute, but eternal. It didn't matter if a person close to me had occupied the pedestal ten minutes ago and been the object of my abundant love. When the emotions changed, it was as if that love had never existed and the hatred I felt today would be the way I felt forever. The means by which I coped with these alternating extremes was called splitting. If I couldn't get what I needed or expected from either Tim or Dr. Padgett because I was in the throes of bitter anger at one of them, I would turn to the other one in his stead. It was the only way I could bear such wildly vacillating emotions about the people to whom I was closest and expected the most.

"Projection" occurred when I assumed my thoughts were their thoughts, my motivations their motivations. If I angrily accused Dr. Padgett of hating me and wishing I'd just "snap out of it," it was because I hated myself and wished I could snap out of it. I was most likely to project my deepest fears and feelings of self-hatred because they were simply too disturbing to acknowledge within myself.

When a person close to me fell off the good-guy pedestal, my initial reaction (through the clouded eyes of my impossible expectations) was rage and betrayal. I felt the horrifying fear of abandonment. Dr. Padgett described the anger coupled with the desperate clinging as "I hate you, don't leave me."

All of these theoretical terms made sense. I became adept at pointing them out and expounding upon them with intellectual ease. I was a prized pupil aiming to please. If I could grasp all the terminology and processes, I could intellectually conquer my problems.

Thinking came easily to me. But it also kept me at an emotional distance. It was as if I were watching a play, discussing the plot, finding the meaning, but forgetting that I was the central character, and that it was real.

This strategy was not lost on Dr. Padgett, who began to mention that the intellectualizing was actually a form of defense. I didn't want to feel. I was using a barricade of jargon to repress all of the childhood feelings and hide behind a facade of sophisticated adulthood.

∞

By the time I'd reached my goal of 120 pounds, I knew that my "diet" wasn't like the two I'd successfully managed after childbirth. Instead it was an echo from my anorexia of 1978: the isolation, obsession, and the detachment from relationships in favor of frenetic activity. The number on the scale told me it was time to begin eating regularly again. Yet the mere sight of a plateful of a nondiet meal filled me with nausea. I couldn't bring myself to eat it, or I would just sample a small portion and shove the plate away, claiming I was full. Eating a candy bar would lead to hours of unbearable self-recrimination as I watched my thighs "expand" before my very eyes. The only relief came with skipping the next meal and doing a triple workout. It was a penance of sorts. Only a scale reading the same or lower granted me absolution.

Tim, aware of my adolescent history and postbaby diets, was concerned. He began to ask if I was taking this one too far. So I began lying, dumping platefuls of mashed potatoes in the trash when he wasn't looking, carefully obscuring it behind a paper towel or discarded cereal box. I'd claim I had the flu or a big snack right before dinner. Lies.

I didn't need a psychiatrist to tell me what this was. I wasn't in denial. I was aware of it but was unable to control it.

Feeling in the grips of something beyond my control, I continued my pattern of openness with Dr. Padgett and filled him in on my discovery.

"Dr. Padgett," I said, "I know I'm at a normal weight right now. I don't look like I'm emaciated or anything. But I'm anorexic, and I know it. I can remember it so clearly from back then, and this is the exact same thing. What do I do?" Humble penitent to the confessor again, I was turning myself in. I expected my father's threatening reaction, my friends' nagging, or Tim's fear.

Perhaps Dr. Padgett knew how I would react to any of these—see the threats as persecution, ignore the nagging or invest it with ill motives, or revel in the fear. So he didn't respond as I had expected. He didn't tell me that I, of all people, should know better and demand that I "better snap to reality and start eating."

Instead he saw the re-emergence of anorexia as evidence that I was, indeed, repressing a child within. And that the child was reacting vehemently. The solution to this most recent problem was not to give lectures on eating habits, but to explore the emotions of my inner child. This anorexic episode was not a coincidence, but just the latest form of defense. Not wanting to eat was linked to not wanting to feel. "Think of your buried fears and irrational feelings as being like those little roly-poly bugs," he said. "You know, the ones that crawl around under rocks. When you turn a rock over and expose them to light, they quickly form a little hard-shell ball. When the threat of exposure is gone, they quickly run under the closest rock.

"You have painful and frightening feelings within you,

so frightening that you'd rather suffer indefinitely, sometimes rather die, than look at them in the light of day. Your defenses are the rocks you hide under. Therapy is a process that seeks to put your worst fears, the roly-poly bugs, into the light, which is exactly what a part of you wants to do. The part you've been displaying here recently.

"But it isn't the only part of you. The other part is so desperately afraid that she'll do nearly anything to avoid the scrutiny. So she finds more rocks the bugs can hide under. The rock of rage. The rock of I-don't-give-a-shit-about-anything. The 'fuck you, Dr. Padgett, I hate you' rock. The rock of suicidal ideation. And now the latest one, the rock of anorexia. This isn't a separate illness, Rachel; it's just one more rock to hide under, one more place to avoid facing the same feelings."

Who is this other part? Who is this inner child he's always talking about? I hate that child! She has destroyed me at every turn, intent on sabotage. She wants to kill me. Now she's trying to destroy therapy just when I've regained control and settled down to some hard work. She wants to kill me. Well, I want to kill her!

"I never said therapy was going to be easy," Dr. Padgett continued. "I never said it wasn't going to be frustrating, stopping and starting, and that sometimes one step forward will be followed by two steps back. Each time we turn over a rock and expose those bugs, those feelings—the bugs—are going to run to another rock and hide.

"But one day, Rachel, there won't be any rocks left. One day we'll turn over the last rock. With no place left to hide, the bugs, the feelings, will scamper away for good. And you'll experience a life you've never believed you could have.

"The rock of anorexia is a big one, very intense. It

might seem as if all is lost and things are getting worse. The fewer rocks there are, the more bugs will be found under the ones that remain. But we're getting closer to those feelings, Rachel. Much closer. Together, the two of us are going to lift up this rock too, like we have all the others so far. This isn't a time to run; it's a time to feel."

Only if that wicked little child lets me, Dr. Padgett. Only if she lets me.

∞

I weighed 110 pounds. The critical mark. Two conflicting parts of me were in a virtual war over the needle on the scale, which had stubbornly clung to 110 pounds for well over two weeks. Perhaps a few pounds under where it really should be, I thought as I stood on the scale—something I was doing several times a day now. But at least I'm maintaining my weight. The episode is over, and I can move on with therapy. But another part of me was overtaking this rational part of me. This "me," restless at the frozen mark on the scale, considered the plateau a failure. This "normal" weight was a mark to be surpassed. Only an increased dedication to the diet and working out could get me to where I needed to be. I was aware of the life-or-death ramifications of self-starvation. But my alter ego of sorts was equally convinced that losing more was a matter of life and death.

Ultimately that other part began to win, and I lost weight once again. Occasionally I passed out, once in front of a client. More than once I was gripped by stabbing chest pains, most likely the result of a panic attack. It reminded me that singer Karen Carpenter had died not of actual starvation, but of a heart attack resulting from her diet. I was becoming frightened as I realized this diet could kill me. It was like being in a struggle for survival against a murderous foe, except I was the one who was fighting for survival *and* I was also the murderer within.

"Dr. Padgett," I pleaded in tears at a session in early February, "this inner child, she's taking over. Can't you do something about her? I can't do anything anymore. I know this is dangerous, but I can't stop her. I want to stop the diet. I really do. Help me."

"I can't stop anyone, Rachel," he answered. "Only you can. You say you want to stop, but a part of you doesn't want to stop. There is no 'her.' There's only you. And you are the only one who can control what you're doing. I can't help you. You have to help yourself."

"Fine, then, fine!" I roared at him, as if someone had flipped a switch and I had been transformed into a completely different being than the one who'd pleaded and begged for help just a moment ago. "You sonofabitch! I don't need your help. I want to take that goddamned inner child and strangle the bitch!"

I was trembling by now. I'd maintained my composure with Dr. Padgett for dozens of sessions. Yet here I was, telling him off, the rage reappearing with a vengeance. I was blowing it once again.

"You can't strangle that inner child," he pointed out calmly. "That child is you. And the only way to destroy her is to destroy yourself."

"Well, she's destroying me," I retorted angrily. "Manipulative little piece of shit. Why can't she just snap out of it and deal with things like a . . ." I stopped short, not wanting to give Dr. Padgett an opening.

"*Like a man?* That's what you were about to say, wasn't

94

it? You want her to snap out of it and show some guts like a man?"

I didn't reply, just sat there, clenching and unclenching my fists, tapping my foot on the floor, glaring at him.

"That's what your father would have said, isn't it? Right down to the last word. To a scared little girl, afraid to stand up for herself. He'd want that little girl, whom he saw as weak and manipulative, to snap out of it and act like a man."

"Fuck you, asshole."

"Ah, another thing your father would have said."

"You don't know your ass from a hole in the ground. You wouldn't know what it's like to be a man if it came up and bit you on the ass. You're a shrink, goddamnit, a fairy profession."

"It's your father talking again."

"What are you trying to do, Padgett? Piss me off enough so that I'll strangle you? You think I couldn't kill your sorry little ass? Think again, you pathetic little faggot. I could probably kill you with my own bare hands. I know exactly where you live. I looked you up in the county tax records. Surprised? You think you'd fool me with an unlisted number? Well, the county's got your name and number, and now I do. I could come to your house in the middle of the night and murder you in cold blood—your wife and kids too. You have no idea who you're fucking with here, absolutely no idea."

My eyes were burning into his, but I could not detect the slightest reaction of fear, intimidation, or even anger. All I could see was sadness.

"I'm not your father, Rachel. What you just said is what you wished you could have done to him when he was abusing

95

you. You wished you could have attacked him back or killed him to stop him."

"I could kill him, you, or anyone else I want to, you fool. I could go out and buy a gun and blow all of you to pieces in a single afternoon."

"You could do that now, maybe. But you couldn't do that then. You were mad enough, perhaps, but you were too vulnerable, too young, too weak to overpower him."

"Don't you *dare* call me weak, Padgett! You wanna fight right now, you asshole? You wanna see who would win? I'd kick you in the balls and have your guts ripped right out of your throat before you'd even feel the pain."

Still no sign of fear or anger from the man.

"You were a child. A child at the mercy of her parents. He could overpower you if he chose to. You weren't the one who could kill with your bare hands. Your father could. And you feared that more than anything. Totally vulnerable. So angry but so unable to do anything about it. And so afraid."

I remained silent.

"If I had been your father, you wouldn't have had to be afraid like that. I wouldn't have laid a finger on you to harm you. Most good parents, most good fathers would never dream of harming their children. Your father was physically strong, maybe, but as a man, he was terribly weak. He couldn't control his emotions, so, instead, he took it out on a little girl like you: too small and too young to defend herself."

The grip of the raging tyrant left me, as if it had been exorcised, the pleading, helpless little girl left in its place.

"Please help me," I said, in a tiny voice. "Dr. Padgett, I'm so scared. I don't know what took over me. I didn't want to say all of those terrible things. I didn't want to hurt you or scare you away. I need you, Dr. Padgett. Please help me.

What's wrong with me? Am I really crazy? She's taking over."

"Who is taking over?" he asked gently, as if to a child.

"The other one. The mean one. The one that always says the terrible things and gets me in trouble. That part of me. She's the one trying to starve me to death. And she's blaming it on me. It isn't fair."

I listened to myself speaking, stunned. Truly, I thought, I must be losing it.

"There's only one you, Rachel. Just one. You're fragmenting here. Dissociating."

"What does that mean?"

Dr. Padgett went on to explain the terms. Fragmenting, or dissociating, occurred when a person did not have a fully integrated personality. Different aspects of the personality would emerge, depending upon the situation. It was a patchwork means of coping.

When gripped by fear, the abusive tough-acting persona would come to fend off the threat and reduce the feelings of helplessness and vulnerability. When she was overwhelmed by the need to be close to someone, the pleading, begging little girl emerged. In many situations, the adult sensibilities and rationality were present, and thus the personalities would be somewhat integrated and subdued. But in times of intense feelings, one of the other two personas would step in, overwhelming me.

It wasn't a multiple personality disorder type of dissociation, he explained, because I was always conscious, at least on some level, of what I was doing and saying. A person with multiple personality disorder, like Sybil, would not have the conscious awareness I did.

But the dissociation set the stage for a fierce internal conflict as the two inner-child personae, like oil and water, battled each other. One clearly female; one clearly male. It was the legacy of abuse, of trying to please both a father and a mother who despised femininity.

Not all of me was a child, however. Some aspects of my character had managed to grow to a more advanced stage of development than others. I was capable, at many times, of interacting quite functionally in adult situations. It was important to explore the childhood personae in order to better understand and one day integrate them, Dr. Padgett told me, but even more important to remember that I was an adult too. As long as I could retain that adult aspect as I explored the others, I could handle the introspection and ultimately work to become whole. If I lost the adult in me, however, and let either of the child personae completely take over, the results could be disastrous.

∞

Handling the two children within me was far more exhausting than handling the two real children I had. But I could not escape the ongoing battle between the two fragmented creatures inside me. Exploring their natures in sessions had brought new life and energy to them; they never seemed to tire. The adult me, however, was exhausted.

Sessions were almost like séances to me. The words and expressions came out of my own mouth, the body language from my own body. But still I felt inhabited by intruders. I wanted calm. I wanted peace. I didn't want to kill these inner children, but I did fervently wish they'd go away for a while and stop tormenting me.

Meanwhile, the needle on the scale kept leaning left until I had only 103 pounds on my five-foot, six-inch frame.

My bedroom mirror was like the fun house variety. At times the weary "adult" would look into it and be shocked at the sight of my ribs, which were grotesquely protruding. My calves were no larger than my ankles, which made my size-ten feet look abnormally huge. My bony knees nearly as large in circumference as my thighs, two huge knobs connecting brittle sticks. When I would raise my arms, I could see every tendon twitch, the clear outlines of bone. My shoulder blades stuck out so sharply it appeared they were on the verge of severing the skin like a knife. My face was hollow, and my eyes were underlined by dark circles. I was a vision of death.

Until suddenly, that same vision would transform. Those same calves and thighs would expand before my very eyes into cellulite-ridden obesity. My face blew up as if inflated, and I could see a second chin appearing. The knobby knees looked fat. Before I knew it, I would be down-stairs in the living room again, jumping and twisting to the instructions of Jane Fonda, the exhaustion of an hour ago replaced by hyperactivity.

Then the evening would come. Tim couldn't even stand to hold me in his arms anymore, much less make love. I'd lost my appetite for sex long ago anyway. He couldn't bear to feel the sharpness of my bones. He'd tried to be supportive by nagging, coaxing, or getting angry with me. But nothing worked. His wife was wasting away, and he couldn't do any-thing about it.

Finally I made the decision. The adult was too tired to handle this anymore. It was time for more serious action. Now that I was in physical danger, I knew it was time to go back into the hospital for the third time in less than a year. It was a decision not made by a child seeking a place to hide, but by an adult seeking a place that could help me live. This time Dr. Padgett agreed readily. Tim, of course, thought the decision was long overdue.

I told a lot of my friends at the church of my decision. Having seen the visible effects of my illness, they supported me fully, offering to help Tim out with meals and child care, as they had during the first two stays, and to visit me. I notified Jeffrey's preschool teacher and Melissa's part-time babysitter that I'd be going in the hospital. I asked that they let Tim know if the kids seemed to be having difficulties, although I didn't explain the true nature of the illness.

Then, finally, it was time to explain it to the kids. The first two hospitalizations had been rather spontaneous, an escape. This time, however, I realized that whatever happened on the psych floor could be harder than handling the responsibilities of home. It was an adult choice, and I was aware of just how painful this separation would be for the kids. Telling them was one of the hardest things I've ever done.

Melissa, only two, seemed to handle it well, most likely because she could not quite grasp exactly what I'd be doing or how long I would be gone.

Jeffrey, however, at four, *did* understand. He remembered my two prior stays quite vividly. His big blue eyes welled with tears as I sat him on my knee and told him.

"Mommy's going to have to go away for a while, Jeffrey."

"Where, Mommy? To work?"

"No, sweetheart. Mommy's going back to the hospital."

He began to cry and shake his head vigorously, shredding my heart at the realization of how much all of this was hurting him.

"No! No! I don't want you to go!"

By now, I was crying too.

"Jeffrey, I don't want to be away from you either. I love you and Melissa more than anyone else in the world."

"Then don't go."

"I have to go, Jeffrey. Mommy is sick. Not the kind of sick where your throat hurts or your tummy hurts or you throw up. A different kind of sick. The kind of sick that makes Mommy really sad sometimes and really mad sometimes—so sick sometimes she can't even eat because she's too upset. In the hospital my doctor will be there and nurses and other people that can help me get better so I won't be so sad anymore."

"I already know that. Daddy told me that the other times you went away, but you didn't get any better."

It was the uncanny ability of a child to cut straight to the truth.

"This is going to be different, Jeffrey. This time I am going to get better."

Jeffrey looked at me for a moment and then asked, "Mommy, are you going to die?"

How could I do this to my children? What kind of a mother was I?

"No, sweetheart. I'm not going to die. I'm going to get stronger and come back and play with you and read to you and even take you to the zoo."

"Will you let us see you? Will you want us to come there? We won't make you cry or get mad, I promise."

Oh, my God. My heart sank. *The poor little boy has been thinking this is his fault.*

"I want you to come and see me every day. You kids aren't the ones who make me sad or mad. It's the sickness that does that. You kids make me happy. And when I'm in the hospital, I'm going to take a great big picture of you and

Melissa with me and put it right on the nightstand where I can always see it. And when I feel really sad, I'll look at that picture. Seeing you helps make me get better."

There we were. Mommy clutching her child, both of us hugging as tight as we could, both of us in tears. He still didn't want me to go, but I think he at least was able to understand that I wasn't going just to leave him. I was going to get better. Yes, I was going to get better. I had two children who depended on me and a husband who loved me very much. And I was going to do anything it might take to be able to be reunited with them and be the kind of wife and mother they all deserved.

Chapter 7

It was an embarrassing reunion.

I took my bags to my room, placed the gold-framed picture of Tim, Jeffrey, and Melissa on the nightstand, and said my tearful good-byes to Tim and the kids. I ambled down the hallway to the smoking lounge.

Scary. I knew this place all too well.

Joe, a second-shift nurse in his midforties, was standing behind the nurses' station counter, sifting through paperwork. When he looked up, he did a classic double take. Joe, who had a quick wit and crooked grin, had been my favorite nurse the first two stays, not exactly a compliment as all the male nurses tended to be my favorites.

"Rachel! So you've come back to join us in Happy Hotel for another visit. What happened to your butt, milady? It's gone."

My God, it's that obvious, isn't it? Hey, he noticed, how wonderful. The battle continued within.

"Umm, yeah. I kind of went on a diet. Sort of went overboard, I guess. So you've got me back again."

Back again for the third time in a year. Did I really need to do this, or was Dr. Padgett just appeasing me? *I want to go home. I want to stay here forever. I don't know what I want.*

"Well, if you behave yourself and don't stir up too much trouble, I might just let you share one of my peanut butter cups. You're practically invisible, ya know."

Not as invisible as I wish I could be right now, I thought to myself.

∞

"No! I won't!"

Howls from the other bed shook me out of my sleep. The sun was just barely shining through the window. What the hell time was it?

Writhing on the bed next to me was a wisp of an elderly woman, her white hair peeking out from under the covers, clumps of it together, some of it obviously missing— a tiny mess of wrinkles with a voice like a police siren. Two of the graveyard shift nurses were standing over her bed.

"Come on, Alice," one of them said. "You know better than to scream like that. You're going to scare this poor girl out of her wits. Let's change your bedpan, okay?"

Bedpan? God, this is depressing.

"Go away! No! No!"

"That's it, easy does it. We're just going to roll you over. Easy does it. Now see, was that so bad?"

Why are they talking to her like she's three years old?

With the bedpan changed, the small figure in the neighboring bed rolled over and went back to sleep. By then

I was far too awake and disturbed to even think about it.

"You have to excuse Alice," the younger nurse said from the door. "She's not always conscious of what she's doing, and she can be a handful. Let us know if she bothers you. We'll see what we can do."

A handful. Like me. Misunderstood. Like me. Giving up on sleep, I pulled my book off the nightstand and began to read.

"You're a very pretty girl, you know." A voice emerged from the rumpled mound of sheets and blankets a few feet away.

"Excuse me?"

"I said you are a very pretty girl. Pretty eyes, such pretty eyes. I'll bet they just drive the men crazy. So pretty."

What could I say to that? I just sat and listened.

"You know, I used to be very pretty. Just like you. Men. All kinds of men. My sailor boy, oh, he was so handsome! Almost pretty in a way too. Knocked me out of my socks, looking at him in that blue uniform. He used to tell me I was the most beautiful woman in the world. And you know what, honey? I believed him."

Alice was smiling now, the shriveled smile of a woman whose dentures were still sitting on the bathroom sink. Despite her thinning white hair and sagging wrinkled skin, I could still see the wide brown eyes now coming to life. She had the marks of a faded beauty.

"My son put me in here, you know. I loved my high-rise, my condo. And the men, oh honey, the men were everywhere. But he decided I was too old, couldn't handle it anymore, and tried to shove me in one of those old folks' homes. What's your name? Why is such a pretty girl like you in a place like this?"

I told her my name and why I was in the hospital.

"Oh, honey, that's just terrible. You're so pretty, and you've got your whole life ahead of you. And you're so sweet, sitting here listening to this old lady ramble. That picture over there—is that your family?"

"Yes, the little boy is Jeffrey. He's four. And Melissa is two. And the big guy is Tim. He's my husband."

"Oh, honey, they're absolutely beautiful. I'll bet they just love their pretty mommy."

"I guess so."

"And your husband. Wow! What a looker. Just like my sailor. If I were five years younger, honey, you'd have to watch out, 'cause I'd be going right after him. You got a man like that, you better hold on tight."

I couldn't help but grin. "I will, Alice; I will. Tim is a great guy."

"Well, whatever's wrong, I hope it gets better. You're way too sweet and you've got too beautiful of a family to be stuck in a place like this."

I found out later that my conversation with Alice was the first time the woman had communicated with anyone in the hospital except in monosyllabic screams. Even when I was moved down the hall to another section with younger patients, I still made it a point to visit Alice every day. I helped her put on her makeup, and I brushed out her hair. She had fascinating stories: a living history of World War II, the trainloads of soldiers pulling into the station, the glamour of the fifties, her life with the "sailor boy" who'd passed away more than a decade ago.

I watched her slowly come back to life. And with her rebirth, a part of me came to life too. She'd called me sweet, and for once, I had actually been that way. We were the two misfits of the east wing, helping each other.

∞

The flashing lights of the fire truck light up the suburban landscape. The smell of the diesel fumes makes me feel sick.

Daddy's enraged. He's taking charge, demanding to know what happened.

Grandma's looking down, her face through the clouds, a horrible scowl on her usually smiling face. She shakes her head and finger to the earth below and yells, "You are a horrible mother! Shame on you!"

Mommy's crying, her face buried in shame. Daddy and Grandma and the firemen are scolding her relentlessly. She's the center, the martyr of the scene.

And off in the distance stand two little boxes. They look like coffins, no, little wooden figures, immobile, stranded there, masklike, frozen in horror. No one pays any attention to them.

It's my older brother. And me.

The drill sergeant was standing over my bed. For once I was happy to see her. It was two in the morning, and I was sweat-drenched, still shaking and hyperventilating.

"Come on now, Rachel. You're awake now. It was just a dream. You need to calm down."

"It was horrible!" I shrieked through my tears, "Horrible! The fire trucks, and Dad was yelling, and Mom was crying, and Grandma was looking down from the dead shaking her finger. And everyone just left us there. What happened? What did she do? Why were we lying there? What happened? *What did she do to me?*"

"I can't make sense of what you're talking about. It's a nightmare, Rachel, a nightmare. You can tell your doctor about it in the morning. You really need to get some rest."

She let me go into the smoking lounge and have a

cigarette. I tried to go back to sleep, but the same nightmare roused me again. I finally gave up and stayed awake, waiting for morning distractions to take over.

∞

During this hospital visit I couldn't believe the amount of emotional pain I was in. I hadn't remembered that from the first two visits. This time I was saw the anguish in the faces of the other patients on the floor. This wasn't a retreat. Each person was going through his or her own form of personal hell, as was I. It was a hell so furious that it wouldn't leave me alone. I couldn't distract myself. The pain was so piercing I could feel it physically pressing upon my chest. I knew the isolation had been by design, and I knew it was working. I was feeling, intensely feeling, and wondering just how much of it I could take.

∞

The little oak crib with the duckling painted on the side. My crib. Jeffrey's crib. Melissa's crib. Unmistakable.

Mommy's frantic. Mommy's mad. She's screaming. "Shut up! Quit crying!"

I'm hungry, very hungry. So hungry it hurts.

"I can't feed you. It's not time yet. Stop crying! Shut up!"

Angry eyes, reaching hands. I see them. I reach back.

I'm flying! I see the wall. I'm flying!

Everything goes black.

I was hyperventilating and screaming again. The sweat and horror had become a nightly ritual. I'd endured over a week of this. I was so exhausted I could barely stay awake, yet too horrified to sleep. When exhaustion overtook me and I closed my eyes, the nightmares invaded with fierce intensity, the subconscious mind seizing control. It was a hell on earth with no escape, not even through sleep. Numb by day, possessed by night, an unending sequence of nightmares, pummeling me with their fury. I speculated on what happened but could never come to any certain conclusions. What was symbolic, and what was a real memory? One thing was certain: if my parents had actually done any of these things, they would never, not even in their dying days, admit to it.

Most of the nurses, even those whom I'd aggravated before, were supportive through this. They could tell I was sincerely trying this time. In the grips of these nightmares and the anguished tears, the nurses would try their best to comfort and calm me, but only Dr. Padgett and I truly understood the intensity of our therapy and what these dreams might be saying.

∞

It was 2 A.M. again. I hadn't fallen asleep, this time awash in guilt. I had been so caught up in my own little world that I had completely turned my back on my family. I had to see them. I had to see them now. I got up out of bed and went to the nurses' station.

The drill sergeant again. I approached her anyway.

"I need to go home."

"It's two in the morning, Rachel. Please go back to bed," she said flippantly, not bothering to look up from her *Cosmopolitan*.

"Didn't you hear me? I said, I need to go home."

She glanced up, irritated. "I don't have release orders for you. And I'm not about to get them at this time of the morning."

"Call Dr. Padgett then."

"He's not going to release you at two in the morning. As a matter of fact, if you keep trying to pull stunts like this, he might not release you for a long time."

Funny, the first two times I'd been in the ward such words would have been music to my ears. I'd feared release then, a return to the adult life of responsibility. I had wanted to remain a child of sorts, dependent forever. This time, however, the words were a warning. If I didn't straighten my act up and display some self-control to Dr. Padgett, he wouldn't release me. Now, I *wanted* to be released. I wasn't thinking as a child; I was thinking as a mother.

Within a week I was released and back home. There would be plenty more fantasies about being an inpatient. Many times I would long to be back in the safe shelter of the hospital. But my third hospital stay was destined to be my last. It had taken three trips, but finally I had opened myself up to the intensity of my emotions and had actually gained something in my stay—not weight, but insight and the drive to keep moving with the journey to get better.

"You're way too sweet and you've got too beautiful of a family to be stuck in a place like this."

Maybe, just possibly, Alice had been right.

Chapter 8

I'd never placed much stock in the theory that dreams were anything but random entertainment. A jumbled mix of details and snippets of words, sights, and sounds. Meaningless. A horror film or fantasy of the mind that ended with the light of consciousness. Exit the theater, and it's over.

But the nightmares in the hospital didn't end with the credits rolling down the screen. They seized me long after I woke up, haunting me. I could not ignore these messages, and they would not stop until I faced them. My subconscious mind demanded to be heard.

Most of my therapy sessions during my hospital stay and its immediate aftermath were devoted to the feelings these dreams brought about. What was the message? Substance or symbolism? Truth or fiction? Or both?

What could the events have been? What did the flashing lights and my angry and hysterical family mean? Guilt? Retribution? For what? Why were the two little woodenlike figures apart from everyone? Was it abuse? Had things gotten so bad that someone summoned the fire department?

In a family that valued secrecy above all else, even within itself, the details of my early childhood were sketchy. My parents seldom spoke about that era of our family's life, although they spoke freely about later years. Was it just coincidence, or were they withholding dark secrets?

I only knew that it was a particularly stressful time for my parents. My father had been working eighty-hour weeks to get his business off the ground, and my arrival (the fifth child in the family) was unplanned. Worse, I was a girl.

I knew that during my infancy my mother was sick a lot. Psychosomatic illnesses always gripped her in times of great stress. I knew that she had always been a stay-at-home mom, but for some reason, even though all of my older siblings were already in school, they hired a nanny to take care of me for a few years. Why?

The EEGs and MRI and CT scans had all shown that I had some type of lesion and scar tissue on the left side of my brain. We never reached any conclusions. But now I found myself wondering why it was there. Was it an aberration? A fall on the playground? Or was it the legacy of abuse?

These were horrible questions. The possibility of abuse existed, but the only people who would know whether or not it had occurred were my parents. And I knew I could never be certain of their answers even if I directly confronted them. If the speculation were false, they would justifiably deny it. But if it were true, they would also deny it. There was no way I would ever know. Just pondering the reality of that dream was a serious accusation.

After discovering many real memories of my childhood, those I knew had occurred, I was beginning to feel furious toward my parents. The embittered rage of the betrayed. Yet I could not bring myself to condemn them based upon sketchy dreams without firm evidence, evidence I would never have.

Dr. Padgett did not say much at this time. He was cautious not to lead me either way—symbolic dream or memory. As much as I relied upon him now, even a few words could have tilted the balance. Instead he focused on the one thing he believed was real in the dream—the feeling memories. He had always been convinced that, in whatever form it may have taken, my early childhood had been far more abusive than I had imagined. Determining the specifics, he said, was not as important as coming to grips with fact that I was abused, and, above all, feeling the emotions that came with that revelation.

Eating came very hard. But Dr. Padgett did not bring it up, even though I had not gained back a single ounce. He strongly believed that if I could face these fears, eventually the need to be anorexic would dissipate.

For me it was no longer an issue of anorexic body distortion. It was the horror of these feelings, the recognition of a sickening reality so revolting that I lingered on the edge of vomiting.

One day I came perilously close to doing so right on Dr. Padgett's office floor. I was writhing, gagging, the bile rising in my throat as I battled the demons of these feeling memories. I shook and shuddered—every part of my body somehow in motion. I grabbed and twisted my hair and bit my fingers in wild kinetic motion. I was crazed, trying somehow to expel these feelings.

"Sit with them," Dr. Padgett would say calmly but firmly. "Sit with the feelings. Don't act them out. Don't run away. Feel them. You can do it, Rachel. Sit still and put these feelings into words or tears. Share them with me. They're only feelings. No one can hurt you now. I'm right here with you."

Words often eluded me, and I could only manage to howl in pain—the bloodcurdling cries of an infant that jolt the mother, wherever she is, to run to her child's aid. No magic words exist to soothe these cries, and Dr. Padgett didn't try.

Instead he sat.

He listened.

He was present and unconditionally accepting. From behind the blank screen I could see the pain in his eyes as he witnessed my suffering. It was a pain he did not try to hide and one I don't think he could have hidden even if he had wanted to. These feelings transcended words and analysis. They simply needed to be felt. And Dr. Padgett simply needed to be there with me, feeling the pain of a parent watching a child suffer and knowing that only time will make it pass.

We would wind up these sessions of raw, primal emotion—unvested with words because the feelings were so early in origin—by gently bringing me back to adulthood.

After one particularly intense session, he chose to unveil pieces of himself. He had two grown children, a boy and a girl. He would tell me stories of his own experiences with these children. His little girl would crawl away, scrambling across the floor giggling as he attempted to change her diaper, him laughing too. He would tiptoe into their bedrooms at night, stand next to the crib, peek in, and watch them in grateful wonder. He would hold his little girl through her tears, his own heart breaking, wishing her pain away, but

114

careful not to let her see too much of this pain because she needed him to be strong. He loved, cherished, and saw the beauty and the miracle in his daughter as much as he did in his son.

As I emerged from the memories, still in muffled tears, exhausted, he would tell me that this was the childhood I always deserved. While we could not rewrite the past, he could meet my need for unconditional love and acceptance. It could never be a substitute. It could not erase the past. But it could help me become whole in the present.

I listened and fantasized about what life would have been like with Dr. Padgett as my father. They were comforting thoughts, but painful as well. The only way I could conjure them up was to plunge deeply into the depths of vulnerability I felt as a young child. As much as he took pains to remind me that I could never be a child again, I fervently wished I could. The distinction between fantasy and reality was one I desperately didn't want to make.

Chapter 9

I was back home unpacking my suitcase from the hospital when I noticed a pink sheet of paper. It was a form with the hospital logo titled "Patient Treatment Plan." Several signatures ran along the bottom, including those of Dr. Padgett, a nurse I assumed to be drill sergeant, and my own. I didn't quite recall signing it, but then again, I'd signed lots of paperwork during my stay. Before tossing it in the trash, I wondered, what had I signed?

It contained a lot of jargon about suicidal ideation. A stress scale, whatever that was, showed overwhelming anxiety. I recognized Dr. Padgett's handwriting in the section marked "physician." He had printed the diagnosis, however. *Anorexia nervosa.* No surprise there.

But there was a second diagnosis this time. *Borderline personality disorder.*

Borderline personality disorder! What in the hell was that? I'd never in my life heard of that term. But it sounded sick, twisted, and demented—crazy. Dr. Padgett had mentioned a number of psychiatric terms in the course of therapy but had never mentioned this one. Yet here it was in his own handwriting. How could I have signed that paper without noticing?

I quit unpacking and headed straight for the public library and the microfiche kiosk. Under the category "Subject—Borderline Personality Disorder," three books were listed, and one caught my eye immediately: *I Hate You, Don't Leave Me.*

Those were the words Dr. Padgett had used to describe the alternating love and hate of my black-and-white relationships. It wasn't just a phrase he had coined but the title of a book—a book that was entirely devoted to a diagnosis the doctor had, for some reason, failed to tell me. *Why hadn't he told me?*

I drove to the bookstore with the library computer printout in my hand. *I Hate You, Don't Leave Me: Understanding the Borderline Personality* by Jerold J. Kreisman, M.D., and Hal Straus. I found the blue paperback on the psychology shelf and spent the rest of the evening and the next morning devouring it.

It was compelling reading, a comprehensive portrait of severe mental illness—one that could cause damaging consequences, not only to the ones suffering from it, but also to their loved ones.

"Borderlines," as they were called, had an overwhelming inclination toward self-destruction. Ten percent of borderlines committed suicide; even more engaged in dangerous, impulsively self-destructive behavior. Chemical addictions and abuse marked the disorder, as well as reckless driving and eating disorders.

118

Clearly Dr. Padgett had been telling the truth when he said that therapy was a matter of life and death. Not only was borderline personality disorder (BPD) serious, but, according to the authors, also exceptionally difficult to treat.

Borderlines were disproportionately represented in the psychiatric inpatient population and were prone to a host of other mental illness episodes as well: major depression, chemical dependency, and anorexia, to name a few. Often the best that could be hoped for was to treat these episodes as they occurred and to possibly control some of the BPD-related behavior such as explosive rages, damaging manipulation, and compulsive acts of self-destruction. Controlled but not cured.

The prognosis was bleak, and a significant number of borderlines were destined to lead lives of turbulence. Lifetimes spent in and out of psychiatric wards, prisons, and institutions. Significant recovery from the illness was rare and almost always meant several years of intensive psychotherapy.

This couldn't be me, could it? There must be some mistake. To discover this answer for myself, I closely reviewed the criteria for BPD in the American Psychiatric Association's *Diagnostic and Statistical Manual of Mental Disorders (DSM)*, the thick book psychiatrists used to determine a mental illness diagnosis.

Diagnostic criteria for Borderline Personality Disorder: A pervasive pattern of instability of mood, interpersonal relationships, and self-image, beginning by early adulthood and present in a variety of contexts, as indicated by at least five of the following:

(1) A pattern of unstable and intense interpersonal relationships characterized by alternating between extremes of

overidealization and devaluation. The black-and-white thinking, the good guy/bad guy phenomenon Dr. Padgett had pointed out. A definite yes.

(2) Impulsiveness in at least two areas that are potentially damaging, e.g., spending, sex, substance abuse, shoplifting, reckless driving, binge eating. (Do not include suicidal or self-mutilating behavior covered in [5]). Promiscuous sex with more partners than I could either count or remember until Tim came along. Heavy drinking and illegal drug use that had slowed with the births of Jeffrey and Melissa but were still present. Midnight runs would probably meet this criterion. Certainly anorexia would. Dr. Padgett was always bringing up my out-of-control behavior. This one was a yes too.

(3) Affective instability: marked shifts from baseline mood to depression, irritability, or anxiety, usually lasting a few hours and only rarely more than a few days. Another definite yes.

(4) Inappropriate, intense anger or lack of control of anger, e.g., frequent displays of temper, constant anger, recurrent physical fights. I had struggled my entire life to keep this one under control, trying to heed Sister Luisa's warning from years ago about the damaging power of words. However, outbursts against Tim had been increasing, and my explosive temper with Jeffrey had driven me to seek help in the first place. Dr. Padgett, who loosened my defenses and thus my reins on my emotions, had witnessed such intense and inappropriate anger countless times. I had to admit this was a definite yes too.

(5) Recurrent suicidal threats, gestures, or self-mutilating behavior. The suicidal ideation and threats were so frequent they had prompted Dr. Padgett to threaten to commit me. The

two runs to the West Side, before and during my first hospitalization, fit this criterion. I wasn't sure whether anorexia fit into this category or not. I'd never made a bona fide suicide attempt, never swallowed pills or put a gun to my head, but I'd thought about it plenty and talked about it frequently. I surmised this was a yes as well.

(6) Marked and persistent identity disturbance manifested by uncertainty about at least two of the following: self-image, sexual orientation, long-term goals or career choice, types of friends desired, preferred values. Clearly I hated myself, although on occasion I could be prone to delusions of grandeur followed by crushing lows. Now coping with the concept of fragmenting (conflicting selves), my self-image was definitely a serious problem. In the area of heterosexual versus homosexual orientation, I hadn't had self-doubt, but I had very serious difficulties accepting my gender. Long-term goals were nearly impossible for me to contemplate, much less to hold, even briefly. This also had to be a yes.

(7) Chronic feelings of emptiness and boredom. I made frenzied attempts to stay busy as hell to escape them, which never seemed to work for long. This point was a no-brainer yes, something I'd known about myself long before I ever entered therapy.

(8) Frantic efforts to avoid real or imagined abandonment. (Do not include suicidal or self-mutilating behavior covered in [5]). The tough, I-don't-give-a-shit part of me resisted identifying with this one, loathing the concept of dependency. But Dr. Padgett had specifically pointed out the abandonment fears on several occasions. I had to give this one a yes, although I preferred to think of it as a qualified yes.

The question now was about my prognosis. I had already been a psychiatric inpatient three times in less than a year and was going to three therapy sessions a week. Was this something I could expect for the rest of my life?

∞

Having arrived for session two hours early the next day, I strolled the grounds of the hospital and surrounding neighborhood, listening to the melancholy strains of Supertramp, trying to make sense of my most recent discovery. Granted, I'd always known I was different, messed up in many ways. But seriously mentally ill? The thought was overwhelming. I had to see Dr. Padgett right away. I couldn't bear waiting another minute.

By the time the session began, my uncertainty and confusion had turned into rage. I immediately walked to my chair, intentionally leaning forward and tightly folding my arms. It was confrontation time. I didn't need any time to collect my thoughts. I started in right away.

"You lied to me! I can't believe you lied to me!"

"Lied?" Dr. Padgett had the innocent look of one who sincerely had no idea what I was talking about.

"You know what I was doing until four in the morning? Do you? I was reading *I Hate You, Don't Leave Me*. It's not just a phrase some shrink coined, you liar. It's a book—about a diagnosis you didn't have the balls to tell me about."

He nodded. Now he knew exactly what I was addressing.

"Borderline personality disorder," he said.

"Yes, borderline personality disorder. I'm sick as hell. I'm a fucking mental case, demented. I'll probably be in and out of this goddamned hospital for the rest of my life. Sitting in here for 120 bucks a throw, ad infinitum. And you were gonna keep it from me, weren't you, you asshole? Just keep on sucking the cash from the little fuck-up until you retire."

"I didn't lie," he said, as calm as I was agitated. "The diagnosis was on the treatment plan, very openly. You read it; you signed it. I haven't lied to you about anything."

I rolled my eyes, tapped a drum roll on the table, and began to swivel the chair back and forth. I wanted to strangle him. I wanted to run. Goddamnit. I wanted to run and never stop.

"Bullshit! This is all bullshit. I signed so much crap in the hospital, filled out so many forms. Who reads it all anyway? A bunch of bureaucratic, psychobabble paperwork bullshit. You're a chicken shit; that's what you are, a spineless chicken shit. From that very first session when you didn't have the balls to give me the test results to my face, just tossed me some goddamned written report on my way out the door. And now I've got some psycho, demented mental illness. I despise you. I wish I never ever met you."

By now the drum roll had reached peak intensity, the chair not only swiveling, but rocking wildly back and forth, my feet tapping the floor, body shaking, ready to explode.

"Rachel, you're an adult. You're not crazy, and you can control your body motion. Stop with the tapping, stop with the feet and the chair, calm down, and listen."

Without raising his voice in the slightest, he had delivered his command with clear authority. Still seething, I stopped moving.

"First of all, you know the rules here. We can't work on your intense feelings when you physically act them out. We need to use words."

"Okay then. Fuck you!"

"That's not what I'm talking about, and you know it. Cussing me out is just another way of acting out. It doesn't tell me what you feel or why you're feeling it."

That one took me aback. It was the first time he had censored my speech and called it "acting out." I felt the cold slap of having stepped over the line. I could feel my face flush, and I was silent.

"Are you listening now? Are you ready to look at this issue now? Is the adult in control?"

I nodded.

"Okay." Even the blank screen couldn't hide his irritation, but under the circumstances he was containing it quite well. "I wasn't trying to hide any diagnosis from you. It was on the treatment plan that you signed; that's not hiding it. We've been dealing with a lot of important issues right now. The diagnosis is an issue in itself, but I don't think it's as relevant as others we've been discussing."

"You don't think borderline personality disorder is relevant? Look . . . How can I say this? I'm really trying to control myself here. I was up until four in the morning reading this book about what seems to be a very serious illness. I meet the criteria. I've gotta say I can't see a whole helluva difference between having BPD and being just a manipulative asshole. Can you really blame me for freaking out?"

"It's a very broad and general diagnostic category, maybe too general, in my opinion. BPD encompasses all kinds of people with all varieties of behavior. It doesn't define you."

"So you're saying I don't really have it? That it really isn't that bad? Maybe mine is a milder case?"

"No, I'm not saying that. You meet the criteria, and you are in a very serious situation."

"So I *am* sick."

"Yes, you are sick. I've never said anything to contradict that. I've always said therapy was a life-and-death matter for you. But you aren't a lousy person, Rachel. At your core you are a good person who's been through an awful lot."

Touchy-feely affirmations. I knew that argument; everyone is good at the core. The eloquent defense lawyer paints the tear-jerking portrait of the neglected, abused "kid of the streets." The lawyer plays on sympathies, tugs on heartstrings, and twists everything around so that somehow the rapist or murderer becomes the victim. Perhaps the lawyer's story of neglect and abuse is true. Sad, perhaps. But to me, it never cut it as an excuse. The dead person is the victim, and the murderer is the murderer.

I was cynical of the core-goodness philosophy since it was so often used as a weak justification for anything goes. What good were morals, what value was to be had in character if everything could be blamed on a bad background? Was everything inexcusable based on somebody's troubled childhood?

I felt very strongly about this and told Dr. Padgett so, fully expecting him to disagree, perhaps even attributing these thoughts to my father's legacy. He surprised me.

"I don't disagree at all with anything you're saying. As a matter of fact, I do believe there's a definite line between right and wrong and that there are people who cross that line and deserve to be punished and face the consequences. And it doesn't matter what happened in their childhoods. I believe in the death penalty in certain cases.

"But you haven't crossed that line. Maybe you've done some things in your life you regret; maybe you've done some things you *should* regret. But you've paid for them dearly and punished yourself much more than you've ever deserved.

"I'm not disputing anything you've brought up from

the book. Yes, there are a lot of borderlines who will never recover. But I believe you are one of those people who can overcome this. Not just control it, but fundamentally change and be freed from it. If I didn't believe that, I wouldn't have committed to therapy. I wouldn't have chosen you."

Chosen me. Words I'd met with cynicism before were just what I needed to hear right now.

"What I'm trying to say is that borderline personality disorder is too broad a category to make any one-size-fits-all conclusion. Most psychiatrists think Adolf Hitler was a borderline, but they also think Marilyn Monroe was too. Can you see the difference there? I'm not going to understate how serious this is for you. It *is* grave. But the nuances and differences in borderline personality disorder are like stations on a radio. A radio can be turned up full blast, to the highest decibels of intensity, but the musical scores you hear when you tune from one station to another can be completely different."

By the time the session ended I felt relieved, albeit only temporarily. The notion of borderline personality disorder was still staggering to me, and something I would be grappling with for a long time. But Dr. Padgett still believed in me, no matter how bleak the prognosis might be.

Perhaps one day, I thought, *I can believe in me just as much as he seems to.*

Chapter 10

The morning sun was burning through the bedroom window, the heat on my face a wake-up call. 7:30. Sounds of the shower were coming from the hall. The sheets were crumpled next to me; Tim was getting ready for work.

I tiptoed past the kids' rooms. Melissa, no more a morning person than I, was still sleeping soundly, a tiny little toddler's snore, her black hair peeking out from her Barbie blanket. Jeffrey was up but content with a dot-to-dot coloring book. I crept downstairs into the basement.

I went to the brand-new scale, digital and state-of-the-art. I'd purchased it ostensibly to monitor my weight prior to the hospital stay so I could keep the pounds from declining. Tim had been amenable to the idea; diligent monitoring was the way I had kept the postbaby diets from getting out of hand. But he had realized quickly that I was using the scale almost constantly to check the progress of my true goal: weight reduction. After seeing me step on it one too many times and disgustedly remark how fat I was getting, Tim couldn't bear to see me step on it any longer or even to see the scale itself. It was a reminder of his wife's emaciation and how helpless he was to do anything about it.

I'd told him that I'd given the scale away. But instead I tucked it into a storage corner of the basement. I would sneak down several times a day to check up on my progress. I had to sneak because it would kill Tim if he knew I was still doing this weeks after enduring the pain and expense of the voluntary three-week hospital stay.

As part of the ritual, I dropped my robe to the floor, took off my pajama top and bottoms and weighed myself. It read 101, a pound less than my weight when released from the psych ward.

All that time, all that pain, all that drive. A three-week separation from the kids. All for nothing. I'm just as anorexic as I ever was.

I had actually been up to 105 a few days earlier but could not live with the number on the readout. I'd skipped breakfasts and lunches, picking at my dinners, tripling my workouts when Tim wasn't around. The big rock of anorexia hadn't waned a bit. It had only become far sneakier.

Then the demon within took over.

Hmm . . . 101, not bad. It's about time. Only two pounds from double-digits. Keep it up! You're not anorexic. They want you to be fat.

The sessions since my hospital release had been dominated by dreams, the borderline diagnosis, and my childhood abuse and feelings. I hadn't brought up my weight, nor had Dr. Padgett. I had even been sneaky with him. I vowed that in today's afternoon session I would turn myself in and come clean.

I slumped in my chair, penitent-to-confessor again. The small little girl voice. The eyes downcast. A bad girl deserving punishment.

"Dr. Padgett, there's something I have to tell you. I weighed myself today. I weigh 101 pounds. I'm still losing weight. I've been exercising and skipping meals and checking the scale constantly, and I've been hiding it from everybody, including you."

I braced myself for admonishment that didn't come.

"What are your thoughts on this, Rachel? What do you think is going on?"

"She's taking over, Dr. Padgett. She's taking over completely. I can't win. I'm trying so hard, and nothing is happening."

"She?"

"The part of that wicked, little inner child, the one who hates me. She's trying to kill me, and she knows she's stronger than I am. She knows I'm weak, and there's nothing I can do about it. Please, can you help me?"

"The only solution is to put food in your mouth. I can't do that for you. Only you can."

"But I could die. Don't you see that?" I pleaded. "You've told me that. How can you just sit there and do nothing? I thought you were like a father to me; I thought you cared, you loved me."

"You're an adult, Rachel. You're twenty-nine years old, and you have two kids. You can control this. You can bring yourself to eat. You just choose not to. I can't make you do that; only you can."

Where is he? Where is the man who said all those gentle

loving words? Why won't he comfort me right now? Why won't he tell me some of those stories about his little girl?

"I don't understand this," I began to cry. "This is horrible for me. Can't you at least comfort me? She's torturing me! How can you be so cold?"

"There is no she; there's only you. One you. And when you can confront your fears, you won't need to be anorexic anymore. I can help you face the fears but not if you don't participate. And right now you're letting the child take complete control."

"I can't believe this. I thought you loved me. How can you just leave me hanging here like this and not do anything?"

A look of impatience flashed over his face then quickly passed.

"This isn't therapy right now. This is acting out. When you are ready to participate, I'm here. But I can't work with you unless the adult is present."

How dare he lead me on the way he does and then turn on a dime.

"You're right. This isn't therapy at all. This is a big scam, a rip-off. You think you can pick my brain, play me like an instrument, sucker me in, and just collect your goddamned fees. Well, fuck you! I don't need your stupid rules and your stupid limits and all the other shit you come up with to pull my strings like a puppet. How dare you call me a child. If I end up dead, it'll serve you right."

"I call you a child when you act like one. You have to decide if I care or not. If you can't believe it by what I've done, then whatever I say or don't say isn't going to make a difference. I think you need therapy, and there have been plenty of times when you've agreed. But that's your decision too. I can't keep you here if you don't want to be."

130

"I don't need you!"

"You say that, but you don't mean it. You need me so much it scares you. You're afraid your need is so vast that somehow it will swallow me alive or drive me away. But it hasn't, and it won't. The only way therapy will end is if you end it. You can leave before it's finished, before your needs are met. You can leave in a rage. But it will hurt you much more than it will hurt me."

The rest of the session was a babysitting of sorts. I raged and roared, rocked and swiveled the chair with frenetic intensity, retorted back with every slicing insult I could think of and every string of profanity I could muster. But Dr. Padgett didn't return the outburst. He simply sat and waited and repeated the same points. He also didn't say the comforting words or tell the loving stories I so desperately sought. When time was up, I rose quickly, hurled the tissue box from the end table against the wall and stalked out. He didn't follow me.

∞

I was still fuming by the time I'd reached my car. I wanted revenge. To land a blow on him that would take him down. But any revenge against him would be empty. That damned blank screen. He didn't even care enough to get pissed at me.

So I reached into my glove compartment, found a pen and pad of paper, and began to scrawl one more attempt at the last word, hoping somehow to destroy him. When I was finished, I walked over to the doctors' parking garage.

Doctors. I hated them all. Such pompous beings, always playing God. The lot was filled with BMWs, Cadillacs, and Porsches with a stretch of vanity license plates befitting the vain arrogance of physicians. *DOCTOR. DOCTR. DR-III. DOC*. Which one could be Padgett's?

Finally I found a red Mazda with a sunroof—*JMP*. John M. Padgett. This must be the car. The reserved-parking-space sign confirmed it. Rich sonofabitch, how dare he exploit me for money! Lifting up the recessed windshield wiper carefully, although I was tempted to break it, I placed my note right in front of the driver's seat where I knew he would have to remove it and read it. I stood there for a minute before I took my pen and scrawled a few more words on the outside of the folded paper.

I know where you live, asshole, and now I know what you drive!

∞

By the time I'd reached home, the anger had faded and I felt some satisfaction in my eloquent revenge. I even ate most of what was on my plate, much to Tim's relief.

By sunset on this late spring day, I was filled with remorse. I wished that I could go back and retrieve the note. But certainly Dr. Padgett had left for home by now. The deed had been done. I needed Dr. Padgett. I didn't want therapy to end. I wasn't sure if I ever wanted it to end; perhaps this is what scared me the most.

But I'd threatened him, harassed him, and left the evidence. I had broken the law. He had the right to exit therapy now, despite his promises, out of sheer self-preservation. I'd gone into that session filled with love, the warm feeling in my heart of being cared for, the burning desire of need. And I had proceeded to leave the session filled with hatred. *I Hate You, Don't Leave Me*. Right down to the last letter. Filled with self-hatred, wishing I were dead, I finally fell asleep. Tim didn't know about any of this. I was afraid that if I told him, he would know what an evil soul lay within the emaciated figure sleeping beside him. The mother of his children. He would leave too.

∞

The adult showed up to the next session.

I was like the parent of an unruly child, dragging her into the drugstore, making her confess to the manager about the shoplifting she'd committed the day before. I knew that there were no excuses, no disorder that could justify what I had done. No child within had done this without my knowledge or consent.

The greeting smile again. How could he do that in light of what I'd done to him?

When we entered his office, there, on the table, sat the white piece of paper with the words scrawled on top, still folded exactly as it had been when I'd placed it on his windshield. I was puzzled.

This time the little girl voice did not come out, nor did the defensive profanity of the tough guy. I neither leaned forward nor slumped backward. I looked him straight in the eyes.

"I'm sorry, Dr. Padgett. I was really out of line. I shouldn't have tried to hurt you like that. You didn't do anything to deserve it. I know I can't come up with any excuses, but I do want to apologize. I'm really sorry. I understand if you can't see me anymore. I crossed the line. I didn't mean that stuff, not really."

He listened to the apology. But as it turns out, it wasn't

as necessary as I thought. When he'd seen the note on the windshield, he had removed it and had figured it was from me. But he hadn't opened it.

Among Dr. Padgett's therapy boundaries was the rule that a patient's emotions, particularly those of the turbulent inner child, should be confined to sessions. So he had decided not to read the note. He did, however, invite me to read the note to him right there, in session.

I declined, telling him that it was basically a repackage of the same insults I'd hurled the day before.

He accepted my apology nonetheless. Instead of the lecture or the terse warnings that were warranted, he changed the topic away from the letter and toward the feelings that had prompted it.

Immediately I was filled with love for him. This was a man who truly meant what he said about unconditional love. This was a man fully committed to keeping his promises.

"Therapy is a lot like parenting," he told me. "A child needs the parent in ways that the parent simply doesn't need the child. The parent may love the child and not be able to imagine life without the child, but it is a different kind of love. The child is wholly dependent on the parent, but it doesn't work the other way around. Healthy and loving parents wouldn't dream of exploiting the child's vulnerability. But abusive parents do. Your parents did. You couldn't help that you needed them so much. But that need brought you pain. You had no other choice but to rely on them. There was no one else to take care of you. But now you have someone else.

"Every child needs to feel safe, to love completely, and not to have that love exploited. You cannot relive your childhood. But you can get what you need here. And you can become whole."

I loved him so much at that moment I couldn't believe how I could have harbored the hateful thoughts that had prompted the note. At times like this I could not imagine how I could have hated him—ever. In times of hatred I sometimes wished I could summon these warm feelings of love. But they always seemed to elude me. Intellectually I knew the goal of therapy was to fuse these conflicting emotions into a whole. But for now I simply clung to these tender moments of intensity, savoring them for as long as they lasted. They were enough to get by, enough to keep me coming back.

A pattern was emerging here, I noticed, an ironic twist on an old biblical saying: "Ask and ye shall receive." With Dr. Padgett the phrase was transposed: "Ask and ye shall not receive; do not ask and ye shall."

When I came in hungering for his tonic words of love and comfort, yearning so much it burned within me, Dr. Padgett was often distant. He repeated his same line, *"If you can't believe I care about you based on all that's happened here, what I say or don't say isn't going to matter."*

It was the times when I least expected it, felt I least deserved it, that he would open up with his warming words of love and comfort. As he would often say, *"Love isn't something to be earned. It's something to be given."*

In the previous session I had accused him of trying to pull my puppet strings. Projection again. I was the one who was trying to control him, and he was not going to let that happen. But slowly I was learning that I wasn't always going to hear exactly what I wanted to hear. Maybe it was truly because, as he said, what I wanted wasn't always what I needed.

Anger and fear temporarily lifted. I went home and spent a peaceful evening playing with the kids and watching mindless sitcoms with Tim. For once I slept well with no nightmares to rouse me from a restful sleep.

∞

I'd gotten into the habit of arriving to the hospital an hour early to take long walks and reflect on what was most pressing in my mind. Strolling through the meticulously kept gardens of the hospital grounds, I rarely had harsh thoughts toward Dr. Padgett. Yet once I entered the office, there was no predicting how I would behave.

Sometimes I walked for an hour or two, thinking kind thoughts. But once I crossed his threshold, I was besieged by rage, and the gentle eloquence I had planned would turn to bombshells of insults.

Outside the walls of the office, I was getting better at emotional self-control. Inside them, however, was another matter entirely. In my moments of loving and feeling loved, I would feel remorse for the bitter attacks of a session or two before. I'd be filled with regret as I looked into the eyes of a man I couldn't imagine wanting to hurt. Yet I knew I had often done everything in my power, not only to hurt him, but also to destroy him. I didn't understand why I could not control myself despite my best intentions. It made even less sense why he continued to put up with me.

At these times his chair became a slowly rising pedestal, and I looked into the eyes of more than a therapist—a saint. I tried to put words to this consuming love that I felt, to let him know just how remarkable and kind I thought he was. To let him know how I felt right then, before the moment passed. In this session I tried once more.

"I've treated you like shit, Dr. Padgett. I've told you off, threatened you, and maliciously insulted you. But you stay here anyway. You keep being kind to me. I don't deserve you."

"You *do* deserve me," he replied. "That's the whole point. Every child deserves parents who give love unconditionally, who don't exploit vulnerability but nurture it with kindness. Not because of anything a child does or says, but because the infant simply *is*. A child shouldn't have to earn this love. It's a birthright.

"I'm not by any means perfect. I don't have to be. All I have to be is good enough. You think this kind of love is rare. But it isn't. It happens all the time for most children. Most parents are good enough parents. And, quite frankly, it's really not that difficult to love you. There is a lot in you to love."

It still didn't make sense. I had been downright hateful to him so many times. What could he possibly see in me to love? I wasn't a child. I was almost thirty years old. His kindness, in ways, was only deepening my remorse.

"Come on, Dr. Padgett. Let's be serious. I've cussed you out so many times I couldn't even begin to count them. I've insulted everything: your profession, your motives, your integrity, your competence, even your masculinity. I've threatened you and your family. How could anybody but a masochist or a martyr put up with this?"

"Have your kids ever thrown a temper tantrum?" he asked. "Do they ever want something that seems insignificant, and yet, to them, it's like the holy grail? And when you don't let them have it, they pitch a fit with everything in their being?"

I thought of Melissa, who a few days before had desperately wanted to use a crystal vase as a teapot for her dolls. My little girl, usually so good-natured, had rolled around on

137

the floor, pummeling her tiny fists, writhing like a possessed creature.

I described the incident to Dr. Padgett.

"What did you do? Did you get angry? Did you scream at her or spank her?"

"No. I might have been a little irritated, but she's just a little kid, and she was awfully tired. I didn't give her the vase, but I pretty much let it pass."

"Have your kids ever told you that they hated you?"

I had to smile at this one. It was the running joke of the preschool mom set. All of us, at one time or another, vied for the title of "meanest mommy in the world."

"Sure," I answered him.

"But you're smiling. Didn't you take it personally? Didn't it hurt you?"

"No, of course not. They don't really mean it."

"Ah, that's where you're wrong," he responded. "For the moment, when they are right in the middle of an emotion, they mean it with all of their being. When they say they hate Mommy, they absolutely mean it—the same black-and-white thinking you do sometimes. That same inability to feel intense anger and intense love at the same time. That cookie or crystal vase is as important to them at the moment as anything—a job, a home, a marriage—could ever be to an adult.

"But the parent can handle this because he or she knows this is simply the way two-year-olds can be. The hate is tempered with the intense and pure love that prompts them to tell you an hour later that you're the best mommy in the world."

I smiled again. Tim and I had long ago agreed that God had made toddlers so sweet at times to make sure their parents didn't strangle them when they acted like little monsters. Survival. Although, really, toddlers were a joy far more than they were a headache. It wasn't hard to love them at all.

"Another question for you. Let's say Jeffrey or Melissa were ten or twelve years old and still dropping to the floor, kicking and screaming every time they didn't get their way. What would you think then?"

"I'd be really worried. I'd think something was seriously wrong."

"Would you hate them then?"

"No, of course I could never hate them. They're my kids."

"So you'd be very worried because you'd know that continuing to act in such a way at those ages could be very harmful for them. But you'd still love them. And you'd be worried precisely because you loved them."

"Yes," I was beginning to see where this was leading. This was a time I preferred to listen rather than speak.

"When you were a little girl, you were afraid to express these strong emotions. You were afraid to leave your bedroom at night or cry out of fear, much less throw a tantrum. In your world it wasn't safe. If you dared to express your anger, your fears, that would not be accepted. You were afraid that if you told your parents that you hated them, they would, in turn, hate you. And you needed them, as all children need their parents. You couldn't risk that.

"So you buried those feelings. You had to out of sheer survival. And, in the meantime, a part of you never grew out of that phase—a part buried out of fear and self-preservation that has never left you.

"What I feel when you lash out as you do, lose control as you do, isn't hatred, Rachel. How could I hate a child? Yes, I worry about you. Because you've grown up in many ways, you have a much greater command of language than you had back then. So the words you say can be quite hurtful to people who don't understand that they come from the child within and not from the adult. This can destroy relationships.

"And, as an adult, you have the freedom and the access to indulge in much greater forms of self-destruction than a two-year-old could ever have. You can drink and use drugs. You can smoke. You can be promiscuous. You can kill yourself if you want to, run into the streets at night, choose to eat everything in sight, or starve yourself. It's dangerous when the raw black-and-white emotions of a child are harbored in an adult's mind and body.

"Your rages might irritate me sometimes. But they don't make me angry. They don't make me want to leave you any more than my own toddlers' tantrums made me want to desert them. This isn't a normal adult relationship with adult expectations. It's a unique one where you're safe to express your childlike emotions and not be judged or reprimanded. It's safe here for you."

I found consolation in his words. And yet I still had difficulty accepting the notion that I was in any way a child. I'd earned a degree from a prestigious university. I had an emerging career. Perhaps it was offtrack right now, but I did have one. I was in a marriage and had two children. At times I had taken his childhood analogies as being rather patronizing. Now they were more embarrassing. Shameful.

"Those are kind words, Dr. Padgett. And I don't doubt for a minute that you mean them. You do have a role, and you are great at that role, a lot better than I would ever have expected. Better than I deserve. But look at me. I'm an adult sitting here. A skinny one, maybe, but still an adult. Sitting in here crying like a baby sometimes. Acting like a child. Don't you think it's kind of pathetic? How could you possibly respect me?"

"Sad, maybe, but not pathetic. In fact, quite courageous in that you're willing to look inside yourself and face what's there. Anything you've managed to do in your life has been like climbing a mountain with a two-hundred-pound weight on your back. How could I not respect that?

"One of the saddest facts isn't that there is still a child within you but that you're so ashamed of that child. What's even sadder is that you have *always* been ashamed of that child, even when you were one. You can accept the childlike nature of your own children, but you can't accept it in yourself. Someday you will, Rachel. Someday you will."

Chapter 11

A warm glow filled me on the way home, that of a child loved by her patient father. One who believed me to be not only lovable, but also courageous. Was I courageous? It was still hard to believe, and yet he wasn't the type to say things he didn't mean.

I'd verbally torn him to shreds more times than I could count. Yet I hadn't quit going to sessions. I hadn't given up. No matter how much I humiliated myself, he was there waiting for me.

Therapy was a bittersweet addiction. There were moments of catharsis, moments when I felt as if Dr. Padgett found a part of my soul that always ached for love and understanding. My need for him was vast, opened wide like the tiny beak of a baby bird awaiting a worm from its mother. I was in the nest alone.

How had I come to need him so much?

The constant transitions were painful—opening up,

baring my soul, only to face the abrupt ending ritual: *"That's about it for today."* From that point on, I had to bear the emptiness, the pain of missing him. Everything I did in between sessions was filler. A way to kill time. I silently marked the days until our next session. I went through the motions of being a wife, mother, accountant, church member. But I was living these days for therapy. It had become not only my lifeline, but my life.

My desperate need for him was limitless and almost embarrassing. Was it really worth those brief moments of feeling loved?

∞

As much as I tried to savor the moments of warmth, they often left me as quickly as they came. By the next session the walls had been erected again. It was simply too exhausting and painful to keep needing Dr. Padgett as much as I did. I had stepped onto a high-speed train powered by my torrent of emotions on an endless journey with no destination. My only option was to jump from the moving train. Death seemed preferable to a life like this.

The session began in silence. There were plenty of thoughts running through my mind. But I chose not to share them. Instead I sat back, silently staring at the books on his shelves.

Go ahead, Dr. Padgett. Make my day! You take the lead for once. I'm not saying anything. I can be a blank screen too.

After ten minutes or so had passed this way, Dr. Padgett finally did say something.

"So what's on your mind?"

"Nothing."

"Nothing?"

"That's right. Absolutely nothing."

More time passed.

"You're burying your feelings, Rachel. They are there, but we can't work on them unless you open up."

"You're the damned expert," I snapped back at him. "You seem to know everything that's on my mind. You seem to know all there is that makes me tick. Why don't you figure it out?"

"I'm not a mind reader."

"Oh, really? You certainly seem to be able to put all kinds of words in my mouth and thoughts in my head that I've never said."

"This isn't therapy," he said firmly. "This is acting out. You aren't apathetic, and you aren't numb. You are deliberately withholding your feelings. You know how the process works."

My tough chick persona was sitting back and calling the shots. She was making Dr. Padgett pursue me rather than the other way around. It was a powerful feeling of omnipotence that fed upon itself. *Come on, Dr. Padgett. Beg for it. Get on your knees.*

Dr. Padgett did not beg. For the next twenty minutes neither he nor I spoke a word. I glanced at my watch. Only fifteen minutes remained in the session. Fifteen more minutes before the dreaded words: *"That's it for today."* I was squandering a session, and I could feel the self-recrimination for wasting our time together welling within me. Panic filled me, along with the anticipated resentment of the enforced end of session. *The sonofabitch was going to let me do this to myself, sit back there and outlast me!*

Suddenly it was his fault. I was determined not to let

him get the better of me. I was determined to have the last word. He'd pay for this.

"You're right, Dr. Padgett," I said coolly. "There are things on my mind. But I have no intention of sharing them with you. You know why? Because you're a manipulative bastard, that's why. A control freak. You want me to get down on my hands and knees, to strip my soul naked so you can exploit it. You want to see me grovel for your attention. Fuck you. I'm not doing it. You can have your rules, but I don't have to follow them. You can't make me talk, you bastard!"

It was projection plain as day. But he didn't point it out, and I didn't choose to see it.

"You're hurting yourself, Rachel. Not me. You need to release your feelings during sessions not afterward. And you've wasted a good amount of that opportunity today."

"I don't need you, asshole," I laughed haughtily. "Don't you see that? I don't need anybody. I'll feel whatever in the hell I want to feel whenever I want to feel it. And I'll say what I damned well please whenever I damned well want to say it. Are you worried I'll call you in between sessions? Infringe on your precious leisure time? Well, don't worry. I wouldn't call you if you were the last fucking person alive and I had a loaded gun pointed down my throat. I'd squeeze the trigger and lay there bloody on the floor with my brains blown out before I'd ever pick up the phone and call an asshole like you!"

Dr. Padgett was looking at the clock that faced him. *Sonofabitch. He can't wait to get me out of here. He can't wait to toss me out of his office and onto the street.*

"I don't need you, you asshole!" I was screaming desperately now, as aware as he was that only two minutes remained. "I don't fucking need you or anybody else! I may as well be dead! You'd like that, wouldn't you? Because then you wouldn't have to fuck with me anymore. I'd be out of your hair. I'd quit trying to suck you dry. You think I'm some kind of loser, some dependent, worthless little psycho. But I don't need you. I don't need a fucking soul."

Dr. Padgett sat expressionless for a moment. Then he said the closing words.

"That's it for today."

Before he had finished the sentence, I had jumped out of my chair, fumbled with my purse and car keys, cursing under my breath, and stalked out of his office without another word.

∞

Sometimes the twenty-minute drive home was a calming transition, a time to collect my thoughts and prepare to re-enter reality. Like an infant in a car seat, I could be soothed by the gentle vibrations and humming engine of a car ride.

Today was not one of those days.

The other drivers on the road exacerbated my anger as I pushed the speedometer needle to fifty-five miles per hour in the thirty-five zone, darting in and out of traffic, returning the angry honks and upturned middle fingers of those I'd tailgated or cut off. My emotions were spinning out of control, and I was riding them until I was in a frenzy.

I managed to get home without incident. Tim wasn't there yet, and I still had a half hour before I had to gather Jeffrey and Melissa from the sitter. *The hell with it*, I thought. *Let Tim pick them up. Let Tim deal with them.* I did, at least, call the babysitter and lie to her, telling her I was running late with a client and that Tim would pick up the kids. I then went immediately to the attic and locked myself in, ready to have it out with anyone who came near me.

I sat there, chain-smoking, steaming with rage. I was waiting to hear the front door open, the boisterous sounds of the kids, the sound of Tim's footsteps below. But I heard nothing. No one was home. Which made me even angrier.

How dare Tim just leave me up here alone? He doesn't give a shit either, the sonofabitch! No one cares how I feel.

I went into Jeffrey's room, grabbing a marker and some wide-lined tablet paper, and began to scrawl out terse notes that I taped throughout the house.

The note on the front door read: *Tim. You need to pick up the kids. I'm upstairs in the attic. Don't even think of going up there if you know what's good for you!*

At the bottom of the stairs I taped another note: *Stay away! Don't mess with me! You don't know what I might have up here!*

The sign on the locked door to the attic said: *I might die anyway, but if you dare come in here, you might all be dead! You don't know what I have up here!*

The implication, of course, was that I had a loaded gun—which I didn't. I knew it was being manipulative when I wrote the notes, but I justified it because I hadn't actually lied. Besides, if there had been a gun around the house, I would have brought it up there. I could get a gun quite easily, and I just might do so.

Once I had taped up all the notes and locked myself back in the attic, I waited quietly for Tim to arrive. As I heard the front door slam, I could envision him reading these notes, the fear and panic in his eyes, tearing them down even though neither of the kids could read yet. The door slammed again twice, the second time accompanied by the sounds of Jeffrey and Melissa, who were busy bickering over something that had happened at the sitter's.

I was beginning to get bored. I was itching for confrontation, and yet Tim had heeded my words. I'd gotten what I'd claimed to want. To be left alone. But now I found myself resenting it. *Doesn't he care?*

A few minutes later I heard pounding on the attic door.

"Rachel!" Tim bellowed, fiddling with the door, trying to pop the lock.

"I told you to leave me the fuck alone!" I screamed back.

"Dr. Padgett is on the phone," he insisted. "He wants to talk to you right now."

"Tell the bastard I don't want to talk to him. I didn't call him."

"Damnit, Rachel!" Tim was exasperated.

"I told you, tell the asshole I didn't call him, and I don't want to talk to him." Even through the door, I could hear Tim sigh.

"Whatever," he said.

That'll show Padgett! I thought. I'd kept my word, I hadn't called him. Either Tim had called Padgett, or Padgett had called me, but I hadn't made the call. *I'll show that bastard that I don't need him.*

Soon Tim was knocking at the door again.

"Please let me in, Rachel," he pleaded gently.

"Did you tell Padgett I didn't want to talk to him?"

"Yes."

"Is he still on the line?"

"No."

Satisfied, I went down the steps and unlocked the door.

Tim's face was white and blotchy, his eyes watery, swollen, and red.

He had been crying. Clearly I had hurt him. However, I was still convinced that it was Padgett who had caused this all, not me.

"You don't have a gun up here, do you?" he asked weakly.

"Maybe I do, maybe I don't."

"Please don't play games with me, all right, Rachel?" Tim sounded too exhausted to be angry.

"Why do you care, Tim? Why would it matter if I have a gun?"

Finally Tim had reached the breaking point and lost his patience.

"Damnit!" he exploded. "I haven't done a goddamned thing to you, and neither has Dr. Padgett! We've got two kids downstairs crying because they want to see you, and they can't understand why you won't let them up here. They've been upset and scared to death since you didn't pick them up at the babysitter's—"

"Why would they be scared? I called her and told her I was with a client. And how the hell did Padgett end up calling here. Did you call him?"

"Hell, yes, I called him! And he wants you to call him back within the next ten minutes, or he's sending the goddamned police."

"Yeah, sure," I rolled my eyes. "The police bullshit. The commitment crap. I've heard it all before. He won't really do it. I will not call that asshole back."

"He will do it, Rachel. And let me tell you something: if the police show up at the front door, I'll let them know exactly where you are."

"You backstabbing sonofabitch! You'd turn me in, wouldn't you? You're in on this with him, aren't you?"

"I don't know what the hell else to do. Look. I've tried to be patient with you. I really have. But you know what? Nothing I can say or do is right. I can't win with you. You think the whole world is out to get you."

"You really hate me, don't you, Tim? You wish I were dead. You wish you could just get me out of your hair."

"I don't hate you," Tim's eyes were welling up with tears, "but let me tell *you* something. I know therapy's been hard for you, but it hasn't been a picnic for me either. You're not the only person in the world who has problems, Rachel. Everybody's got problems. And I tell you what, there's only so much of this I can take. Sometimes I wonder if *I'm* losing it. Sometimes I wonder if maybe *I* might not be better off dead."

The last statement shocked me into reality. Had I really pushed Tim that far?

"Okay, I'll call Dr. Padgett. All right?"

"Thank you," he said, crying hard by now and turning to go back down the steps.

He stopped midway. "Can you do something else for me? Would you please say hi to the kids? They're really upset."

"Okay."

Before I had the chance to make it downstairs to the telephone, Jeffrey and Melissa had bounded up the steps.

"Mommy!" Melissa shrieked happily, throwing her pudgy little toddler arms around me, squeezing me tight.

Jeffrey stood back for a moment, looking into my eyes.

"Mommy," he said with great concern, "please don't cry, okay? Please don't cry. Everything's going to be okay, right? Everything's going to be okay. You don't have to cry."

Four going on twenty-four. A child who needed comfort was instead comforting his mother.

What had I done?

∞

Armed with a fresh glass of ice water and a full pack of cigarettes, I called Dr. Padgett's emergency number. I reminded myself that, technically, I wasn't calling him. I was simply returning his call. I knew the answering service routine well by now and wondered if the people at the service were beginning to recognize who I was.

"Dr. Padgett's service."

"Uh, yes. I'm a patient of Dr. Padgett's. I need to talk to him."

"Is this an emergency?"

Always that question. Why did it always have to be an emergency for me to be able to talk to the doctor after hours?

"Yes."

I gave the woman my name and phone number and sat, waiting for the phone to ring. Five minutes passed. Ten minutes. Fifteen minutes. Twenty minutes. *Is this another power play? He demands that I call him within ten minutes and then makes me sit here and wait for twenty minutes for him to call me back!* Any inclination to be apologetic had passed.

Finally the phone rang. Although my hand rested on the receiver, I deliberately let it ring five times before I picked it up. I'd be damned if I was going to let him know that I was sitting and waiting by the phone for him.

"This is Dr. Padgett."

A moment of cold silence.

152

"This is Rachel."

Volleyed back into his court. Silence on the other end of the line.

"Tim said you wanted me to call you, so I'm calling you."

"Tim was very upset. So were your kids. You hurt them when you do these things, you know."

No, Dr. Padgett. You are the one who hurts them. You are the one who makes me do these things. "Well, everything's okay now, Dr. Padgett."

"Do you have a gun?"

"Maybe I do, maybe I don't," I answered with deliberate vagueness. "Maybe I could get one if I didn't."

"No games, Rachel," he said firmly. "You played games all session; you won't play them now. Either you tell me the truth about the gun, or I'll call the police."

A tempting proposition. But then I remembered Melissa's desperate hug of relief and the fear in Jeffrey's eyes. I'd already put them through enough.

"No, I don't have a gun."

I braced myself for a lecture on my shameful manipulation, on having panicked everyone with the threat of a gun that didn't exist. No such lecture ensued.

"Are you in control?"

"Yes. I'm . . . in control."

"Then I'll see you at tomorrow's session."

Another pending good-bye. I couldn't take it. The need washed over me again. I couldn't let him go.

"I'm sorry, Dr. Padgett," I sobbed into the receiver. "I'm so sorry. I'm such an asshole. I'm blowing it. I tried to scare you. I'm such a fuck-up."

"I think you should be making your apologies to your

husband and kids. We'll talk about this tomorrow."

"But what if something happens?" I cried desperately. "What if I lose control again? I can't help it. The child just takes over. I'm scared. Please, can't we talk about this now?"

"You can control yourself when you chose to. No one can do it for you. You can ride these feelings out. We'll talk about them tomorrow in session."

"But Dr. Padgett!"

"Tomorrow in session. Good-bye, Rachel."

"Good-bye."

I hung up the phone and sat numbly. Tim tapped at the door.

"Can I come in?"

Wordlessly, I unlocked it.

"Did you talk to the doctor?" he asked gently. "Are you feeling better?"

"I talked to him. I don't know if I feel any better, but I'll be okay. And I'm sorry for putting you and the kids through all of this. I really am."

"You don't have to apologize for anything, Rachel." His eyes were still swollen and red, dark circles forming beneath them. Worry lines had aged his face. "All of us just want you to get better."

∞

The tough chick threatened to emerge again at the next day's session. It was tempting to repeat the events of the day before. To say nothing, play the game. My pride made it difficult to admit that I had manipulated my family and Dr. Padgett as well. Thus I did not apologize, nor did I revert into the helpless little girl mode. I did, however, force myself to say what was on my mind.

"It isn't that I don't need you," I began. "It's that I *can't* need you. It hurts too much to need you. It's dangerous to need you. I fall apart. I lose control. I turn into some kind of a madwoman, some kind of a crazed child. I managed for thirty years without you, and now look at me.

"This isn't the kind of person I am, Dr. Padgett. I've never done these kinds of things before. I'm worse than I ever was. It isn't you. I need you too much when I let my guard down. It was better when I didn't need anybody."

"It wasn't better," he pointed out. "You needed someone then. You've always needed someone. The need isn't going to go away until you are satisfied. You came to therapy thinking that life wasn't worth living. You came wanting to die. You came because the tough denial of need was more than you could tolerate."

"It was a fluke. Sure I wanted to die. But it wasn't the first time I wanted to die. I wouldn't have done anything. I don't have the guts to kill myself, Dr. Padgett, and you know it as well as I do. I listened to the priest, and he talked me into coming to the hospital. It wasn't something I sought out. And I honestly believe that if I hadn't come to the emergency room, if I hadn't started therapy, it would have passed. I would have been tough enough to withstand it and keep going."

"Maybe you would have lived. Maybe you'd live to be eighty years old. But what kind of quality of life would you have? You'd just be enduring life instead of enjoying it."

"Life sucks. Don't you understand that? Life sucks for everyone, not just me. It's just that some people are deluded enough to think that it doesn't. The world is a lousy place, Dr. Padgett, filled with rotten parents who abuse their kids and con artists and assholes who will screw you in a minute if you let them. Backstabbers, hypocrites, and rapists. The bad guys are always winning, and the good guys are getting screwed."

"The triumph of evil?"

"You bet, the triumph of evil."

"What about love?"

"Love is weak. Love is delusional optimism. It's a fairy tale. Hate always wins."

"So you think that hate is stronger than love?"

I was astonished that he could even ask such a foolish question.

"Of course. Hate is not only stronger than love, it kicks love in the ass every single day. Cheaters aren't supposed to prosper, but they do."

"So, then, how is it that you think you've survived so far in this world filled with hate? How is it that you've managed, with the two-hundred-pound weight of these emotions on your back, to somehow survive? You're in a strong marriage, you're a good mother by your own admission, and you've managed to succeed in many ways. How do you think that happened?"

Another foolish question with an obvious answer, I thought.

"Because, once upon a time, I was really tough—before I came in here. I knew not to be dumb enough to trust anyone else so I wasn't crushed by disappointment. Then I come in here and start trusting, and look what happens. I'm a basket case. A crying, weak manipulator. I hate myself this way. I want to be tough again. I wish I'd never come here."

"So you were tough at twenty?"

"Yes."

"At thirteen?"

"Yes."

"At ten?"

"Yes."

"At *two*?"

Pride forced me to lie on this one.

"Yes. . . ."

"There's no such thing as a tough two-year-old, and you know it. Once upon a time you trusted your parents with all your heart. You were completely vulnerable to them because you had no other choice. Once upon a time you believed in love so much so that you rescripted your entire past to put love in where it didn't always exist. A two-year-old can't fight fire with fire. A two-year-old is completely at the mercy of the adults around her."

The tough chick facade had broken down, and I was sobbing.

"But they screwed me! Can't you see where that got me? I learned the lesson everybody learns in the long run. I just learned it earlier."

"Love is infinitely more powerful than hate," he said gently.

"That might be your opinion."

"No, that is fact. You want to know how you really got by, really survived this far?"

I nodded.

"You survived by seizing every tiny drop of love you could find anywhere and milking it, relishing it, for all it was worth. Your parents weren't all hate or all abuse. There were tender moments, whether or not you choose to remember them now. There were those moments, however brief, when you felt safe. You felt loved, and you savored every minute of it and held it closest to your heart. And as you grew up, you sought love anywhere you could find it, whether it was a teacher or a coach or a friend or a friend's parents. You sought those tiny droplets of love, basking in them when you found them. They are what sustained you."

These were completely new concepts to me. My sobs abated as I simply listened.

"For all these years, you've lived under the illusion that, somehow, you made it because you were tough enough to overpower the abuse, the hatred, the hard knocks of life. But really you made it because love is so powerful that tiny little doses of it are enough to overcome the pain of the worst things life can dish out. Toughness was a faulty coping mechanism you devised to get by. But, in reality, it has been your ability to never give up, to keep seeking love, and your resourcefulness to make that love last long enough to sustain you. That's what has gotten you by.

"Therapy isn't easy, Rachel. I never claimed that it would be. I never said it was going to be less painful than it is or that it wasn't an arduous process. But what waits for you on the other side of the rainbow is a life so different than you could ever imagine, so much more satisfying, that when you get there, you'll see that all of this has been worth it."

Tiny drops of love. At that moment I wished that I could simply open up completely and soak in that love like a sponge.

But no words, no simple solution would suddenly bring the walls crashing down and allow me to become instantly trusting and open. One more stone, however, had been cleared away, letting in one more tiny glimmer of light to sustain me and keep me on the journey.

Chapter 12

It was an unseasonably cool June day as I sat on the porch swing with a mug of hot coffee. I was reflecting on the year that had just passed, one year to the day since my first fateful trip to the emergency room. My first anniversary of losing it.

At this time last year I'd never heard of a psychiatrist named John Padgett. I'd never dreamed I'd be embarking on a journey that would involve three sessions a week for twelve months.

As I watched Jeffrey and Melissa furiously pedaling their Big Wheels on the sidewalk, my heart ached. Again. It was Friday, which meant I had to wait four days until I could see the man to whom I felt pathologically addicted. During these empty times, sometimes it was all I could do to go through the motions of being a wife and mother.

Granted, I'd always known I was different, not in a positive way, but in a shamefully twisted one. If only I could believe Dr. Padgett, that this past year of hell was the price I had to pay to free myself from a lifetime of anguish. Somehow the three-page summary of the psychoanalytic process did not capture what had transpired over that year. It had referred to confronting buried, fearful issues in therapy as "temporary anxiety." *Temporary anxiety? More like a living nightmare.*

I recalled the way Tim and I had scoffed at the notion that anyone would need three to five years of therapy to get better. Such assessments, we'd thought, were for the Woody Allens of the world: the hopelessly neurotic, the deranged psychos, the horribly abused. Certainly not me. Yet here I was, in therapy for a full year already, barely able to manage a long weekend without Dr. Padgett. I couldn't imagine ever reaching a point where I could handle life on my own.

Is this how I was going to spend the rest of my life? Was I just a classic borderline personality disorder case, forever dependent on her therapist and psychiatric drugs? Was I going to become the crazy lady in the attic?

I imagined myself as the hollow shell of an elderly woman, incarcerated for years in an institution, dutifully visited by her children. Jeffrey and Melissa would vaguely recall the vibrant young woman they knew when they were toddlers.

What a year it had been. Sixty-one days in a psychiatric hospital, one out of every six days since last June.

But that wasn't the worst of it. I'd spent twice as many days when I accomplished absolutely nothing. Running in the streets after dark; taking the car on rambling, reckless drives; screaming into a pillow while locked in the attic or my bedroom; threatening myself, Dr. Padgett, or Tim. There were also the days when I could only drag myself to therapy or spend hours confined in my room with pen and paper.

A minipharmacy of little brown plastic bottles decorated my dresser—the anti-anxiety pills I swallowed six times a day, the nightly doses of antidepressants, and all the half-empty vials of medications my physiology could not tolerate. The prescriptions were so expensive I couldn't bring myself to throw them away. Yet I could not remember the last time I had awakened happy, the last time I had genuinely laughed, or the last time I had truly enjoyed myself.

Former pleasures meant nothing to me anymore. Life was a series of tasks to be endured, and even the simplest ones were painfully arduous. It took everything I could muster to cook a meal, wash the dishes, or do the laundry. My income was virtually nonexistent. My occupation was therapy.

I did not want my children to be cheated anymore than they had been by the sixty-one days I was hospitalized, the hours spent locked in my room feverishly writing, and the times I was physically present but emotionally absent. So I dedicated any energy I could summon to them. I hugged them, cuddled them, read to them, and took them to the park or zoo. Perhaps my life was a living hell. But I was determined not to let it make their childhood the hell that mine had been. While my love for them was real, I sometimes wondered if they could see that my loving smiles were an act, barely masking the despair I felt within.

Nonetheless, it was the best I could do. It had to suffice.

Jeffrey and Melissa were now racing down the sidewalk, squealing in joyful exuberance, giggling as they repeated the ritual of "ready, set, go!" Their tiny legs pedaled as fast as they could to the imaginary finish line. They seemed carefree, now three and five, just enjoying a breezy summer's morning. Could they somehow manage in spite of all that had gone on?

Certainly the turbulent events of the past year had to

have affected them in ways that might not show itself fully until years later. Dr. Padgett, never one to airbrush reality just to appease me, acknowledged a possible effect and that the long separations were hard on the kids.

To him, it was a relative phenomenon, a lesser of two evils. Whatever pain my absences and emotionally turbulent therapy had inflicted on them, it paled in comparison to the longer-term damage that would be inevitable if I did not do whatever was necessary to get better. A mentally ill mother going through the hell of therapy was not easy on Jeffrey and Melissa. But a mentally ill mother who refused to get help and remained ill indefinitely would be far more damaging. And, he told me emphatically and unequivocally, the greatest devastation of all would be if their mother were to commit suicide. That, he maintained, would condemn them to an inner hell worse than even I had endured.

I sometimes believed that Tim and the kids would be better off without me. But I could never take the chance in case Dr. Padgett was right about suicide. Often I wished I had never met Tim—not because I didn't love him, but because now, with two young children and a husband depending on me, I could not bring myself to make the final exit.

I'd recently turned thirty, an age I vowed I'd never live to see. I had hoped that somehow I'd have crashed before then. The accidental pregnancy and subsequent marriage and family, however, had forever denied me certain choices.

At times I resented this ultimate punishment—being sentenced not to death, but to life. At other times it seemed too fateful to be a mere coincidence. The pregnancy could have easily been the result of a one-night stand, a drunken evening with a man whose name I couldn't remember, or one of my many abusive relationships.

But it hadn't been. Instead it had been Tim: strong, sensitive, and loyal, who was there when the Russian roulette game of unprotected sex reached its inevitable conclusion. So I didn't have an abortion. I had a family of my own. Perhaps it was part of a master plan to keep me alive.

Now I no longer had the option of running or taking my own life. All I could do was to keep going to therapy, keep enduring the pain, hang on, and survive.

Jeffrey and Melissa pulled their Big Wheels onto the grass and started begging for Popsicles. They seemed content, although worry sometimes clouded Jeffrey's eyes. In many ways he was perceptive beyond his years. Had I caused him to be wiser than he needed to be?

Melissa selected a cherry Popsicle and bounced back out into the yard, picking a bouquet of dandelions. Jeffrey, however, continued to stand on the porch, looking at me, as he licked a grape one. *What was he thinking?*

I remembered Tim telling me what Jeffrey had said on the way home from a hospital visit a few months before: *"Daddy, Mommy isn't really going to get any better, is she?"* The same thought I'd had frequently. The same thought that Tim had left unspoken between us. But did a preschooler have to be tormented by it too?

God, if you exist, please spare these kids. I promise I'll keep going to therapy. I'll do whatever it takes, but please help me. These kids deserve to be happy, not worried about me. I know I haven't prayed in year. But if you will, please give me a sign that there's a purpose to all of this suffering.

Jeffrey finished the Popsicle, neatly placed the sticks in the gooey wrapper, and set them down on the porch. He sat next to me on the swing and wrapped his arms around me.

"You know what, Mommy?" he asked.

"What, sweetheart?"

"You're the best mommy in the whole world."

Eyes glazed with tears, I looked up to the sky. I would make it through this. I would live. I *had* to live. Perhaps my prayer had been answered. Perhaps this little five-year-old clutching me tightly was the sign I'd been asking for.

∞

At Tuesday's session, I spoke about all the thoughts I'd had on the front porch.

"The only thing that keeps me going," I concluded, "is the kids. I love those kids, Dr. Padgett. If nothing else, I'd like to think I'm a good mother."

"How about you?" Dr. Padgett asked.

"What about me?"

"How about staying alive, getting better for yourself?"

"I'm not the concern here, Dr. Padgett. Jeffrey and Melissa are. They're kids. They're innocent. They need to be protected."

"You were a kid too, Rachel. An innocent one. In a lot of ways you didn't have anything to do with this either. *You* weren't protected."

"My time is up, don't you see? I had my chance to be a child, and it's over now. If nothing else, maybe the next generation can live happily ever after. If I can help these kids do that, maybe my life will have a purpose."

"You're afraid to admit the truth of your feelings, aren't you?"

"What truth?" I answered, irritated once again that he was trying to put thoughts in my head. "I've just told you everything I feel."

"Not everything," he shook his head.

"What else am I supposed to be feeling?"

"You're afraid to admit that you resent your kids just as much as you love them. That, in a lot of ways, you wish they weren't around."

"How can you say that?" I replied, astonished. "I love those kids!"

"I didn't say that you don't love them. I didn't say you aren't a good mother. What I said is that you aren't seeing the whole picture. You also resent those kids, and sometimes, deep within you, you wish you could react as violently to them as you do to me. You're afraid of those feelings. Very much afraid."

Can't he ever just take what I say and leave it at that? Can't he just take my word for it instead of dissecting every syllable and interjecting his own version of my vile motives and thoughts?

Okay, so I beat Jeffrey once. Is this man going to use it against me forever? Maybe I'm crazy, maybe I'm an asshole, maybe I'm immature and manipulative and all of those other wretched traits on the psychological profile and in the borderline personality disorder books. But I'm a good mother. Does he have to take that away from me too?

"What's on your mind, Rachel? Tell me what you're thinking."

"I'm thinking that you're very wrong about me. I'm a good mom."

"I don't always think I'm right," he replied calmly. "But on this one I do."

"Well, guess what, Dr. Freud?" I retorted. "On this one you are wrong. Dead wrong."

"You're very defensive about this. You won't even

consider it. Once again you're seeing the world as black and white. You're afraid that if you have such feelings, you can't have them and still love your kids. But just because you disavow the emotions, they aren't going away. And if you hide from them out of fear, you only make the inner conflict worse."

"Psychobabble bullshit!" I cried. "You're accusing me of wanting to hurt these kids. I did it once, so you think that you can hold it over my head for the rest of my life. As if it isn't hard enough to look back on a childhood, something I never had a problem with until I started working with you, by the way, and see all kinds of abuse I didn't think about back then. Now you want to accuse me of doing the same horrible things to my own kids. And then you sit there, poker-faced, stoic as hell, and act like it's no big deal!"

Dr. Padgett sat silently for a moment then replied.

"No," he said gently, "*you* are the one who won't let the abuse incident go away. You are the one who won't forgive yourself for it. Not me. That's why you can't even bear to get in touch with the very real feelings, deep within you, of resentment toward your kids."

"You're convinced I'm an asshole, aren't you?" I spit the words back at him. "Rotten right down to the core. So rotten I'd even hate my own kids. But you don't have any idea what it's like. I'm good to those kids, Dr. Padgett, no matter what kind of a crazy borderline asshole you think I am. Sometimes I wake up wishing I were dead so bad I can taste it, but I don't take it out on those kids. I hug them, and I cuddle them, and I treat them fairly. I listen to them and play with them, and I'm as goddamned good a mother to them as any normal mother around. It's the hardest fucking thing in the world to keep being a good mom despite this hell inside, but I'm doing it, goddamnit. And then you tell me I'm some kind of Mommie Dearest. Well, you're wrong. I'm a goddamned good mother, and I'll continue to be—even if it kills me!"

"That's precisely my point," he replied. "It *is* practically killing you. There's no doubt in my mind that you're a good mother. But you're doing it out of fear and buried guilt. You take those violent feelings—the resentment you refuse to face—and you twist them around and turn them toward yourself. You treat your children well at your own expense. In ways they literally drain the life right out of you."

"So you're telling me I should quit being a good mother and be a violent, angry one? You're telling me to think only about myself and not about them?"

"No, I'm not. It doesn't have to be all or nothing. You can acknowledge your feelings of resentment without ever having to act on them. You can be angry with them. You can even fantasize about being violent toward them without hurting them in the least. And it doesn't mean that you love them any less. If you're open about the feelings, we can work on them. They won't frighten you as much. But if you keep them buried, they become larger-than-life, which only makes it that much harder to be a good mother."

"So you're saying there's nothing morally wrong with wanting to beat the crap out of my kids? Which, by the way, is what *you* say I'm thinking not what *I* say I am."

"Exactly. There's absolutely nothing morally wrong with thinking about it. Just with doing it."

"Haven't you ever heard the biblical saying 'impure thoughts are as impure deeds'?"

"I have, but I don't buy it. Haven't you ever heard the one about 'actions speak louder than words'?"

Always a comeback. I could never be right with Dr. Padgett. I wasn't going to play that game, so I sat back, arms folded, glaring at him. I'd never debated competitively, but I could outdebate almost anyone I'd ever met. Except Padgett.

"I remember one time when my kids were small," Dr. Padgett continued, ignoring my silent treatment. "I took them to see a cartoon movie. I thought it was a great movie and one they'd really enjoy. But in one part a puppy was abused. When we walked out of the theater, both kids were in tears. They'd barely speak to me. It was only a minor piece of the plot, but it was the only part they thought about.

"Children are much more in tune to abuse and much more empathetic than adults are. Because they're vulnerable. Cartoon or not, they related to that puppy. And I felt terrible. I'd made a big mistake in taking them to see it. Because I forgot what it was like to be a kid."

Padgett making a mistake? *And admitting it?* I leaned forward and tuned in more closely.

"You are an adult, Rachel. And a good mother. And it's harder for you to be a good mother than it would be for a lot of people. You aren't just dealing with the two kids you have. You're dealing with the fragmented child within you. To that vulnerable child, the mere thought of abuse is tantamount to doing it. The mere fantasy of violence or anger is no different than if it were real. But there is a big difference between fantasy and reality. The inner child condemns you for having normal human emotions of anger and frustration."

"Okay, okay," I blurted out. "Sometimes I do resent them. Sometimes they make me mad as hell. Sometimes I just have to run upstairs and let Tim handle things because I'm afraid of what I'll do. And sometimes I wonder what life would have been like if I hadn't gotten pregnant. If I hadn't been such a goddamned slut, so stupid about birth control. But I feel guilty as hell when I think this way. Actions have consequences."

I paused, thought a moment. "Sometimes I even wonder what life would be like if I'd had an abortion and just walked away from Tim instead of deciding to get married. I wouldn't be dealing with kids, my career would be much better off, and I wouldn't be trapped in a situation like this."

I had to stop as the bile rose up in my throat, and I fought back the urge to vomit. My entire body was shaking. Dr. Padgett waited silently for me to continue.

"What kind of a selfish bitch am I? What kind of horrible mother would even speculate on how her life would be better if she'd had an abortion? What kind of a hateful, ungrateful, despicable mother would think like that?

"And Tim is probably the best thing that ever happened in my life. He's been a rock through all of this. A lot of guys would have hit the road a long time ago. But he hangs in there. He loves me. Damnit, Dr. Padgett! I don't deserve anyone as good as Tim. I don't deserve those beautiful kids. They've all kept me alive by loving me no matter what I've done. How dare I even think about hurting them, leaving them, or wondering what it would be like if they weren't in my life—even thinking life might be better. How horrible!"

I was crying hysterically now, shuddering at the evil thoughts spinning through my head. Ashamed of getting pregnant through my own promiscuity and negligence. Ashamed of wanting to run from my responsibilities and having the audacity to resent my own family who gave me nothing but love.

"It's totally natural to think these things, Rachel. Especially in your position. Motherhood wasn't a decision for you. It was the consequence of impulsive actions. Maybe in ways you weren't ready for it. But let's look at the facts and not just the feelings. You have faced your responsibilities and done so admirably. You've had many more obstacles to overcome, but you haven't given up. And no matter what thoughts and feelings you've had at times, you haven't acted on them.

"Maybe if you had it to do over, you would have done things differently. But you've accepted the fact that you didn't. And it isn't a total loss. It might be more difficult to mother your kids as they grow up while you try to grow up yourself. But it isn't impossible. Whatever thoughts you've had, they haven't driven you to abuse so far, and they aren't going to do so just because you discuss them."

With that time was up.

I was frozen in my chair. It took a few moments to get up; my mind was spinning in so many directions I had difficulty fishing for the car keys.

Finally, numbed and overwhelmed, I rose, mumbled a quick good-bye, and headed for home.

∞

On the drive home I speculated on Dr. Padgett's notion that feelings had no moral consequence—only the actions taken in the throes of them. It contradicted my Catholic upbringing. I could envision the elderly priest standing in front of a sixth-grade classroom full of adolescents and repeating the phrase: "Impure thoughts are as impure deeds."

In those days I'd cowered in the confessional, afraid to mention the thoughts I was having, afraid to confess to the masturbation I knew to be a mortal sin. I'd emerged from the confessional deliberately withholding my thoughts and actions. And I knew the consequence of acts of deliberate omission. Deliberate omission—a mortal sin.

Why had I never confessed those thoughts? Was I too ashamed to utter them aloud? Or was I afraid of committing an even greater sin, that of confessing a sin that I knew I would repeatedly commit again, thus making a sacrilegious farce of the sacrament?

Dr. Padgett's philosophy on relative morality, the lack of moral implications to thoughts and feelings, was a comforting one indeed. I'd spent a lifetime chastising myself for what I felt were demented thoughts—a lifetime of shame so great I could not bear to share it with another soul. To believe Dr. Padgett would be a tremendous burden lifted from me, and part of me fervently wished I could do so.

Intellectually it all made sense. Intellectually I had already made the decision to discard much of the Catholic doctrine I had been taught. For several years I hadn't practiced Catholicism at all and had gone so far as to wonder if God even existed. But changing my beliefs on an emotional level was another story. Regardless of how I viewed Catholicism and its tenets today, I had spent nearly all of my childhood in Catholic schools. Its impact on me was just as entrenched as that of my parents.

Which was it? Was Dr. Padgett right? Or was he advocating a lesser morality, one designed to appease me and absolve me of guilt when such absolution was not deserved? Were impure thoughts and shameful feelings amoral or immoral? Was he easing my conscience at the cost of my soul? Was he leading me into temptation, away from the church I had only recently re-entered? Was I being forced to choose between my therapy and my religion?

A year ago I had been obstinate in my opinions about almost every aspect of life, including my own interpretation of Catholicism. I had steadfast views on parenting, morality, marriage, and family. I could argue my viewpoints with such rhetorical flourish that I could often convince others to adopt them. But mostly, I now realized, I had been trying to convince myself.

Now no ground was solid. I questioned everything. The more deeply I probed the issues, it seemed, the more deeply conflicted I became, the hazier and increasingly elusive the answers seemed to be.

In one year everything I thought I believed had been challenged. And I began to wonder if I could ever believe anything again.

Chapter 13

It had been a rough evening. Vicious, resentful thoughts about Jeffrey and Melissa exploded in my mind like hand grenades. I was torn between analyzing these thoughts and defusing them as quickly as possible. Yet another Pandora's box had been opened. So many boxes, so many issues, all unresolved. My mind was spinning.

Once Tim arrived home I retreated to the attic, fell asleep, and didn't re-emerge until morning. Yet another evening when the kids didn't see Mommy. Is this what they deserve?

Was this abuse?

I was determined to resolve the conflict between Dr. Padgett's views and my religious upbringing. I needed to believe in something.

So I walked into the Wednesday session with a clear and predetermined agenda. If Dr. Padgett were going to espouse such views, he would have to support them convincingly. I could not simply take this one on his word. The moral stakes were too high. Today Padgett's brain was going to be picked apart; his motives were going to be assessed.

I had barely settled in my chair before I started the interrogation.

"Are you Catholic, Dr. Padgett?"

"Why would that be important to you?"

Answering a question with a question. His same old trick. This time I'd stand my ground.

"I asked you a question," I replied, ignoring his question. "Are you Catholic?"

"We need to explore why you want to know."

"No," I answered tersely. "*We* don't. *We* need a straight answer to a very direct question. I'll repeat it in case you missed it the first two times. Are you Catholic?"

"I'm not going to answer that."

"Are you Christian?"

Silence.

"Do you believe in God at all?"

Silence.

"Look, Dr. Padgett. I know your little power-play game. I have to answer everything; you don't have to answer anything. I'm not going to play it today. I think, for as long as we've been in therapy together, I deserve at least one straight answer to a simple, direct question."

"Therapy isn't about what I believe, Rachel. It's about what you believe."

"But that doesn't stop you from spouting off your own versions of morality, does it?"

He looked genuinely puzzled.

"Yesterday you said that there were no such things as impure thoughts—which directly contradicts Catholicism.

174

About 25 percent of this country is Catholic, Dr. Padgett, so if you're going to contradict them, you'd better be prepared to say where you're coming from."

"There are no such things as impure thoughts," he replied. "People can't always control their thoughts and emotions—only how they choose to react to them."

"I don't believe you! You're pretty damned convinced of your views, but you won't say a word about where they come from."

"Why would it matter if I were Catholic?"

"Because, if you were, then you would know exactly why your views contradict the stuff I was taught growing up. And if you're not, then we might just not be on the same playing field."

"Playing field?"

"Yes. For all I know you might just hate Catholics. You might not believe in God at all. You might think all of it is really just a bunch of mindless, anti-intellectual, fundamentalist crap. And I need to know that if we're going to work together."

My rabid defensiveness about a religion I had so often questioned myself surprised even me. I was confused, angry, and on a roll.

He said, "My religion, if I have one, whether I believe in God or not, isn't the issue here."

"There you go again. The blank-screen shit. Maybe you don't believe in anything; maybe behind that blank screen there's just a big pile of nothing."

"I don't see any benefit in sharing my views on organized religion with you. As a matter of fact, I can only see harm in it."

"Harm?" I laughed incredulously. "You think that

talking about God and religion is harmful? What? Is therapy a religion now? Are you supposed to be God?"

"I didn't say I wouldn't discuss religion—only that the discussion needs to focus on your views, not mine."

"I spent my entire childhood in Catholic schools, Dr. Padgett. And the teaching on impure thoughts was very clear. Impure thoughts are as bad as impure deeds. Are you saying the whole Church is nothing but a lie?"

"What do you think of that teaching? What do you think about impure thoughts?"

"You know what I think? I think you're on such a power trip, you don't want me to believe in God. You don't want me to have a religion because you want me to bend down and kiss your ass and worship *you*. I think you're trying to manipulate me into thinking exactly what you think and calling it gospel. That's what I think!"

Out of the mouth of an agnostic, yet I spoke the words like a tent-revival zealot.

"I think," Dr. Padgett said slowly, "that you are confusing me with your father. Your father was the one who equated opposing viewpoints with intolerable disrespect."

"Don't bring my father into this one. He was a staunch Catholic. He knew what he believed in and wasn't afraid to say it the way you are."

"And your father beat the hell out of you, tormented you, and exploited your vulnerability as a child. Maybe he was staunchly Catholic, but I don't see how you could say his actions were moral."

"You're intimidated by people with strong beliefs, aren't you? What kind of a man are you anyway? A touchy-feely, wishy-washy wimp."

"That's your father talking, Rachel. And you know it.

You're the one who was intimidated by strong beliefs and scared to death to question. You're the one who isn't sure what you believe in, and that's perfectly okay."

"So you're saying I'm too much of a wimp to believe in anything? To stand for anything?" I retorted defensively.

"I'm saying that you're confused and conflicted right now. You aren't sure what you believe. Not only about religion but also about life, about how you feel about your gender, about being a parent, about how you feel about your own parents. A major part of this process is to look back on your whole framework of thinking without the distortions and re-emerge as the person you're destined to be."

I sat back, defeated. "I'm tired of reassessing, Dr. Padgett. I want to believe in something. I don't know what I stand for anymore. I can't even trust my own judgment. It would be a lot easier for me if you'd just answer my question so I could know whether your challenge to a major Catholic doctrine is valid or not."

Dr. Padgett reclined a bit and sighed.

"I can't tell you what to think, Rachel. I'm here to help you sort out the questions, not to give you the answers. You're the only one who can provide the answers. If I try and influence you with my own viewpoints, then the person who emerges won't be you. You're the one who has to make all the decisions. My role is to help you do that, not to do it for you."

The vulnerable, whining child entered the picture.

"But Dr. Padgett! Why can't you help me make the decisions? You don't always keep the blank screen. You told me about your kids, didn't you? Why can't you tell me about religion?"

"The purpose of the screen is to benefit you, Rachel, not me. I thought that revealing the fact that I have two kids of my own was beneficial to your progress. Just as I think revealing my religious beliefs would be detrimental.

"This is a critical issue to you. It's going to take some time for you to sort it out. I'm not going to influence you in any way about beliefs you have to reach on your own."

"But you're telling me to turn my back on my religion. You're telling me not to believe all that I was taught."

"What I'm telling you, Rachel, is that you need to revisit the entire issue. You need to take a new look at your religious upbringing in the same way you've taken a new look at what happened in your childhood. Only this time without the distortions and without the black-and-white filter. This time you need to face it as an adult."

"But what if it turns out to be different than what you believe?"

"What if it does?"

"How can you understand me if my views are different than yours?"

"If that were the case, how could I understand your issues of femininity without being a woman? How could I understand mental illness without being mentally ill myself? I don't have to be the same as you, Rachel, and you don't have to be the same as me. What matters is that I care. What matters is that I have the ability to respect who you are as an individual and the ability to empathize with how you feel."

Another master plan, another predetermined agenda had gone awry. I'd sought direct answers and asked for quick solutions only to be presented with more questions.

I was weary of introspection. Yearning for simplicity, I found only more complexity. Slowly and painfully every layer of perception and distortion was unraveling. I feared there would be nothing at the core. A black hole.

Dr. Padgett had been right. My father—and my mother—had discouraged questioning. They saw introspection as a pathological weakness. The childhood flashback from the couch session focused in my mind. I was a six-year-old, lying in bed, awake and frightened, looking out at the seemingly infinite darkness outside my bedroom window. My grandfather had just passed away, and we had been discussing the concept of heaven and afterlife at school. Heaven seemed comforting. But, even then, I could not accept it.

I had wondered what happened before I was born. For thousands of years life had existed, but I had been alive for only six of them. What had I been before then?

In the haunting darkness the answer had kept coming to me. *Nothing. I'd been nothing before I was born.* Endless questions had consumed me with fear. *What was nothing? What was I for the thousands of years I didn't exist?*

Death scared me because I feared nothingness. If I had been nothing before I was born, then I could imagine that I would be nothing once I died. I'd been absolutely horrified, paralyzed in my bed. But I could not cry or seek comfort because I knew what would happen if I did. It had happened before.

My parents thought it was nonsense that a six-year-old would harbor such thoughts. I could remember their answers the few times I did dare share my fears.

"You know what your problem is, Rachel? You think too much. That's positively stupid. People go to heaven or hell when they die, and you are already born, so what difference does it make what you were before then? You're too smart for your own good. Your mind is playing tricks on you. It twists around with terrible thoughts. What is wrong with you? Quit thinking about those things this instant!"

As convinced as I was that I was paying the price for too much thinking, I could not stop. The worries horrified me, and I was ashamed of them. So I kept them to myself. I'd spent innumerable sleepless nights looking out my bedroom window as if it were a prison cell.

This is how I'd learned the value of rhetorical argument and obstinate opinion. Convincing those around me—and especially myself—that my thoughts were absolutely right. If my mind began to wander again, I found a way to distract it. Stay busy. Get drunk. Get laid. Anything to escape the chamber of torture that was my mind.

And now Dr. Padgett was asking me to reopen that chamber, to question everything again. To enter that frightening black hole of infinite smoke and mirrors where nothing was solid and everything was an illusion.

Suddenly I was aware of my surroundings again. I had no concept of how much of the session I'd spent in my own world. Dr. Padgett was still sitting there, apparently having decided not to interrupt my thoughts.

"What are you thinking about?" he asked when my eyes once again focused on him.

"Nothing," I replied. "I'm just tired, Dr. Padgett. Really, really tired."

"Well," he said, "that's about it for today. We can pick up where we left off tomorrow."

Perhaps that was "it" for the session, but I knew it was not "it" for my thoughts. The questions had only just begun. I was grateful for the antidepressant Desyrel I took at night. It would thrust me into a deep sleep.

The sluggishness of Desyrel. Once asleep I couldn't be aroused by the buzzing alarm clock or the early-morning bustle of Tim preparing for a day at the office. It took a real effort—or a horrifyingly explicit nightmare—to stir me.

Yet the alarm had not rung nor would it for hours. No nightmare had roused me, and I was stirring nonetheless. Strange. One eye half-open, I looked at the clock. Two o'clock.

I was uncomfortable for some reason. Warm. Damp. My skin chafed.

Had one of the kids spilled something on the bed? How could it still be so warm? A little less groggy now, the dampness of the sheets irritated me. I ran my hand across the mattress sheet. It was soaked. So, for that matter, were my pajamas. I sat bolt upright as I smelled my moistened finger, and the reality hit me.

I had wet the bed.

Tim was sleeping soundly, and his side of the king-size mattress appeared to still be dry, so I gingerly moved the blanket aside and climbed out of bed, not wanting to disturb him and not particularly interested in letting him know I'd wet the bed.

I was mortified as I peeled off the soaked silk pajamas, rinsing them in the bathtub to get rid of the stench. Changing the sheets would mean waking Tim, so I spread a thick towel over the wetness instead. Embarrassed as I was, the feelings of dizziness and nausea from the Desyrel made this cleanup an arduous task.

I could not recall this ever happening before. I had never been a bed wetter, although I could remember nights as a child lying in bed, scared to death that I might fall asleep and pee in the bed. I was frightened by how my parents might respond, how ashamed they would be of me. Undoubtedly this must have had something to do with therapy, with regression. Nearly everything seemed to. As the sedated grogginess overcame me again, I vowed I would address it with Dr. Padgett in my next session.

∞

One of the things that struck me as most frustrating about therapy was that nothing ever seemed to progress sequentially.

Nearly every intense session ended with Dr. Padgett's closing words: *"We can pick up on this next session."* Yet, more often than not, that same issue might not be picked up for weeks or even months as we devoted the next session to something else entirely.

I'd left yesterday's session prepared to pick up the topics of religion and existence and afterlife in the next session. Instead I'd peed in my bed. And walked into Thursday's session sheepish and horribly embarrassed. I'd planned on the academic roundtable and yet, once again, found myself to be the little girl cowering shamefaced in the confessional.

I knew enough to know that any event so disturbing, so clearly in the forefront of my mind, was that which most warranted exploration. But sitting in Dr. Padgett's office, swiveling my chair, biting my fingernails, tapping my feet, not daring to look him in the eye, the words escaped me.

The session began not in the silence of being unable to put my finger on my thoughts, but of being absolutely revolted at the notion of discussing them. I hated such sessions, and Dr. Padgett knew it.

"What's on your mind?"

Little girl voice, eyes still downcast, deciphering the carpet pattern.

"Nothing."

The chair swiveled more vigorously now, my feet tapped a quicker beat, and I was biting not only my fingernails, but also the ends of my hair.

"It seems like something is on your mind. Why don't you stop the motion and put it into words?"

He's right. Why don't I? Why can't I?

But my silence continued, and my hyperkinetic display of nervous anxiety and tics just kept intensifying. The more I deliberately withheld what was on my mind, the more anxious I became and the harder and more humiliating it became to attempt to reveal my thoughts.

Every shred of rational sense told me that I should just go ahead and bring it up. And yet the little girl had me mute, intent upon saying nothing, filled with shame and humiliation.

Finally I spoke. All I needed to do was say a few words, so I blurted them out as quickly as possible.

"Ipeedinmybed," I mumbled unintelligibly.

"Excuse me?"

"What are you trying to do, humiliate the shit out of me? You asked me to say what was on my mind, and I said it, and now you're going to force me to repeat it?"

From vulnerable little girl to the hardened tough guy.

"Honestly, Rachel," he said sincerely, "I really couldn't understand what you just said."

Back to the vulnerable little girl in a flash.

"I peed in my bed," I repeated, still in a barely audible near-whisper but at least decipherable. My eyes were still riveted on the carpet pattern. I couldn't bear to look up.

"How do you feel about that?"

"Really bad, really embarrassed. I don't want to talk about it. Let's talk about something else, okay?"

183

"You know we can talk about anything you want, but this seems to be pretty important to you."

"Well, it's not, okay? Forget I said it. I didn't say a goddamned thing. All right? It doesn't mean shit."

A battle of the inner children. The adult me was barely present and astonished to witness my behavior.

Silence again. Dr. Padgett was not going to lead me anywhere.

Finally I burst out again. "I'm so ashamed of myself. I peed in the bed. On the sheets, on my pajamas. Everywhere."

"Why don't you look at me?" he asked calmly.

"I can't! You're probably disgusted with me. You think I'm stupid because I'm making a big deal out of it."

"You can't know what I'm doing," he said gently, "unless you look up at me and see for yourself."

How could this be so hard? I was not a wallflower, not shy. I was known for my I-don't-give-a-shit-about-what-people-think-of-me attitude. Indeed, I had always prided myself on being tough, courageous, always looking people straight in the eye. *Like a real man does.*

Jesus Christ, where did that last thought come from?

Still I couldn't bring myself to raise my eyes. The thoughts within me were spinning wildly in momentous vacillation. How could I be aware of it and still let it go on?

"I hate myself," I managed to say. "I wish I could just crawl into a hole and die."

My God, you are overreacting, you disgusting little piece of filth! You just want attention. It's no big deal.

I was overwhelmed by the desire to pee again, right in my chair. And mortified by the possibility.

"Why don't you look up at me?" he said again. "I think it would help. I'm not angry with you."

"Well, you should be. You should spank me!"

"That's what your father would have done."

"That's what you should do. That's what I deserve. That's what would make me feel better."

"I'm not going to hit you. Why don't you look up at me?"

"You don't get it. I want you to hit me! You don't understand, do you?"

"Why do you want me to hit you?"

"Because I'd feel better, okay? Because it would help me get over this."

"Help you get over feeling embarrassed because you wet your bed?"

"Goddamnit! Don't rub my nose in it. What are you trying to do, humiliate me?"

"No. You're trying to humiliate yourself."

"You wanna fight me, you fight like a man! I know you want to; you're dying to. Beat the crap out of me! Damnit, I *want* you to!"

"Why would I want to do that?"

"Because I'm crazy. Because I'm shameful and I don't deserve to be alive. If you don't hit me, maybe I'll just hit myself."

Here was an instance where the borderline personality disorder diagnosis became a self-fulfilling prophecy. I'd had plenty of plunges into the depths of self-hatred. It had manifested itself in many self-destructive ways. But I had never embarked on what could be considered outright self-mutilation. Having read quite a bit about it, I began to imitate what I'd read, slapping myself in the face, digging my fingernails into my arms and scratching. It didn't feel natural, but I was a borderline, and I was convinced that this was what a borderline would do. Maybe it would help.

"Rachel."

"I hate myself! I hate myself! I wish I were dead." I was crying hysterically now, twisting and writhing in the chair, eyes rolling and practically spinning in my head, slapping myself harder, digging my nails in just a little deeper.

"Rachel, look at me now!" His was no longer a gentle request but a command. I'd pushed Dr. Padgett as far as he was about to go, and I recognized the authority in his voice.

I looked up into his eyes, which were set and determined. He was not hiding his impatience.

"You're yelling at me!" I cried. "Don't yell at me, Dr. Padgett! Please. I'm so sorry."

"That's enough!"

I was stunned by the sharpness of his tone. Enough to stop the slapping, the scratching, and the motion completely.

I didn't say a word, just kept looking at him.

"This isn't therapy. This is acting out."

"I was just saying what was on my mind," I whined.

"You're letting the child take over. The adult isn't present. And you're doing more than just talking; you're abusing yourself, humiliating yourself. It feeds on itself. And you need to stop it, right now."

Summoned, as if by a hypnotist's finger snap, the adult reappeared.

"I'm sorry, Dr. Padgett. I just couldn't control myself."

"You let the child take over," he repeated, still a firm edge in his voice. "You can't do that. It's important to get in touch with the child within you, but it's just as important that you maintain a sense of perspective. Otherwise you're not exploring your feelings; you are literally immersing yourself in them, getting lost in them. It's dangerous to do that."

"I know."

With twenty minutes left in the session we began to explore what had just happened, the feelings and perceptions, the distortions that lay beneath it.

Dr. Padgett pointed out something I had noticed but was loath to admit. I had not only continued in the self-humiliation, but I had, in some ways, taken a perverse pleasure in it. My silence and subsequent skirting of the issue were not rooted in the desire to *avoid* humiliation and embarrassment, but to *increase* it. I took a certain pleasure in feeling ashamed. Once I had gotten a taste of it, unless and until he stopped me, I just hungered for more. Sick. Twisted. And totally true.

The pleasure. The increasing sense of shame paired with the increasing desire to urinate. It all came back to me. When I was a little girl and masturbated almost nightly, the pleasure was sexual. But I didn't know it to be sexual. I only knew it gave me some relief and enjoyment. I knew it was shameful, and yet that shame only enhanced the excitement. I didn't know what sexual feelings were. Rather my fantasies were of urinating, peeing, or, more accurately, of having an overwhelming need to pee but being denied the opportunity.

The more harshly it was denied, the more badly I needed to go, the more intense the excitement and pleasure.

Another recollection came to mind—the first time a boy fondled my breasts in high school. It was at an afternoon matinee at the neighborhood theater. I was frightened and disturbed by what I would discover later was an orgasm. By then I had a fair idea of what sex, of what making out was. But at first I was horrified that it made me feel like I wanted to pee and the climax was identical to the shuddering feelings I had when I masturbated to the cruel urination deprivation fantasies I had as a young child.

At the time I had quit thinking about it and began to seek the thrill of orgasm from any boy who would give it to me. Revisited in this context, however, my earliest notions of sexual climax were very disturbing.

I was not yet ready to openly share these thoughts and conclusions, although I realized their truth. Instead I listened as Dr. Padgett shared more observations and conclusions of his own. It is normal at a certain phase in a child's development, he explained, for girls to harbor deep feelings toward their fathers. Deep *sexual* feelings. Normal children, sufficiently loved, grow past this phase at about age five or six. But in the face of my normal sexual desires—Freudian desires that I had previously thought were pure fiction and perversion—my father humiliated and abused me. I had established a link, a distorted but close association, between pain/degradation/shame/humiliation and excitement/pleasure.

Part of the humiliation and shame centered around my own genitalia—the fact that I had a vagina rather than a penis. My brothers and father peed like men, standing up, while I was forced to shamefully squat. My parents did not favor girls, so I was ashamed to be one. My urination deprivation fantasies were based upon truth.

Often my parents, patience gone, not wanting to deal with their children anymore for the evening, would send me to my room with strict orders to stay there, not to come out— *or else*. On a few occasions when I tried to sneak out to use the bathroom, I could remember them yelling at me to get back into my room *immediately*. Their tone of voice frightened me. It was an indicator of a beating that was to come.

And so I would stay in my room, my fear and the intimidating tone of my father's voice shaming me. It made me need to urinate even more.

But I could not. I could not leave the room. If I wet the bed, as I had wet my pants in my preschool years, I knew I would be subject to a harsh, humiliating beating. The thought of it, in a distorted, twisted way, excited me even more and made me burn with the desire to pee even more. It reached the point where, lying in bed at night and holding myself between the legs as small children do, I discovered that the presence of my hand there led to even greater excitement and pleasure.

I did not tell Dr. Padgett much, if anything, about this memory during that session. Indeed, it would take a long time before I would be able to revisit the issue and even longer before I reached any kind of resolution about it. I was still dubious of Freudian theory that attributed sexual desires to five- and six-year-olds, but I had no doubt there was a strong link between humiliation and excitement for me. It was the vulnerable little girl who had felt those feelings of simultaneous shame and sexual pleasure. And it was the tough guy in me who found them repugnant and thus sought to be beyond intimidation, beyond humiliation, and beyond vulnerability—to be, in essence, the boy Daddy and Mommy wanted me to be.

It was a crude, distorted form of self-preservation I had developed out of necessity—and a pattern so entrenched it would take years to break.

But at least I had taken the first step, painful as it had been. At least I was aware of it. In this particular instance I was, for once, more aware of it than even Dr. Padgett.

Chapter 14

Regression.

It was embarrassing, painful, and shameful. I would sit in a therapy session, thrust out of the realm of reasonable, intellectual discourse and into a world of a little girl's inconsolable tears and fears of events that transpired years ago.

It was a world of wild and raging tantrums that even my three-year-old daughter had begun to outgrow. I would whine and plead, demanding the impossible, like wanting Dr. Padgett to forgo his much-needed vacations and weekends so that I wouldn't be "left alone." I was reduced to a toddler, practically tugging at his pants leg and grasping at his ankles, refusing to let him go.

Regression invaded my sleep too, as I woke up in a puddle of my own urine for a second, third, and fourth night.

I endured the embarrassment and my childishness, believing I had lost Dr. Padgett's respect. And I certainly couldn't respect myself. The normal theme of healthy adult relationships was give-and-take. Yet frequently I chastised myself as someone who only took. I was certain that no one could possibly give me everything I wanted and needed.

Regression, as painful as it was, was a necessary evil. I longed for therapy that was intellectual and philosophical. But the unavoidable reality was that I had to feel. Not just the vague and sometimes hard-to-define emotional discomfort and anxiety of the adult, but the raw passion and pain that fueled this anxiety—the explosive, clinging, irrational feelings of the inner child herself. Dr. Padgett insisted this was necessary. Deepest within me, I knew he was right. Despite this knowledge, it was never easy, never smooth as my emotions vacillated wildly out of control, hemmed in by the limits of therapy like a handball crashing against one wall and then the other.

At times, no matter how driven I was to open up and expose these childhood feelings, I could not access them. I'd leave these sessions feeling empty, numb, and frustrated, the dull ache inside me untouched as if nothing had been accomplished. At other times the fragmented inner child would dominate the session. It was a bitter struggle of emotional explosions and one-sided confrontations as Dr. Padgett sought to rein in the pervasive inner child and maintain some degree of contact with reality.

I would leave these sessions exhausted, often ashamed of the verbal outbursts and outlandish behavior I'd displayed. My loss of control and brush with the edge of sanity frightened me.

Dr. Padgett was a skilled navigator, steering me from extremes. Sometimes he coaxed me out of total repression; sometimes he firmly reprimanded me back to reality.

The characteristics of the fragmented inner child were

becoming more clearly defined. Like a portrait of diametric opposites. In my writings I named the two of them. When I was in the throes of spinning conflict, I would script playlike dialogue where the pair would vent their feelings and confront each other, the adult me as a moderator. Like much of what I wrote, I was careful to hide it in the bottom of my sock drawer. If anyone else saw these thoughts, they would think I was unequivocally insane.

Even my closest friends from the church—even Tim—never knew the distorted inner workings of my mind. Had they known, I don't think I could have faced them again. This was a matter between me and my therapist. And it was yet another way that I was vulnerable to Dr. Padgett to a far greater extent than I had been to anyone else in my life. He knew the darkest secrets within me. It forced me to trust him as I had never trusted anyone before.

I was far more familiar with the tough half of the inner child, whom in my writings I'd dubbed Toughie or TC for Tough Chick. This was the hardened facade I had maintained for years. TC was the swaggering presence the sisters ousted from the classroom and remanded to the hallway. TC lived by an I-don't-give-a-shit credo, too tough to be hurt, too independent to care, and too streetwise to ever trust a soul. To TC, trust was an open invitation to be screwed.

TC was male in every way but one. He had somehow been trapped into a female body. He was the portrait of manhood as I saw it in my childhood, one who loathed weakness and sentiment, as my father did.

The other fragment was the vulnerable one, whom I dubbed Vulno in my writings. I was not nearly as familiar with this one, whose presence seemed to have been given life through therapy. Where TC had erected a barricade of walls in self-protection, Vulno was the antithesis, a font of raw openness. Vulno trusted everyone and could not make sense of those who would not return such trust with love. It was as if the vulnerability itself, the willingness to be screwed over, would somehow protect her. She was ruled by emotion, always thirsting for love, seeking it everywhere with anyone, and suffering great pain if it weren't forthcoming.

Vulno was intimidated by power. She did not seek it. She was content to be a follower if that would gain acceptance and love. She was as dependent as TC was independent, and she would give herself up completely if she could only, somehow, be taken care of.

Vulno wished that Dr. Padgett would simply take over. She feared disagreement, as if in doing so, she would anger her loved ones and drive them away. Her only means of asserting herself was through whining, pleading, and begging for mercy or pity.

Neither fragmented identity was admirable. Both were extremes. Neither appeared very worthy to me or, for that matter, lovable. But at least I could respect the tough side, which is, perhaps, why that side openly manifested itself far more frequently than the vulnerable one. How Dr. Padgett could ever believe that these two fragments could somehow integrate, find common ground, and accept each other was thoroughly beyond me. They hated each other, and getting in touch with these conflicting feelings inevitably led to turbulent and confrontational sessions. I went along with Dr. Padgett in attempting to explore the nuances of these fragmented identities. But secretly I was more inclined to believe, and even hope, that it would be a battle to the death with one fragment emerging dominant and victorious while the other was banished to permanent oblivion.

Given a choice, I had to say I preferred that Toughie be the survivor. TC, after all, had gotten me this far. I couldn't imagine giving up that part of myself, my greatest protector and mechanism for survival.

∞

Unlike those who seemed to perpetually circle the parking area to find the closest slot, I eyed an oasis of empty spaces in the farthest corner of the hospital lot. As the July sun burned on the asphalt pavement, wavy lines of heat rising from the blacktop, I sat in my car. The air conditioner was broken, and I baked as I kept watch, making certain no one was around. When the coast was clear, I got out and opened the trunk, retrieving two large garbage bags filled with children's toys. I'd be too visible in the elevator and opted for the stairs.

The inundating pain and excruciating embarrassment of a series of regression episodes in sessions had left me gun-shy and numb, unwilling and unable to brave the territory of childhood feelings again. For the past two weeks the sessions had been numb, distant, and unproductive as I desperately clung to intellectual and philosophical pursuits to avoid being seized by the monstrous inner child fragments.

While Dr. Padgett could understand my reasons to avoid regression, he also felt that until I re-entered the world of childhood feelings, I would not make further progress. At his suggestion I'd agreed to try play therapy, a methodology he and others had successfully used with children.

With young children of both genders in my household, the materials were easy to obtain. Once Jeffrey and Melissa had fallen asleep for the night, I'd tiptoed through their rooms, selecting toys they hadn't touched for months, with a careful eye for those that reflected a gender preference, as Dr. Padgett had suggested.

At ten o'clock, while Tim was absorbed in the news, I had sneaked my bags of goodies out to the car and hidden them in the trunk. Like the writings, I had no intention of Tim seeing the bags either. That would have required explanations I was far too embarrassed to give.

Dr. Padgett had given me his customary smiling greeting, as if such fare were routine for adults, but I felt uncomfortable nonetheless, assailed by second thoughts. Alas, I was already there. I had managed to bring the bags in, so I might as well go along with it.

Wordlessly I emptied the contents of the trash bags onto the carpeted floor. A big plastic fighter plane with a number of badly worn G.I. Joes. A toy machine gun with a broken trigger so that it no longer made any noise. A laser gun complete with sounds and flashing lights. A rubber hunting knife. A miniature football. A stuffed puppy that Melissa had managed to unstuff with too much loving. A blonde, curly-haired ballerina doll that had gained an impromptu punk-rock look when Melissa first began experimenting with scissors. A few more dolls and stuffed animals. A miniature plastic tea set decorated with crayon scribbles.

The largest and most prominent of the toys was a stuffed clown, nearly three feet tall and still looking new. For some reason it frightened Melissa, and she'd banished it from her bed and into the recesses of the closet.

The toys lay scattered on the floor like garage sale leftovers.

"So what am I supposed to do with this shit?" I asked, arms folded, defensive and embarrassed. "You know, Dr. Padgett, this was a really stupid idea."

"You agreed to try this," he replied with no trace of admonishment in his voice. "Just pick up whichever ones you want to, play with them as you wish, and say what's on your mind."

"I'll tell you what's on my mind. I feel like a complete asshole."

He didn't reply.

I picked up the laser gun first, now loaded with fresh batteries. Dr. Padgett, I decided, deserved to be annoyed. Lights flashing, the sounds of sirens and rat-a-tat bullet fire filling the office, I aimed the gun directly at him. No reaction. He didn't even flinch.

I then turned the gun toward the dolls, firing relentlessly.

Dr. Padgett remained a silent observer, and I began to be immersed in the play—entering the child's world. I lined up all the dolls against the couch next to me, then loaded the fighter plane with disabled G.I. Joes. I dropped imaginary bombs on the little girl toys, then swooped low in flight, tumbling them to the floor like dominos. I stood the dolls up again, then snapped the football at them, scattering them on the floor. In a way I was cognizant of the message I was sending with my style of destructive play—using the "boy toys" as weapons to torment the "girl toys." But I felt a certain euphoria as well, a fire within that took on a life of its own.

Finally I sat back in my chair, arms folded once again, and stared him down with a you-asked-for-it-you-got-it kind of glare.

"Any thoughts on this?" he asked softly.

Is this man a complete idiot or what? Didn't he just witness this whole massacre? I hate being a girl. I hate dolls. So what difference does it make?

"Gee, Sigmund," I retorted sarcastically, "can't you fig-ure this one out?" Obviously I wasn't going to get a rise out of him. Once again he was infuriatingly patient and simply re-iterated the question, ignoring my caustic remarks.

"What are your thoughts on this, on what just hap-pened here?"

Sighing, I stated the obvious.

"I hate the girl stuff. I like the boy's stuff. Period. I just made a complete asshole out of myself, and we're just hitting on things both of us already know. I knew this wouldn't work."

"Whose dolls are those?"

"Melissa's, of course, you idiot. Do you think I have a son that plays with dolls?"

"Would you have a problem if he did?"

I rolled my eyes. Visions of Dr. Padgett's son, hope-lessly effeminate, flashed before my eyes, although I had never seen him and had no idea what he was really like.

"Maybe you wouldn't have a problem with your son doing it, but I sure as hell would."

"What about Melissa? Does she play with the dolls?"

"Yes," I had to admit but added defensively, "but she plays with Jeffrey's stuff too. My little girl plays with what-ever she wants to play with."

"Are you bothered when she plays with dolls?"

"What kind of a question is that?" I retorted. "Of course not. She's a little girl for chrissakes!"

"Did you buy any of these dolls for her? Have you ever bought her any dolls?"

I knew where this line of questioning was leading. He was trying to establish my complicity with doll play. Tempted to come back with a verbal assault to throw him off the track, instead, for some reason, I had a change of heart and decided to be honest. Was Vulno popping in on the scene again?

"Yes, I buy my little girl dolls. Is there anything wrong with it?"

"Of course not. But I see an inconsistency here."

Which I'm letting you see, you bastard. Quit rubbing it in!

"You don't have a problem with your own little girl playing with dolls—or being openly feminine either. You can accept the fact that Melissa is a little girl, and it doesn't bother you at all. Her femininity, her preference for dolls doesn't make you love her any less, does it?"

"Of course not. I love that little girl more than anything in the world."

"But if you love her, a little girl who acts like a little girl, then it must be possible for you to love being a girl. If you couldn't, you could not possibly love her."

My eyes narrowed.

"Leave my daughter out of this! She can be anything she wants to be. Being a girl is fine for her, but it's not fine for me. I know it's inconsistent. I know it doesn't make sense, but I don't give a flying fuck! You aren't going to trap me into liking being a girl, you understand? You're not!"

With that I picked up the little ballerina, holding her by her botched haircut, and smacked her with my fist as the little arms and legs swung back and forth, each blow becoming more violent. Finally I hurled the doll against the wall, her pudgy arm separating from her body and landing with a clatter on Dr. Padgett's desk.

My entire body was shaking, and I was overwhelmed with the urge to vomit and filled with a sudden rush of remorse.

Dr. Padgett rose from his chair, gathered the two pieces of the doll, and set them on his lap. He looked at the broken doll then at me. No blank screen. His eyes were filled with sincere sadness.

"I'm sorry," I mumbled under my breath. "Very sorry. I broke it. I broke it. It was a nasty, hateful thing to do. I'm sorry."

"You don't have to be sorry, Rachel," he said kindly.

His words did little to comfort me as my eyes began to glaze with tears, still focusing on the smiling little ballerina with the bad haircut and missing arm.

"You're mad at me," I cried inconsolably. "You should be mad at me. I'm an awful, twisted person. I broke the doll. I was so cruel, so mean. I'm so sorry."

"I'm not mad," he replied with a sigh. "I'm sad. For you, Rachel. You treated that doll the way you were treated, broke it the way you were broken. You weren't born hating being a little girl. You were taught to hate being a little girl. But you *were* a little girl. So you grew up hating yourself, imitating the same violence and destruction aimed at your femininity that someone else inflicted on you. It makes me very sad that it happened, and if I'm mad at anybody, it's at the kind of person who could do that to a little girl."

Looking at the shattered ballerina, I felt her pain as if it had been me being crashed into the wall instead. And realized that, in ways, long ago it *had* been me. I began to cry in soft moaning sobs, a hollow portion of my soul crying to be touched, a part of me that had been taken away. I longed to be held more than anything else, to crawl up into Dr. Padgett's lap and sit there while he rubbed my back and stroked my hair. It was an impossible expectation that, for once, I realized and accepted as impossible.

Still the need to be cuddled was burning within me. I reached for the toy clown, the one that had so frightened Melissa, and clutched it, crying my tears into its soft permanently smiling face. A stuffed clown. Genderless. Comforting.

My arms wrapped around it tightly, as if it could hug me back.

I could not hug Dr. Padgett. By his strict limits I could not so much as touch him. And yet, as he had the broken ballerina doll nestled in his lap and I snuggled up with the clown, I felt, in ways, as if the doctor were actually hugging me. Neither of us said much for the rest of the session; we just looked into each other's eyes. His image was blurred by my tears but not so much that I couldn't see the traces of tears in his own eyes. Painful and frightening as it was to have gotten in touch with my childhood feelings, there was also a warmth there, a closeness of being connected, of being comforted as we both realized the sadness of femininity beaten and shamed away.

I wished that the session would never end, and I could sense the same in Dr. Padgett. But inevitably the words came.

"That's about it for today."

I gathered the toys into the bags as Dr. Padgett fumbled to reassemble the ballerina's arm, making it whole again. *Maybe someday he can do the same for me.*

The toys, including the ballerina, remained in the trunk of my car for several months. Except the clown. Hidden by towels, bags, or anything else I could find, the clown was shuttled back and forth and became my therapy companion for many sessions to come.

Chapter 15

The toy session had been one of those rare, compelling moments of catharsis. I was filled with warm feelings of love, acceptance, and empathy. My connection with Dr. Padgett was almost like a high. I spent the evening observing my children, enthralled by their innocence and beauty, grateful to be their mother. Grateful, for once, to be alive.

While regression had worked for me on this one occasion, giving me the euphoric feeling of closeness I so fervently desired, regression of the unproductive and extreme variety dominated my next several sessions. It was all or nothing. If I didn't feel that unique cathartic warmth all the time, then Dr. Padgett was cold and cruel. Vulno and TC sometimes shared, sometimes alternated during the next sessions.

Dr. Padgett had cried for me, and I desperately wanted it to happen again. Thus would I go into long diatribes of pathetic, helpless, and hopeless self-pity, just waiting for the emotional reaction that did not come.

When he didn't respond in the way I'd wanted, TC took over with tough defense and cynical assessments of his motives. The doctor had led me on once again. *He* was responsible for this disgusting display of vulnerable help-lessness. *He* was deliberately withholding the warmth from me in his never-ending effort to control and dominate. The man who had given me comfort—whom I had loved with all my being in the immediate aftermath of the toy session—now became the object of my hatred.

I wanted him to cry again, but he wouldn't. Soon, deprived of that emotional reaction, I hungered for even more than his tears. I wanted to be held, to sit in his lap, have him stroke my hair like any good father.

∞

Tim, who at one time had been profusely complimentary about my looks, had, in the aftermath of my diet, taken to being guarded in his comments. He could never be certain just how I might react to the most innocuous of statements. When he said something nice about how I looked, it would backfire as I'd immediately pinch my thighs, clutch imaginary fat, and emphatically insist how fat I was. It didn't take a licensed psy-chiatrist to figure out that the last thing on earth Tim would want to say was that I was looking good because I was *gaining* weight. Appearance became, between us, an unspoken issue.

But subtle changes were taking place. The five pounds I'd lost after my last hospital visit had slipped back on, and I'd added a few more. At 112 pounds I was still too thin but not quite so emaciated. My ribs were less prominent now, and there was a little softness about me. It wasn't nearly as uncom-fortable to sit in a church pew. As the autumn leaves began to turn, so, too, were my own "colors" beginning to change.

I had discovered the merits of resale shops. A bean counter at heart, I loved buying a sweater for three dollars instead of fifty at the mall.

When I discovered the racks of size-five clothing at the Goodwill, I could afford to experiment with new looks and new styles. Now the old blue suits remained abandoned in the closet as I opted for lacy, flowing dresses. I developed a passion for floral prints, for the soft and colorful. Cottons gave way to silks.

It began to matter to me how I looked. Although I didn't wear makeup every day, I wouldn't dream of going certain places without it—to church or a client appointment. Frequently I found myself searching through my new "used" wardrobe, devoting some time to the choices, pulling out the iron, the curling iron, the makeup palette just for a fifty-minute session with Dr. Padgett.

As trained as he was to notice the smallest of nuance, certainly the doctor noticed this as well. It was a crisp day in October when he ultimately brought it up.

I'd walked into the session in a cream-colored sweater dress with elaborate lace and tiny embroidered flowers on the collar. I wore matching pumps and a cream-colored bow in my thick, black hair. I was fully made-up, including lipstick, something I'd never worn even in my man-chasing days. I carried myself differently, with smaller, almost floating steps, and I crossed my legs at the knees instead of the ankles.

I looked good, and I felt good because I knew I looked good.

Still I was astounded when Dr. Padgett opened the session with a compliment. Like direct advice, direct compliments were something he rarely, if ever, doled out.

"That's a beautiful dress you have on," he said, not in a leering way, but as a perfect gentleman. "You look very attractive today."

Certainly this is what I'd wanted him to think but not necessarily what I'd expected or wanted him to say.

It reminded me of when I'd been a child, pedaling a bike without training wheels, riding solo without being aware of the fact that Daddy was no longer holding on, steadying the seat. Then Daddy cried out, "You're doing it yourself! Way to go!" Meanwhile, now aware that I was pedaling solo, I was gripped with fear, and the bike soon crashed to the ground. It was Daddy's fault for saying anything. Daddy had spoiled the moment.

"Why should that matter to you?" I snapped back, a bit guilty at having rejected his compliment and yet somehow driven to do so.

Even the "master of the mind" was visibly surprised by this one.

"I was just commenting that you look very nice today—as you have in the last several sessions."

"Is this a come-on? What do you want from me?"

"No, actually. It's an objective statement. You really do look nice."

"What's that supposed to mean? You just want me in dresses all the time, don't you? To be some little Barbie doll, some Stepford Wife. You know, just because I'm wearing this doesn't mean I don't hate being a woman, if that's what you're trying to prove!"

Where is this stuff coming from?

"I'm not trying to prove anything. I'm just making a comment," he replied.

"Actually this is a horrible color on me. It makes me

look fat as hell. Oh yeah, that's right. You want me to be fat."

"I want you to be happy, and I want you to be able to accept yourself for who you are."

"Why don't you just come out and say it, Dr. Padgett? You want me to be able to accept myself for being a woman. Well, I might have to live with it, but I'll never ever like it."

Dr. Padgett settled back in his chair. Obviously this was going to be an intense and confrontational session. If he'd had the stereotypical psychiatric goatee, he might well have been tugging on it now.

Why am I being such a bitch to this man? He was only being nice.

"You thought I'd be a pushover just because I walked in dressed like this, didn't you? Well, I'm just as tough as I've ever been. This is just a costume. And the last time I'll ever be wearing a dress to this place."

"You think I respect you *less* because you're wearing a dress?"

"Bingo!" I said, uncrossing my legs, taking off my pumps, and planting my feet on the coffee table. "That's exactly what I think."

"You are what you wear?"

"You are what you wear if you're wearing a dress. I'm announcing the fact that I'm a woman."

"And because you're a woman, somehow I think you're a pushover? You're saying I think you deserve less respect?"

"Yes!"

"Why can't you be a strong person and a woman too?"

"Don't patronize me, okay? You wouldn't get it. You can say all you want to, but you don't know what it's like to be stuck being a woman. You have no idea. You're a man."

Dr. Padgett redirected the focus, "What is it precisely

that you hate about being a woman?"

I countered with a litany of reasons. He would not render me speechless on this one. It was something I'd been thinking about for as long as I could remember.

"There were those stupid frilly dresses that you couldn't play in instead of the pants boys always got to wear. Boys got to pee standing up, and they could do it anywhere.

"Boys did fun things: they played sports, climbed trees. Girls did prissy things like fooling with dolls. Boys were direct. Girls were catty. Boys were strong and tough. Girls were weak and had to cry to get their way.

"Boys who stuck to their guns were assertive; girls who did so were pushy little bitches. Boys were steady and strong, while girls were overemotional and oversensitive.

"And no matter how much I, as a girl, might have learned in high school or college, there would always be a man who'd think I couldn't hack it because I was female."

Content that I'd made my point undeniably and unequivocally, I smugly leaned back in my chair.

"That's your father talking again," he sighed.

"No, not just my father. My mother too. My mother thought the same things. I know she did."

"I don't doubt that she had as many distortions about her gender as you do. But they're stereotypes. Every single one of them. There are men who are emotionally weak and women who are emotionally strong. These are individual qualities; they don't have anything to do with gender."

Time to move away from the topic of emotional stability and strength. Besides I had plenty more ammunition to make my case.

"So, are you so blind, then, that you don't see men who discriminate against women? Men who refuse to believe that a woman is capable no matter what she accomplishes just because she's a woman?"

"Now you're talking about discrimination. I'm not going to deny that it isn't a part of our culture, but it's still wrong. It's a distorted view. One that, hopefully, some day, will go away."

"So you're saying there's no difference between women and men?"

"Not at all. I'm saying that most of the issues you've brought up are gender neutral. Assertiveness and strength aren't the domain of one sex or the other. Neither are intelligence, competence, or emotional stability."

"All I know is one thing," I replied, ignoring his points. "It would be a cold day in hell before my father would ever step into a shrink's office."

"And that's a good thing?"

"Yes, it's a good thing. Maybe you respect women because you are touchy-feely and emotional yourself. Maybe my dad was right; you shrinks are nothing more than frauds and pansies."

A verbal kick in the balls, I thought smugly.

"Maybe your father felt that way because he was afraid of his own feelings. Did you ever think of that?"

"Maybe that's your own brand of self-delusion. My dad was tough. He didn't sit around and wallow in his problems. He pulled himself up by his own bootstraps. He was strong. He wasn't afraid of anything."

"Strong enough to abuse an innocent, vulnerable little girl," he said softly.

"I heard that!"

"I intended you to hear that. You're confusing toughness and brutality with strength. An easy mistake to make, considering what you were exposed to while growing up. But wrong nonetheless. Not every character trait that is stereotypically male is desirable, anymore than the stereotypically female character traits are."

"Then what? Am I supposed to be like my mother? Crying all the time, manipulating the hell out of him, out of us? Totally helpless. Hysterical. Unreasonable. And then she'd point the finger to her triggerman and let him fight her battles. She could just bat her little eyelashes and get him to do anything she wanted. Pathetic. Manipulative."

I was exhausted and depressed by now and wasn't up for any more combat or debate.

"Look, Dr. Padgett. I don't know what to think. I don't know what the answers are. My head is spinning. I'm tired. I'm sick of fighting you on this one. I came in here all dressed up, hoping that you'd notice, but then I turned into some kind of raging bitch when you said what I wanted you to say.

"I try to be tough, but I'm really just as emotional, just as manipulative as my mother. Ruled by hormones. Let's face it. I'm screwed. And stuck. Why don't we just drop this one and move on to something else, okay?"

"This is your therapy," he said gently. "We don't have to talk about what you don't want to talk about. But your conflict about your gender is something that isn't going to go away. And, at some point, you're going to have to come to grips with who you are and who you want to be."

I nodded, tears coming to my eyes. Indeed, I was conflicted on this one. And just as deeply convinced that there was no way out of it. I looked down at the collar of my dress and fiddled with the lace. As much as I hated to admit it, I did like the lace. I liked the dress. And I didn't hate *everything* about being a woman, just most things.

Dr. Padgett began to tell one of his parenting stories. His little girl, then a toddler, all dressed up on a spring day, had modeled her pretty dress to him, spinning in circles until she nearly fell down just to show him how she could make the dress twirl. She'd playfully run out of his reach as he'd tried to hug her, giggling at the game of chase. And he had looked at her, her proud and impish smile, her pretty dress, thinking she was the most beautiful thing in the world. He'd been so proud to be her father, so grateful to have a little girl.

Visions of Melissa danced through my mind as I listened. Melissa was also a big fan of pretty dresses, although she was just as comfortable and content in a hand-me-down pair of her brother's sweats.

One day Tim and I had spied on her as she was absorbed in a game of Barbies and G.I. Joes. The Barbies had been teaching the G.I. Joes how to fly the fighter plane. Then she sat them all down for tea. Melissa, a little girl proud to be exactly who she was, undeniably feminine and yet not in the least prissy. Just free to be who she wanted to be. Had I been just like Melissa at one time in my life?

As always, it boiled down to the same questions: If things had been different, who would I be? Beneath all the facades and distortions and faulty coping mechanisms, who was I?

I remembered the moment when Melissa was born. I recalled the sinking feeling of utter disappointment when the obstetrician announced I'd had a girl. I'd played the game, going along with it, ashamed of the disappointment I didn't dare admit. I'd bought the little dresses, the dolls, and the pink fuzzy animals. As much as I had hated being a girl, I had vowed not to pass that legacy on. But I had been afraid that I'd never be able to love this infant in the same way I loved my son.

I had been wrong. The little girl captured my heart. Dr. Padgett had once speculated that the event that brought me to the hospital and therapy in the first place was watching Melissa grow past infancy. Perhaps seeing Melissa proudly wearing dresses at the age I had forsworn them, happily feminine at the age when I was ashamed of my girlhood had triggered something within me. Something I had yearned for but had missed.

Maybe it was a positive sign. Maybe, someday, I could be as content and comfortable with myself as Melissa. Maybe, buried beneath it all, was a little girl who desperately wanted to be a little girl.

I sighed. *If only Dr. Padgett had been my father.*

Chapter 16

Over the next week or so I spent hours reflecting on the past, rummaging through dusty boxes in the basement to find old photographs, mementos, anything that might stir my memory and help me revisit my childhood. I fished through old letters and junk mail, mountains of programs for special events. I'd always chided Tim for being a pack rat, but seeing all this detritus forced me to admit I wasn't much better.

Finally I found a small, white box, partly smashed by the other boxes stacked on top. Although it was labeled "Baby Pictures," I found few of them. As the fifth of five children, my parents, like most, had lost the urge to memorialize my every step, crawl, and silly face.

Nearly all of the pictures in the box were studio portraits, an annual ritual for my parents. Me at one year old. At two years old. At three years old. I'd been wearing dresses in all of them, since I couldn't refuse them. Baby-fine curls of dark, downy hair crowned my head. Little pudgy elbows peeked out from frilly sleeves.

I'd been an attractive child, with almost a porcelain china-doll quality.

Nonetheless, these weren't portraits I'd want hanging on my wall. I wasn't smiling in any of them. My lower lip protruded as if I were on the verge of tears; my face was strained. Tiny lines furrowed my forehead, a creased knot of worry gathered between my brows. By the three-year-old portrait, these distress marks seemed permanent. My clear, blue eyes were open wide with an unmistakable terror and inconsolable sadness.

I'd seen these pictures before, but I had never paid much attention to the child's expressions. The photos served as veritable proof that my early childhood was indeed as painful as I had been admitting.

I moved on to another box, this one filled with mementos from my grade school years. A chronicle of annual family expeditions to destinations across the country. Unlike my early childhood, these events were well-documented. I had to chuckle as I looked at the wardrobes of the time. I was at least smiling in these pictures, the ear-to-ear goofy grin of a dyed-in-the-wool class clown.

At first glance a stranger would see a happy, healthy, all-American family: the seven of us all together, scenes of national parks and landmarks in the background. Of the children I was the smallest one, scrawny, built straight up and down, clad in the same getup as my brothers. In those days I had been frequently mistaken for a boy. It thrilled me and mortified my mother.

I came upon a slew of pictures from my early adolescent days. I had abandoned the plaids and settled on a simple wardrobe. A white T-shirt and a pair of Levi's, the James

Dean look. My mother, at her wit's end, afraid what people would think, attempted to lure me into more feminine attire. She purchased bags of flowery girlish clothing at the local mall. But they remained buried in my closet untouched, tags still attached.

The last box contained a folder of writing projects from fifth-grade English. Reading through them, I was struck by the extent of my writing style and vocabulary.

Soon, however, another pattern emerged. I told every creative-writing story in first person, and every single first-person character was male.

A sick feeling lumped in my stomach as I forced myself to read on, stunned by my clearly disturbed writing patterns. How could my teachers have read these essays and not been convinced I was emotionally disturbed?

The Rambunctious Rebels
Rachel M.
Grade 5

"Speed up the steak, Gertrude," I called. "They'll be coming any minute now!" It was the day the Frontens were coming over. Mr. and Mrs. Fronten were coming for the night.

"I wonder how in heaven they got a babysitter for those ten monsters of theirs?" I added. "Why don't we have children? Well, I'll ask them if we should adopt a few."

Dingdong. The doorbell rang. The door opened, and Mrs. Fronten walked in. Then Mr. Fronten walked in. I was about to shut the door when I got a horrifying surprise. In walked Mary Anne, John, Joe, Jim, Sue, Mary Beth, Tim, Bob, Barbara, and David.

"Get the aspirin, Gertrude," I whispered in my wife's ear. "I'll need it!"

The experience then started.

"Bobby, what's this?" Jim held up a five-hundred-dollar vase. Then Jim got angry and crashed the vase against the wall and then started to knock down and break all of my lamps. (Jim was known to get hysterical.) Then all the kids joined him in the destruction.

"Arrrgh," I cried. "Out I say! Leave, all of you!"

The parents exited with two kids' collars in each of their hands. I gave Jim and Bob a swift kick out the door. The rest of the kids left quickly.

Ten thousand dollars worth of property, destroyed.

The End

Then there was this excerpt from an autobiographical essay, "My family's funniest moments"—kernels of family folklore as they had been told to me.

I hated everybody when I was two weeks to one year old. I wouldn't stop crying, and I wouldn't set foot in anyone else's house. I would sit in the doorway until we went home.

Packed with violence, conflict, and male self-identity, the pictures and the essays told the stark story. How could no one have noticed? How could no one have cared? The pain of those years revisited me, my eyes blurred with tears as I shuffled through them again and again in numb shock.

∞

I brought several stories and pictures into the next session, reading and showing them to Dr. Padgett as he listened intently.

When I was done, I looked up into his saddened eyes.

"How did they let this go on, Dr. Padgett? How could they have just ignored it like nothing was happening? How could they?" My voice was breaking with tears.

He didn't have an answer to that one. How could I have expected one? I didn't have one either.

"You know," I continued, flooded with memories, "I got straight Fs in behavior. Straight Fs! My teachers used to write novels on the back of my report cards. I never got in trouble at home for it. Never! My mom would tell me she wasn't going to show it to my dad, just sign it herself. Do you really think my dad went for years without seeing a report card? God, Dr. Padgett! I used to think it was so cool that I didn't get in trouble. Now I look at it, and I can't believe they just sat back and let it go by. If your daughter would have been getting those kinds of grades, those kind of comments, would you just let it go by?"

"No, I wouldn't," he said gently.

"This is horrible! I was a completely rotten kid, disturbed as hell. It's so obvious now, and they didn't do a thing!"

I expounded on a host of recollections, tears streaming down my cheeks. The time my father hung over the fence at a third-grade softball game, screaming at me when I'd strike out or drop the ball. He yelled instructions that I was far too embarrassed and upset to follow. The other parents stared at him in shocked disgust, making me even more ashamed.

After the game I told him I didn't want him to come to any more games. He hadn't fought my request or even questioned it. For the next nine years, through Catholic league ball and high school varsity sports, through tournaments and championship games, all the other players looked up to the bleachers to see their cheering parents.

Mine never showed their faces again.

I rode my bike to practices and hitched a ride to games with someone else's parents. The orphan athlete.

For years I'd been convinced that this had been my doing, the result of a shamefully disrespectful ultimatum uttered by an eight-year-old after a particularly humiliating softball game.

"God, Dr. Padgett," I cried. "That was fucked up! They completely ignored *years* of my life, something very important to me. People used to kid around that I didn't have parents at all. None of the other parents acted like that. And you know what? He never ever apologized for treating me that way, and my mom went right along with it.

"Would you have taken me literally, a little kid, and just quit going to games after that?"

"No, I wouldn't," he said. "Then again, I never would have humiliated you to make you want to ban me in the first place."

Memories like waves of raining bombs. Each one landed on me with a blast and a shudder. In high school I'd discovered Mogen David, also known as Mad Dog, a cheap but potent wine popular with teenagers. I had my first taste during the summer after my junior year. It had a nasty bite to it, but it gave me a warmth inside I'd never felt before.

During my senior year I'd been involved in theatrical productions, and I'd sneaked backstage with the props and lighting crews, taking swigs off the bottle of Mad Dog in between sets at weeknight rehearsals, getting high enough to forget my lines or to slur them at times. I'd drive home on these school nights, loaded to the gills. I deluded myself that a stick of Dentyne would somehow cover it up, although I was staggering and had wine spills on my clothing.

They never noticed. Or at least they never spoke a word about it.

I'd get drunker and drunker. They still said and did nothing. They mentioned it just once when I'd come home one night so drunk I'd thrown up in a flowerpot in front of the house. Even then there'd been no chastisement—just a few remarks about my killer hangover being punishment enough.

Back then I'd thought all of it was cool. My parents had been cool. As long as I kept to myself at home, did not openly disagree, followed the house rules, and showed up by curfew, it didn't matter what I did. Raising hell at school, getting loaded, getting high, screwing around—anything was fair play as long as I was a Stepford Child at home.

I'd solved that dilemma by simply never being home.

"They didn't give a shit, you know that?" I cried hysterically. "They just didn't give a shit. I was fucking up my whole life. I was crying for help, screaming for help, and they never did a goddamned thing. As long as my grades were top-notch, as long as I brought home the trophies and ribbons and plaques, they didn't give a shit what else happened. As long as I was gone, out of their hair.

"I used to think they were so proud of me. I really thought I was earning a place in their heart. But you know what, Dr. Padgett? They didn't give a shit about me. They only cared about how everything reflected on them. I could have ended up dead; I could have ended up pregnant; I could have ended up anything, and they wouldn't have given a shit about how much it might have hurt me. Only that it would look bad on them. Spoil the image of the perfect fucking all-American family!"

It was impossible to continue. I was so choked by tears

that I could barely catch my breath to manage the words.

Dr. Padgett took over. "It hurts, I know," he said, kindness in his eyes and voice. "They didn't care as much as you thought they did. They didn't love you as much as you thought they did. In many, many ways you raised yourself, Rachel."

"And fucked up my life!" I nearly screamed. "I could've been anything in the world. But I took the easiest route I could. Skipped half my classes in college because I was hungover or high or so exhausted from sleeping around that I couldn't make it.

"*Now* look at me. I'm pretending to be an accountant, but I hardly have any clients. I'm a loser, Dr. Padgett. I've blown my whole life. What if I would have tried back then? What could I have been?"

"You raised yourself as best you could, Rachel. It's amazing what you accomplished under the circumstances. You could have been a high school dropout. You could have killed yourself years ago. You could be in prison now. You could have completely given up.

"But you never did. You kept on trying, and what you managed to accomplish is almost a miracle. You graduated from college and got that degree. You're married, and you've stuck with that. You're a good mother, and no matter how much hell you've been through, you've never walked away from those responsibilities."

"But I blew it, Dr. Padgett! Can't you see that? I'll bet *you* showed up to all *your* classes; I'll bet your kids have. Everybody else buckled down and tried to learn something. But I wasted the biggest opportunity of my life, getting stoned, getting drunk, and getting laid, like it was some kind of game."

"You had no other choice, Rachel. You *had* to do those

220

things. There was too much going on inside of you that you couldn't handle. The drinking, the drugs, the sex, they were all ways of coping. Faulty ways? Yes. Self-destructive? Yes. But you were compelled to do those things."

"I was sick, right? Are you going to pawn off all this shit on the borderline personality disorder again? I can't buy that. I wasn't a kid anymore, Dr. Padgett. And sick or not, disturbed or not, I am responsible for what I did. I can't lay it all on BPD."

"You were responsible for what you did, Rachel. You've already paid the price. You danced on the edge, and it's a miracle you survived. But you did. You could have died, but you didn't. If you'd have committed a crime, you might be in prison. But you've already paid for all of your actions. You've borne the consequences and driven yourself into the ground with them.

"But it's the past, Rachel. You got through it somehow, some way, intact. You aren't a drunk anymore. You're off the drugs. You've been faithful to your husband since the day you married him.

"Sure," he said, "it's natural to regret some of your mistakes. But it's pointless to destroy yourself with them because you honestly, sincerely couldn't help them. You raised yourself, and you didn't do a perfect job. But you should never have had to do it in the first place. It's time to forgive yourself, Rachel. Your life is ahead of you. You can get what you need here, what you've always needed, and you can go on to have the peace of mind you never believed possible. This is your second chance. This is what counts from now on."

At session's end I was completely drained, torn between utter exhaustion and fresh bursts of anger and pain as I revisited the past and saw what it had truly been like. As

I mourned the loss of my childhood and what I thought it had been, I felt anguish over all the opportunities I'd missed.

∞

It was an unseasonably damp and overcast November. I had no interest in dinner, either cooking or eating it. I was still consumed with the discoveries of the day's session.

Opening the damper to the fireplace, I decided it was time for the first fire of the year. I set up the logs and lit the Duraflame starter block, sitting back, feeling nothing but hollow emptiness as it began to flicker and then catch on. The burning fire and the dancing flames entranced me. Fire. The great power of warmth. The great power of destruction.

Sufficiently warmed, I decided to put away the essays and pictures I'd brought to session. I wondered why I was even keeping them.

Then I spotted another box with my mother's handwriting scrawled across it: *Rachel—Awards.*

Awards. That's all I was good for to them, I thought bitterly. The tokens of honor meant nothing to me now. Absolutely nothing. If anything, they were reminders of the bitter charade my childhood had been.

Opening the box, I looked through the mountains of blue, red, and white ribbons, the many certificates bearing my name. Sports play-offs. Math competitions. Foreign language contests. My high school diploma and National Honor Society certificates. A blur of accomplishments that were now worthless pieces of paper. Trash. As I dug my hands through the contents, I was overwhelmed with the desire to crumple them up and throw them away.

Looking at the fire in the hearth, I was seized by an

idea. One by one I crumpled up the awards and threw them on the fire, a bittersweet sensation of remorse and revenge filling me as I watched them blacken and turn to ash in the roaring flames. The words were melted into oblivion as the fire consumed them. Ribbon after ribbon after ribbon. Certificate after certificate. My high school diploma. All up in flames.

I went into the basement to grab some more and burned them as well.

I was taking my college diploma off the wall and was in the process of removing it from its wooden frame when Tim walked in. He had been out in the garage, tinkering with the transmission of our car.

His face paled as he looked into the fire and saw the remnants of the ribbons and burning parchment.

"What in the hell are you doing, Rachel?" he asked, shocked.

"Burning this shit," I mumbled angrily. "All of it. It's all shit!"

Tim ran to the fire just in time to see the flames swallow my high school diploma.

"My God! That's your diploma." He turned to me, then noticed my college diploma in my hand, already removed from its frame, ready to be next.

"No! I'm not going to let you burn your college diploma too. No way! You've lost it, Rachel. You need to call the doctor. Something. Anything! But there's no way in hell I'm letting you burn your degree."

"Why?" I pouted. "It doesn't mean anything. Doesn't mean shit! Nothing!"

"Look, Rachel," he said firmly, grabbing the hand that held the parchment, physically restraining me from moving toward the fire. "I don't know what happened in your session today. I don't know what this is all about, or what's going on in your head right now. But you are out of control. Do you realize what you've just done? You've just burned your accomplishments away. You're going to regret this."

"No, I'm not," I lied. In reality I was already beginning to regret it. But the deed had been done. There was no way to take it back now.

"Give me the diploma, Rachel," he insisted, still clutching my arm.

"No!" I sounded like a three-year-old.

"Give it to me *now*."

Finally I did.

"I'm going to hide this, maybe take it to the office, until you get your shit together," he said, irritated, and left the room.

Why was he so mad? This wasn't his shit; it was my shit! I earned it. I can burn it. God, what have I done? What came over me?

Tim was right. It was time to call the doctor.

∞

"Is this an emergency?" The person at the other end of the phone was female.

God, I hated that question. It made me feel like I was really crazy. Maybe I *was* really crazy.

"Yes," I answered in a small voice.

"The doctor should call you back shortly. If you don't hear from him in fifteen minutes, you can call us back."

It was a ritual I'd come to know all too well. Locked up in the bedroom as Tim handled the kids' dinner downstairs. A pack of cigarettes, a glass of ice water. I'd done this too many times. Waiting desperately for the phone to ring, I kept my hand resting on the receiver. Pathetic. Absolutely pathetic.

I picked it up on the second ring.

"Hello, this is Dr. Padgett."

"Umm, yes, Dr. Padgett?"

Silence.

"Are you there?"

"Yes."

"Umm," I struggled for an explanation. Why had I called?

"I just lost control. I did something really, really stupid. Destructive."

"What happened?"

"Well, I was looking through a bunch of awards. Ribbons, certificates, that kind of stuff. And I got pretty upset. You know, about all of it, what we talked about today. And, umm, I threw them in the fire and burned them."

"You *what*?" he asked.

"I burned the ribbons and my diploma in the fire."

"Why on earth did you do that?"

He wasn't making this easy. Surely he had to understand. He knew how meaningless those awards had seemed in light of everything.

"I was angry. They didn't mean anything to me. They don't. They're just worthless pieces of shit. Like me."

Come on, Dr. Padgett. Comfort me. You know how awful I feel about this.

"That was a completely self-destructive thing to do," he reprimanded me sternly. "I can't believe you would do something like that. It's plain stupid, Rachel. Absolutely pointless and self-destructive."

"I know that," I whined. "Don't you think I know that? Don't you think I regret it? You know how upset I was. It took me over, just took me over!"

"There's no point in calling me now, Rachel. I can't help you now. What's done is done, and you're going to have to live with the consequences."

This stunned me into pleading tears. "But can't we talk about it, Dr. Padgett? Please. I'm very upset. My whole childhood doesn't mean anything to me anymore. Can't you help me?"

"The time to call," he said firmly, "was *before* you chose to burn everything. Then I could have helped. But there's nothing I can do once you've acted out. If calling me when you're really upset before you go off and do something can stop you from doing it, fine. But I'm not going to continue this conversation after you've already done it."

"Is that all you have to say?" I shrieked into the phone, trying to buy more time, trying to eke out some words of comfort. "Can't we talk about this some more?"

"We can talk about it in session. Good-bye, Rachel."

"But Dr. Padgett!"

"Good-bye, Rachel."

I did not say good-bye, slamming the receiver down instead. Why had I called him anyway? I felt worse than I had before. I sat on the bed, staring at the phone, consumed with regret. Finally I went back downstairs to the living room. The fire had subsided, and the charred remains of the awards were scattered on the hearth. I rushed to the bathroom and proceeded to vomit.

Chapter 17

I slept in late the next morning. By the time I went down the stairs, Jeffrey was already up, a mountain of Legos strewn across the living room floor as he fastidiously assembled an elaborate fort. Hearing my footsteps, he turned around.

"Hi, Mommy!" He smiled at me, then wrinkled his nose. "Something's smelly in here."

Inhaling deeply, I discovered he was right. One of the drawbacks of a fireplace was the pervasive smell of logs burned to ash. It was delightful coming out of chimneys at the onset of winter but a bit rancid when confined to an enclosed room.

Jeffrey, of course, was accustomed to the usual fireplace smells. But this odor was more pungent. As I approached the hearth, the noxious fumes intensified.

Now that the logs had burned completely to ash, my impulsive act of destruction was far more apparent. The charred remains of the parchment were like blackened dried leaves resting on top of each other. The ribbons, made out of something synthetic, had melted into tarlike globs. A few hints of blue and red remained, traces of lettering here and there. A half-burned piece of fabric with the words "first place" stared at me with tarnished gold letters.

Before Jeffrey could take a closer look and start asking questions, I found a trash bag and started scooping up years' worth of mementos—destroyed forever by my own impulsive childishness.

Afterward, clutching a cup of fresh coffee as Jeffrey continued building his fort, I asked myself why? *Why had I done this?*

Had it somehow inflicted revenge on my parents? No. The stuff had been in a box in my basement. How would they have ever known?

Had these awards really been meaningless to me? No. I had to admit that they had never lost their meaning, not even when I was frantically burning them.

I knew deep down the act had not been as uncontrolled as I'd made it appear. Selecting what I would destroy had not been an entirely random process. I had burned a number of blue ribbons from intramural events and activities that had not meant as much to me. But I had spared the ones from the championships, the seventh-grade free-throw contest, the science fair—the ones that had the most sentimental value. As I had grabbed the fistfuls of ribbons, frenzied though I was, I'd still had the presence of mind to scrutinize them.

I'd burned my high school diploma, but I'd spared my college parchment. I was relieved when Tim came in and commanded me to hand it over, but I never would have burned it. I was more interested in Tim seeing that I was about to do it than actually doing it.

The answers were ugly—but nonetheless true. Right out of the borderline personality disorder books. Manipulation. Testing the limits. I had not been content to merely share my sorrows in the confines of a session. Dr. Padgett had given me some support in session, but it hadn't been enough. I'd left greedy for more. Burning those awards had been sheer craziness. And I'd known that even while doing it.

Tim, of course, had reacted according to my expectations. He'd been visibly consumed with worry about me. He'd demanded that I call the doctor, which was exactly what I'd wanted to do.

But Tim's reaction was of secondary importance. The self-destruction was somewhat symbolic, contrived to get the reaction of the one who was now, unquestionably, the center of my life—Dr. Padgett.

Much to his credit, Dr. Padgett had known this the minute I'd called. So he had deliberately avoided the reactions I had most fervently desired to elicit: raw anger, pity, overwrought worry, or words of comfort. He decided not to discuss it on the phone at all. We both knew my act was a direct result of manipulative instinct. Whether or not I would ever be able to lose this consuming desire to manipulate to get what I needed was something I didn't know.

∞

My hidden secrets were not well concealed. The psychological profile had been right, as had the books on BPD. I *was* manipulative, desperately clinging, and prone to tantrums, explosiveness, and frantic acts of desperation when I did not feel the intimacy connection was strong enough. The tough chick loner act of self-reliance was a complete facade and had always been so.

The facade had been my means to conceal those secrets from anyone else, to conceal them from myself. But it wasn't working with Dr. Padgett, as it had never fully worked for me.

I now forced myself to recognize that fact.

Other self-disclosures were easy fare compared to the one I knew I had to reveal in the next session—the confession, not of my action, but of the motives beneath it. For once I entered a session saying precisely what I had planned to say, what I had rehearsed over and over in my head—that I hadn't been completely out of control. That my absurd act had been contrived. And that, most critical of all, I had done it with the specific intention of manipulating Dr. Padgett's response.

For a man who had withstood all my insults, had countless evenings interrupted by my emergency calls—my attempts to stretch the limits and extend therapy beyond the three weekly sessions—this would have been an opportune time to say, "I told you so."

Yet I now understood both him and the context of our relationship well enough that I didn't expect such a response, as warranted as it might be. And true to form, I did not get it.

Nor did I expect profuse words of praise for my willingness to admit that I was desperately ashamed. Not only did I not deserve praise, but I was beginning to realize what would and would not be of benefit to me. A reward for revealing the motives behind the act could be construed as indirectly condoning and encouraging it. So I was not disappointed when I did not receive that either.

Instead the blank screen was firmly in place as Dr.

Padgett simply listened and let me develop my own perceptions and conclusions.

"How can you put up with me?" I asked him sincerely. "You know as well as I do that I've been trying to manipulate you, slinging everything at you that I can muster just to get a reaction. How come you tolerate it? How can you?"

I detected the trace of a smile.

"This," he said, "is why the therapy relationship is structured differently than any other. This is why the limits are in place, why we only meet for three hours a week, and why I don't conduct therapy over the phone. It's not a miracle that I can do this. I can get angry, disgusted, hurt, and insulted just like anyone else.

"But I'm not with you twenty-four hours a day. I'm not distracted by anything else when I'm in here, and believe me, if I ever was, if something were going on in my life that would absorb me so that I couldn't fully focus on you, I'd cancel the session. This isn't like any other adult relationship. I'm here to meet *your* needs. Within these limits I can do that without getting hurt. You can irritate me sometimes. I'll grant you that. But that's about as far as it goes."

An image popped in my head that brought a smile to my face.

Dr. Padgett's own grin broadened, "What are you thinking about?"

"Oh, I dunno. I can just see you right now, in line on the last day of the month at the motor vehicle bureau. Waiting for half an hour until you finally get to the counter and then some bureaucrat with an attitude tells you that you're in the wrong line and didn't bring the right stuff. And you getting pretty miffed about it and telling her a word or two about what you think of the state bureaucracy and the people who work for it."

He chuckled. Obviously I was not the only one in that office who'd ever been ticked off by the motor vehicle bureau.

Laughter and smiles. They'd been absent from my life for such a long time now. It was a part of me that Dr. Padgett hadn't had much chance to see. I missed being able to laugh and smile. I sat back, watching his grin, drinking it in, observing every detail of it, every nuance.

"What are you thinking now?" he asked, still smiling.

"Just that you have a great smile," I answered.

"So do you, Rachel. I like to see it."

I blushed but beamed with satisfaction.

"You know," he commented, "therapy can be very hard work. Very intense and painful. But that's not all it has to be. Sometimes it can be enjoyable."

"But I'm supposed to be here because I'm sick, aren't I? I'm supposed to be working on things, getting into issues. This is supposed to be serious." My smile faded, and soon I was intensely introspective, my brow furrowed once again.

Dr. Padgett's smile faded as well, an act of courtesy and respect for my feelings as much as anything else, I suspected.

"I have to tell you something else," I finally spoke. "I know I'm supposed to be here to try to get better, to get healthier. But sometimes I'm scared to tell you when I feel good. Sometimes I even look back to the days when I was in the hospital going crazy with nostalgia or something. Like I wish I was that sick again. Pretty crazy, isn't it?"

All sorts of secrets were flowing out today.

"You're afraid that if you start to get better, aren't so sick, somehow I'll care about you less?"

"Yes," I nodded. "It doesn't make any sense at all. I really, honestly want to do my best here. I want to make as much progress as I can. I want to do what I'm supposed to do.

I want to be your best patient, your prized pupil. I want to do right."

"You want to be my best patient or my worst patient. Because you're afraid that if you're anything in the middle, I might not care about you as much."

"Yeah, I'm afraid some new patient will come along." I was interrupted by the phone, an exceptionally rare event. Dr. Padgett always held his calls during sessions. I couldn't recall an interruption before.

"Could you hold that thought, please?" He smiled and went to his desk to pick up the phone. "Hmm . . . Uh-huh . . . Uh-huh . . . Well, you're going to have to tell her to get down from there. . . . Call security; use the restraints. Uh-huh . . . Go ahead and increase the dosage to fifty milligrams. I'll be by later for rounds. . . . Okay. . . . Good-bye."

He hung up the phone and went back to his chair.

"So," he said, "you were saying . . ."

"I have nothing to say!" I shot him an icy stare.

God, how juvenile. You're manipulating him again. You know he has other patients. You know he's the medical director of the psych ward.

Still I couldn't go back to the point I'd been at just a few minutes ago. I felt abandoned and betrayed. Undoubtedly he'd been discussing another crazy in the psych ward, someone who was just like what I used to be. Once upon a time I'd been on the critical list. Now I was second priority. Session-interruptus.

I had a pretty clear notion of what had gone on. But I asked the question I knew damned well he wouldn't answer anyway.

"Who was that?" I asked, the scowl of a jealous lover on my face.

"You know I can't talk to you about other patients."

"Why not?" I insisted, unwilling to back down. "If it's important enough to interrupt my session, then I have a right to know."

"You don't have a right to know," he said, slightly exasperated. "You're blowing this out of proportion. I took a short call, and now I'm back. You know I rarely ever do this."

"You're thinking about her, aren't you?" I pouted. "You care about her more than me, don't you? Maybe you'd care if I went home and swallowed a whole bottle of Xanax, huh? Maybe you'd care if I somehow killed myself, and you had to go to my funeral, and it was too late!"

Get down on your knees, damnit, and apologize! Tell me how much you care about me. Tell me you care about me more than her, more than any of your patients.

As always, he wasn't playing the game.

"I took a phone call, Rachel," he said firmly. "That's all I did. You're making more out of this than there is, and you know it as well as I do. I can understand that it's upsetting to you, but you are blowing it way out of proportion. Anything I'd say right now isn't going to make a difference. You're going to have to look at our relationship, look at our history, and decide for yourself how much I care about you."

"Boy," I seethed, "you've got a helluva lot of nerve. Telling me how this is my time for you to focus on me, no distractions. Bullshit! Hypocritical bullshit! I've got to follow a gazillion of your stupid rules and limits, and you can do whatever you want. After all, it's only me. You are the biggest sonofabitchin' prick I've ever met in my life. You owe me a goddamned apology."

"That's enough!" It was the closest I had ever heard him come to raising his voice. "I don't owe you an apology.

I'm sorry if you feel inconvenienced, but I haven't done anything to deliberately hurt you. You, on the other hand, are deliberately trying to hurt me. You aren't expressing feelings; you are attacking me. And I don't deserve a single word of what you just said."

It was hard to imagine the warmth of his smile that had been there only minutes ago. His eyes now opened wide, Dr. Padgett was sitting uncharacteristically forward, visibly irritated, more than a small hint of anger peeking through. It was enough to knock me right out of my tirade.

"I'm sorry, Dr. Padgett," I uttered humbly. "You're right. I was attacking you. And you didn't deserve what I had to say. I honestly didn't mean to hurt you."

He relaxed a bit and regained his composure, but the smile did not reappear. "No. That's not totally true. I accept your apology. I believe it's sincere. But the fact is, you very much meant to hurt me."

Before he had only reprimanded me in the aftermath of self-destruction. This was the first time he had in response to an attempt to hurt him. Funny, I had tried so hard for so long to get to him, to land a sucker punch. I felt almost certain by his reaction that this one had actually hurt, that perhaps I had finally found the vulnerable spot. Yet there was little satisfaction at all in it. An empty victory.

I realized that, sitting across from me in his chair, Dr. Padgett was a living, breathing human being with feelings of his own. I felt awash in remorse.

"I'm really sorry, Dr. Padgett," my eyes were looking directly into his. "I mean it. I was trying to hurt you. I admit it. But I really don't want to. You mean so much to me; you really do. I know you care about me, and I care about you too. Sometimes I wish that there was something, anything, I could do for you. I know I can't take back what I said. But I really, honestly feel badly if I hurt you. I know you don't deserve it."

"Apology accepted," he said, then glanced at the clock. "That's about it for today."

∞

It was an abrupt ending to an intense session, begun with the intention of confessing my own unreasonable motives, ending with me acting upon those very motives once again, rendering the confession hollow. My outburst and his startling reaction had taken place at an inopportune time in the session. There was little time to soften the blow.

So much of how Dr. Padgett chose to react involved purpose, planning, and self-control on his part. I doubted that he'd intended to show his emotions or to let me, the self-admitted master manipulator, see that I had touched a nerve. It had been a rare occurrence of spontaneity. Frustration and hurt boiled over the surface for my eyes to see.

In a way it frightened me. I'd become complacent in the acceptance that no matter what I said or did, the blank screen could always absorb it. Dr. Padgett's patience was infinite. As much as I'd tried to get to him, I couldn't and thus had felt assured that he could be true to his promise, that I could never succeed in driving him away and that he could continue to see me because he was somehow superhuman. Perfect. An altruistic, turn-the-other-cheek demigod and martyr.

Now I wasn't so sure. Perhaps his patience was wearing thin. I couldn't blame him if one day he decided he'd had enough. Was I en route to destroying this relationship too?

And yet there was a certain degree of comfort and relief

to be derived from this new realization that Dr. Padgett was human. Imperfect. He was neither superhuman nor infinite in his patience. Dr. Padgett had stayed with me not because he was a professional, not because he was a tightly self-controlled martyr, but because he really was committed to me. And he'd been hurt, not because he'd fallen off the pedestal of perfection, but because he cared.

One of the most difficult aspects of the therapy limits, the fifty-minute hour specifically, was my compulsive need for closure. Black and white. If I left a session touched by his kindness and feeling the warmth of connection, it carried over into the interval between sessions. The security in being loved.

Sessions that ended abruptly, however, left me in a state of rage, isolation, and despair. These feelings, too, spilled over into the next hours and days. I could not conjure love and warmth as the rage and despair became seemingly eternal.

More often than not, I had acted on these feelings, sometimes through hostile notes on Dr. Padgett's windshield, threats, or impulsive acts of self-destruction—or any way I could overcome the sense of abandonment. Until I was some-how convinced of the bond I had with Dr. Padgett, through an emergency phone call or another session, I'd been virtually trapped in this state of disconnectedness, hungering for his reassurance.

This session, too, had ended before I had the chance to elicit Dr. Padgett's reassurance. Filled with remorse that I had attacked him and regret that my apologies were too brief and insufficient, I had only two words to rely upon: "Apology accepted." No closing profound insights, no reassuring words of kindness, and no offer to extend the session.

It was tempting to engage in yet another act of self-destruction, to find some way to summon his attention and have him reassure me. And yet, for some reason, I did not. Maybe it was because my confession and willingness to accept the manipulative instincts within me were more sincere than I'd thought, even after my voracious attack.

Then again, maybe I was able to feel the bond and sense of connectedness to him without the kind of closure I had needed before.

Maybe, just maybe, I was beginning to grow up.

∞

"I'll bet you were expecting a late-night phone call, weren't you?" I grinned, a child proud of her newest accomplishment.

"Why would I expect that?" Dr. Padgett said, returning my smile with one of his own, a wordless expression that let me know beyond a doubt that I had been forgiven.

"Well, you know," I said, blushing a bit, "that was a pretty wild session yesterday. I left pretty upset. And you didn't seem to be too happy yourself. Usually a recipe for disaster."

"What made you react differently this time?" he asked.

"I'm not exactly sure," I answered. "I mean, I thought about it. I thought about doing something stupid, but I didn't. For some strange reason, I felt secure. Like I knew that, even with the way session ended, everything would be okay. That you really meant what you said when you accepted my apology."

"How does that make you feel?"

"Pretty good, actually. You know, if it had been six

months or a year ago, I would have gone off, locked myself up in the attic, gone off running, whatever. But I didn't. And, actually, last night went pretty well. I played with the kids for a while, cooked a good dinner. I slept great. I can hardly believe it!"

He smiled, sharing in my satisfaction—the same all-consuming, contagious smile he'd showed me yesterday. I was proud of myself, and so was he.

So many accomplishments filled all those past years, and yet none of them had satisfied me in the way that this one did—so simple and natural for other people but so difficult for me. I was like a child finally able to kiss Mommy good-bye without a fuss, content in the knowledge that Mommy still loved her and would be back.

In the vernacular of psychology, I'd gained an understanding of "relationship constancy," an understanding that a strong relationship could weather its moments of anger and irritation and temporary separation. It was a lesson Dr. Padgett had tried to teach me from the very first session and one that, eighteen months later, I was finally beginning to understand and accept. It represented a graduation of sorts into the next realm of issues, a visible sign of progress.

I spoke at length about this as Dr. Padgett listened with the satisfaction of a teacher whose lesson had finally been learned.

"Growing up," he said, "is actually a pretty ambivalent process. On the one hand there is the natural desire to separate from the parent, to move on and be able to handle more responsibilities. A three-year-old sees her older sister riding a two-wheeler and wants to be able to do it herself. A ten-year-old sees that sister driving a car and is no longer as content with the two-wheeler.

"But every once in a while, that child needs to be reassured that she hasn't grown up *too* much and that her parents realize how much she still needs them. A good parent can give that kind of reassurance without thwarting the natural and healthy desire to grow more independent.

"When you were growing up, that reassurance was missing. So, as hard as you tried to achieve your independence, it was a double-edged sword. You wanted your parents to loosen the reins, but you were afraid that they'd just let go of them entirely. With every move toward growing up and independence came a fear of abandonment. It's a scary feeling for any kid, especially in the teenage years. One of the reasons teenagers rebel is to test the limits to make sure they are still there. But for you it was particularly difficult. And something you never really got over."

I nodded, absorbing all his words. They made sense.

"It's the same thing in therapy," he continued. "You want to grow; you want to move on with your life. But you fear wanting that. As if, somehow, if you need me less, I'll care about you less. But that isn't true for me any more than it would be true for a parent. Your feelings may waver, but mine don't. I didn't care about you in the beginning because you were in a life-or-death crisis and needed me more. I cared about you because you are you.

"And I don't care about you any less just because you need me less. It doesn't make a difference whether you're acting like the best patient or the worst patient I've ever had. It doesn't change the fact that I care about you. This is a parent's kind of love. Unconditional."

"Dr. Padgett," I said, "I've got a question, probably a dumb one, but I'll ask it anyway."

"No question is ever dumb here."

240

"I know. Anyway. Umm, I know I think about you all the time, in sessions, in between sessions. Sometimes it seems like you're on my mind every waking hour. Sometimes, even in my sleep, my dreams have you in them. But what about you? Do you ever think about me when we aren't in session together? You know, not all the time or anything—I know you have your own life, and you have other patients—but sometimes?"

"What do you think?" he asked gently, not in the least bit sarcastic.

"I know what I *want* to think. I want to think you do. At least every once in a while."

The blank screen descended for a brief moment.

"You're right," he answered, an uncommon direct response to a direct question, one I had not figured he would answer. "I care about you, Rachel. It's only natural that I would think about you at times, even out of session."

"Do you think about me when you go on vacations?" I asked hopefully.

Dr. Padgett only smiled. I was pushing it, and both of us knew it. I didn't need to hear the answer to that question. The first answer was more than sufficient.

Of course any rational person would assume that, given the frequency, depth, and intensity of a therapy relationship such as ours, a therapist would sometimes think about a patient in between sessions. For anybody else it might have been an eminently dumb question. For me, however, it was anything but dumb, and the fact that Dr. Padgett was willing to answer sincerely and not chastise me for my stupidity reassured my newfound sense of relationship constancy. The question wasn't for the benefit of the thirty-year-old woman who posed it but for the child that resided within her.

"A part of you wants to run away from therapy, wishes that it could be over, wants to push it along and have it all done with," he said. "But another cannot envision it ever ending."

Why does this man always have to spoil the most tender of moments by saying things I didn't bring up, things I absolutely don't want to hear?

"I guess," I answered coldly, not wanting to accept it, but not wanting to argue the issue either.

"It's okay, Rachel," he reassured me. "It really is. Growing up can be scary. The notion of adult responsibility can make a teenager wish she were a little girl again.

"But a good parent realizes that even though this girl can drive a car and hold a job, even though she's reached a state of maturity where she is physically capable of having a child of her own—emotionally that teenager still needs the parent to be a parent. The parents don't throw the child out; the child reaches a point where she is *ready* to move off on her own. A good parent is pleased when this time comes because it is evidence that the child has grown up, not because the parent wants to be rid of her.

"You might not be able to envision it now, but a time will come when you need me a lot less than you need me right now. It won't mean that you love me less, but you'll want to move on to the next chapter of your life. There'll come a time when you'll be better off on your own without me than to stay in therapy."

I felt like Judas at the Last Supper, righteously and vehemently denying Jesus's prediction of the imminent betrayal.

"No, I don't think so. No way," I stammered.

"I'm not going to abandon you, Rachel. I'm not going to

leave you. No, exactly the opposite. You are going to leave me someday, when you're ready."

I could not even imagine the prospect of leaving him. A jolt of anxiety shot through my stomach.

"I don't want to think about that, Dr. Padgett," I said. "And I don't see how it's relevant here at all. Why are you bringing this up now? Do you want to push me out the door? Is this some kind of a message or something?"

"I'm not pushing you out the door."

"Then why are you bringing this up?"

"Because, deep down, you fear it. It's a catch-22. If you don't make progress, you feel there is no hope. But if you do make progress, you fear growing up—you fear leaving this."

"The fact is, Dr. Padgett, I know I can leave anytime I want," I replied, holding in the rage that was starting to build.

"You can leave out of anger; you can leave this process before it's finished. We both know you can run. We both know it wouldn't be in your best interest to leave abruptly, before you get what you need."

"Maybe I'm not getting what I need here," I pouted, knowing it was a lie but saying it nonetheless. "Maybe this is all a hoax, maybe it's hurting me more than helping me, maybe you're a fraud!"

"You just can't see the gray right now," he sighed. "Black and white. You can only see two outcomes. You leave here angry, or I leave you against your wishes. But you can leave here someday, very satisfied, wanting to move on. It will be your decision."

"You know, your timing is absolute shit! There's no reason to even discuss this until the time comes."

"The purpose of therapy is not to keep you here forever. It's not to make you dependent on me. That would be exploitation. In many ways from the very first session we've been working toward the day when therapy would no longer be necessary for you. If I didn't believe that, I'd only be hurting you, not helping you."

"So," I asked incredulously, "what it boils down to is that the purpose of therapy is to end it?"

"Yes."

"And I'm supposed to totally trust you, get closer to you than I have to anyone else in my life, tell you everything, share all my feelings, take down my walls, so that one day I have to say good-bye? I can't think of anything more cruel, more painful."

"It's the furthest possible thing from cruel. Of course there's some pain to it. There's a lot of pain right now in thinking about it, actually, because you're far from being ready to leave, far from getting what you need."

"I hate good-byes," I vowed. "I don't want to say good-bye. I don't even want to think about it."

"Good-byes are painful, I'll grant you that. But it's a bittersweet pain. Sure, it hurts. But there are positive feelings in terminating too, if you do it when you're really ready and not before. New hope. New freedom."

"It hurts too much!" I was beginning to cry, the fear of leaving Dr. Padgett sweeping over me. "I don't see how you can bring this all up so casually. I can barely make it over a weekend without you. When you go on vacation, I can barely survive until you get back, and here you are, talking about saying good-bye for good. Maybe the thought doesn't hurt you; you've got dozens of patients besides me; you'll just fill in the slot with another one, but it almost kills me."

"Who's to say it won't be difficult for me too?" he asked gently, his deep brown eyes looking into mine. "Of course it will be a sad day for both of us, but a positive and hopeful one too."

"You mean it's hard for you to say good-bye too?"

"Just like a parent," he nodded, "watching his daughter drive off all packed up for college. So proud of her to have made it to this point of independence and yet at the same time sad with the pain of missing her and having to come to grips with the reality that his little girl has grown up."

I pondered the thought for a while, recalling Jeffrey's first day of kindergarten, Melissa's first day of preschool. The two of them had been scrubbed and combed, Jeffrey in his tiny, blue uniform shorts and shirt, Melissa in a little dress with an apple on the pocket. After helping them strap brand-new book bags on their little shoulders, I'd snapped a dozen Kodak shots of their shining faces. But under those beaming smiles was a reluctant look of fear that silently begged for reassurance as they'd waved good-bye, ready to file into the school behind their teachers. To enter a new world where I would not be privy to their every interaction. Waving back to them with a confident smile that said "Everything will be okay!" I could see contented relief on their faces as they turned to walk through the doors of the school.

Then I'd been alone with all the other mothers who had waved those same confident reassuring good-byes. Amid the burden of endless diaper changes and late-night feedings, we had all wished for this day. And yet, now that it had come, we had the same bittersweet feeling Dr. Padgett had mentioned. We'd felt proud that our little ones had reached this state of growth and yet a bit empty, lonely at the prospect that their lives and ours would never be quite the same again.

"It must be hard on you sometimes," I said, "having to get so close to patients and having to say so many good-byes."

He nodded in agreement, then added, "But it's the most satisfying work I could ever imagine doing."

I had often wondered why Dr. Padgett chose to subject himself to such abuse, to witness such agony, day in and day out. But it was clear that it was a decision he never regretted. He was one of those fortunate people who had found a way to make a living in a way that truly fulfilled him, a way that made the world a better place.

Whatever his reasons for choosing psychiatry instead of cardiology, whatever his reasons for having chosen me as a patient, I knew that his choices were my good fortune.

Chapter 18

Christmas of 1992 meant another two-week break from sessions as Dr. Padgett took a vacation. I struggled along in his absence, pouring my thoughts every night onto a dozen yellow legal pads, attempting to fill that hollow spot that yearned to see his face and hear his calming voice.

In the meantime I tried to immerse myself in the hectic rush and ritual of the Christmas season. Last-minute shopping. Baking cookies for family and friends. The Christmas Eve choir concert. Attaching the final bows on the presents at two in the morning. Being roused Christmas morning by an exuberant Jeffrey and Melissa before the sun even rose.

And extended family get-togethers.

It was the last of these rituals that I feared the most—a heavy dose of family dysfunction heightened by the stress of the season. The flowing wine and whiskey eggnog loosened my family's lips to speak harsh words that stung like hornets.

Except for the previous Christmas, a point in between hospitalizations when all agreed I wasn't up to the task, Tim and I had been the official extended-family Christmas hosts. This year, as I busied myself preparing the turkey, fresh rolls, and casseroles with the help of Tim's mother who'd come into town for the occasion, I vowed I would not let my family get to me.

Despite our location in a declining urban neighborhood and perpetual drafts through ancient windows that could never be completely sealed, ours was an ideal house for Christmas. With its oak staircase, high ceilings, pine woodwork, and original hearth, it exuded Norman Rockwell and old-fashioned Christmas traditions.

I had timed the meal to perfection, inviting everyone to come at 5:30 P.M. with the intention of having dinner on the table at six. My father was always a stickler for promptness, and my parents rang at precisely 5:30.

At quarter past six, however, they and Tim's parents were still the only guests. No one else had bothered to call.

It was a Marsten family Christmas all right—people showing up when they got around to it, without a hint of consideration or mention of apology. The meal grew cold, my father drinking wine and talking politics with Tim and his dad, my mother and Tim's mom in the kitchen. My mother droned on in an endless litany of name-dropping and wealth references for the benefit of Tim's mom, interspersing the occasional caustic comments about sons- and daughters-in-law who, of course, were entirely to blame for her children's inexcusable tardiness.

"I remember when we sent Rachel to Europe," my mother was saying. "You remember that, don't you, Rachel? Rachel had just graduated valedictorian and went with a group of her high school friends. Who was that one girl, Rachel? I just can't remember the name—her father was chief of surgery at St. Anselm's—what was her name?"

"Jenny," I answered flatly. *What's your point, Mom?*

"That's right, Jenny," she said, then turned aside to Tim's mom. "Jenny graduated second in the class. Her parents were kind of snobs and a little bit bitter about it, but Jenny and Rachel got along pretty well actually."

Tim's mom politely nodded. Like her son, she was a terrific listener with infinite patience.

My mother knew as well as I did that Tim's parents didn't have much money. His dad was a mechanic who worked long hours in his own shop in a rural part of the state, making enough to get by but certainly not enough to even dream about trips to Europe and expensive prep schools. Tim's mom was a part-time teacher in a rural school district. This recital of wealth and stature was another of my mom's backhanded attempts to underscore the fact that she had not approved of her youngest daughter's marriage to a small-town man who did not possess a college degree.

What she didn't realize was that money and status did not impress me or Tim's mom. What Tim's parents lacked in financial resources, they made up in the obvious love and closeness that had filled their home. Tim's mom had also graduated valedictorian of her high school class, but she was too polite to mention it. Instead, with a patience that astounded me, she simply listened with what appeared to be genuine interest.

"There was Jenny," my mother continued, "and there was that little blonde girl, you know, the one from the basketball team—Rachel was captain of the basketball team. Oh, who was she? Her dad was CEO of the utility company, pretty down-to-earth for having that much money—although his wife was pretty much of a bitchy snob, kind of thought she was better than anyone else. Come on, Rachel, help me out on this one."

"Lisa, Mom," I said, barely able to contain my impatience. "It was Lisa."

At that moment the doorbell rang. My second-oldest sister, Sally, and one of my brothers, Bruce, had arrived at the same time, families in tow. Truly I'd been saved by the bell. With four more adults and their three small children now in the house, her story would have been lost in the din anyway.

Everyone exchanged hellos and handshakes but no hugs. Our family wasn't much for hugs.

Having turned off the oven, uncertain when I could serve the dinner and not wanting to choke down dry turkey, I turned it on again. Soon my oldest sister, Nancy, and my brother Joe showed up with their families. The house was now crowded, humming with the low roar of simultaneous chatter and the squeals of young cousins running about the house.

"So you don't even have dinner on the table yet?" asked Nancy, who had arrived last. "It's 6:30. I thought you told us we'd be eating at six. I figured dinner would be on the table. Frank got called in to the hospital this morning. He hasn't had a thing to eat all day."

Damned right, I told you dinner at six. And you were supposed to be here at 5:30. Nope, she's not gonna wreck this Christmas; she's not gonna do it.

Both moms were helping as I rushed to speed up the meal I had been forced to slow down. There were ten other adults in the house. But besides Tim, who was making sure that everyone was comfortably seated and had a drink in their hands, no one else lifted a finger to help. Nancy, Joe, and Bruce had parked themselves at the kitchen table, making sarcastic remarks about my cooking skills—a running family joke that was getting rather stale to me.

"Rachel," my other sister, Sally, was standing in the doorway. "Is *soda* all you have for these kids? You know we don't let *our* kids drink it; it's pure sugar. Don't you have anything else here?"

Yep, Sally, my kids drink soda with every meal. It's just right to wash down the cake and candy dinners they have every night.

"I dunno," I said, exasperated. "Maybe I have some juice in the refrigerator."

Sally just stood there in the doorway, her hands now on her hips, impatiently waiting for something.

"What do you need, Sally?"

She rolled her eyes, "I thought you might get my kids some juice. It's your house."

I retrieved the juice and continued to prepare the meal, the turkey almost ready. As I fumbled with the roaster, Nancy was mocking Sally's fastidious supermom attitude about her kids. All of us were used to this exchange. Nancy and Sally had been cold to each other for years, both unceasing in their attempts to sway the rest of us to one side or another of a feud that had lasted for so long no one could remember its origin.

Finally all of the food was ready to be served. The third generation took their places in the kitchen, Sally's kids swiping sips from their cousins' sodas when their mom wasn't watching, all of them giggling at the bodily function noises that so obsess kids of that age. Unaware of the feuds and envy that so bitterly separated their aunts and uncles, the kids were just having a good time. *At least someone is*, I thought.

The rest of us crowded around the dining room table, supplemented by a foldout card table disguised with a table-cloth and centerpiece. It was a tense scene indeed. The wrong seating arrangements had been known to provoke a holiday civil war. Sally and Nancy, of course, had to be at separate ends of the table. I hadn't assigned specific places, and yet all of us scrambled to accommodate the two of them, adhering to the unspoken rule that had been a part of family gatherings for as long as I could remember.

Joe's wife, Jackie, had, like Tim, failed to meet my mother's standards of wealth and education, and the hostility wasn't helped by the fact that their marriage was on the rocks. In addition, Jackie, in the throes of clinical depression, had chosen to leave Joe for a while and had just moved back in. If it was difficult for my mother to accept Tim, who was beneath her unspoken standards of marriage material for her daughter, Jackie was in a worse position. She was a woman, vying for the affection of one of my mother's precious sons.

Ever since Joe and Jackie began to date seriously, my mother, along with my sister Nancy, had spared no effort in trying to break their relationship apart. Joe was bitter about it and, regardless of the problems that the two may have had, was defensive about jabs taken at his wife.

Thus began the awkward game of musical chairs. Everyone in my immediate family knew the rules by heart, but Tim's parents and the spouses were confused, sensing the tension and following our lead. Jackie's presence added a further complication. Neither Nancy nor my mother could be seated too close to Jackie and Joe if there were to be any peaceful enjoyment of the meal whatsoever.

While my sisters headed for the polar ends of the dining room table, husbands in tow, Joe decided to be seated with his wife right in the middle, refusing to be banished to the card table. Whereupon my mother, sulking, took her place apart from my father and sat alone at the card table. Nancy soon got up and joined her, dragging Frank along. Finally we were all seated, and dinner was served.

Thanks to Tim's mom, who had provided recipes and cooking tips for me, the food was excellent. The turkey was still hot and cooked to perfection, the baked-from-scratch yeast rolls were golden brown, and their aroma filled the room. The casseroles were mouthwatering, the fresh vegetables and salad just right. Tim smiled at me as both of us attempted to relax for a moment and simply enjoy the feast.

"Did you use saturated fat for this casserole?" Sally asked, inspecting it as if it were toxic.

"I don't know," I sighed. "I think I used butter. Plain old butter."

Sally spooned her helping back into the serving dish as Nancy flashed Bruce a knowing look as if to say, "Here she goes again." Sally simply scowled at Nancy, rolled her eyes, and reached for the turkey platter.

My father, as usual, dominated the dinner conversation, a blessing thus far as he could be very witty when he was in the mood. It didn't seem to matter to him that his wife was sitting, veritably pouting, apart from him at the card table. He was used to such displays. They never made him angry; he either patronized or ignored them. Women, after all, were that way.

Meanwhile my mother picked at the food on her plate, refusing to join in the general conversation. She sat quietly, resentment clouding her face as she occasionally stared at Jackie.

Jackie was, simply put, a wreck.

Trembling, fully aware of the unspoken dynamics that filled the room, she sat, head down, focusing on her plate, picking at the food, and consuming as much wine as she could without drawing attention to herself.

It was a minefield just waiting to explode, the tension palpable. Tim and I tried to steer the conversation to polite small talk, any innocuous topic, anything safe that would not trigger the imminent powder keg.

Dad, however, bolstered by a few glasses of wine, was not much for small talk. In fact I often wondered if his tendency to be tactless was intentional. No matter how many times my mother had told me how terribly Dad felt after one of his tactless tirades, it had never seemed to bother him. Yet another case of family revisionism, delicately shaded by Mom.

"So did you pass the real estate exam?" he asked Jackie as he reached for another roll.

Damnit, Dad. You already know she didn't. Why are you asking?

"No," she answered, embarrassed. "Just missed it by a few points."

Let it drop, Dad!

"How many times is that for you now, Jackie? How many times did you try?"

"It was her third try, Dad," Joe retorted angrily, answering for her. "Okay?"

It was hard to judge whether he was defending his wife or himself.

Dad ignored his son's attitude and continued his questions as if they were innocuous small talk.

"So," he continued, "are you two back together now or what?"

Nancy and Mom were beaming, Joe seething, Jackie staring at her plate, the tears welling in her eyes while the rest of us squirmed uncomfortably. None of us had the guts to tell the man it was none of his business and not the sort of thing you discuss at Christmas dinner. Silence hung over the table as I fervently wished the conversation would drift elsewhere.

Dad, however, was not one to pick up on such non-verbal cues, nor was he one to let a question go unanswered.

"Are you married," he went on, "or just playing house? It's hard to keep up with you two."

Finally Tim got up the gumption to intervene, albeit as diplomatically as possible.

"Did you hear we're supposed to get a foot of snow tomorrow?" he asked.

Dad ignored Tim as his tone became even more forceful. "I just don't see how anyone can call themselves married and live in two separate places. She isn't working? She can't even pass a real estate exam for chrissakes. She calls herself his wife and lives off his money, but she doesn't even see fit to stay under the same roof with him. And I just have to wonder what kind of a son I raised that would let her take off, keep paying all the bills, and not set his foot down."

Jackie, unable to stand any more, left the room.

Joe, after flashing an angry look at my father, followed her.

Nancy was smiling, eating all of this up. Sally continued to eat her turkey, as if nothing had been said. Mom was still pouting in the corner as if all of this stress somehow hurt her more than it did anyone else, not minding the jabs at Jackie but miffed that Dad had brought *her* son into it.

The rest of us nervously swallowed our dinner in

silence, the sounds of the kids in the kitchen a soothing background music. Tim's parents were simply stunned, although politely concealing it.

And I'm the one in therapy, I thought. If that wasn't ironic, I didn't know what was.

Thankfully, by ten o'clock the house was peaceful again, just Tim, his parents, the kids, and me.

As we had waved good-bye to the last of them, only my parents bothered to say thank you, as if the bitterness of the whole experience had somehow been my doing. No wonder my mother no longer wanted to host these Christmas gatherings.

But it hadn't been the worst Christmas ever. It had been a typical Christmas dinner, much calmer, in fact, than some others. Like the rest of my family, I had become accustomed to it. It was life for us, the definition of the family gathering.

And yet I was devastated by this dinner, witnessing it through a new lens of reality. It wasn't as if such scenes had been confined to the holiday season. What had transpired before my eyes was not only a replay of a dozen Christmas pasts but also a mellowed-out replay of family dinners nearly every night of my childhood. It was a picture of just how screwed up, just how dysfunctional our "all-American family" had always been. It was yet another portrait of life and truth I wished I didn't have to see but knew I had to accept.

Jeffrey and Melissa, in their flannel pajamas, had finally begun to settle down after all the hyperenergized excitement of a house full of cousins. Barely able to keep their eyes open as they sat under the Christmas tree, re-acquainting themselves with new toys, they were obviously content and sleepy. Somehow they'd escaped all the toxic words and interplay of the evening. They'd had the time of their lives.

Dear God, I prayed, *please never let our family turn into what my family was. Please let our family be like Tim's and not mine.*

∞

Ever since I had started therapy, visits with my family had disturbed me. During a visit and in its immediate aftermath I was convinced that I had prepared myself for it, that I was immune, that I had come to understand them for who they were. But it almost never failed; by the next day a deep depression would set in.

Only after several occurrences did I see the connection between family gatherings and my horribly down moods. Apparently, as much as I consciously tried not to let things bother me, my subconscious was greedily absorbing every nuance of the dysfunctional family dynamics.

I had dreaded Christmas for precisely this reason, knowing it would literally take days to get over such a dose of family exposure. And Dr. Padgett was on vacation and could not be reached, not even by emergency call. It had given me a real bah-humbug attitude about Christmas.

My dark mood of despair after Christmas dinner had lasted a few days and seemed only to worsen as the week went on. Thoughts of running and of suicide overwhelmed me. I was beginning to panic, as was Tim, fearing that this incident might be the one that pushed me over the edge permanently.

Undoubtedly, had such feelings arisen at any other time, I'd have called Dr. Padgett right away. All I had, however, was a slip of paper with the name of another psychiatrist to call if there were medication problems or a serious crisis. I wasn't sure whether my feelings constituted a bona fide crisis, but I was sure I had no interest whatsoever in talking to some doctor I'd never met before who couldn't possibly understand what I was going through.

It was a bitterly cold night three days after Christmas when I was consumed with the desire to go on a midnight run. As suicidal as I may have been, however, death by freezing was not what I wanted. And deep down I knew that if I engaged in such an impulsive act of self-destruction, Dr. Padgett wouldn't be around to pick up the pieces. Instead I picked up the car keys and decided to go for a drive, claiming the need for milk and bread to appease Tim, who wasn't at all convinced but let me go anyway. He, too, had run out of ideas to lift my spirits.

Passing the church, I decided to pull into the rectory parking lot. Although I'd seen the pastor frequently since the initial hospitalization incident and would occasionally update him on the progress of my therapy, I hadn't gone to him for help for fear that doing so might have confused the issues.

Alas, Dr. Padgett was unavailable, and I desperately needed someone. I sat in the car with the heat on and the engine running, deciding whether or not I should bother Father Rick, uncertain whether I was up to facing the priest, who, from all my upbeat accounts, probably thought all was going well.

I compromised.

I picked up the car phone and dialed the rectory number. I could see his silhouette through the second-story window as he answered the phone.

We exchanged pleasantries and Christmas greetings and were about ready to hang up on what appeared to be a trivial call when I finally mustered the gumption to tell him that, once again, I was in trouble.

"Let me check my appointment book and give you a call back," he offered. "Are you at home?"

"No. Actually I'm on the car phone."

I heard a barely audible gasp on the other end of the line. The man had seen me at my worst. He probably figured I was parked on the shoulder of a bridge somewhere.

"Where are you?" he asked anxiously.

"In the rectory parking lot," I admitted.

What kind of an idiot drives three blocks to make a phone call? I wondered.

"I'll meet you at the front door in just a minute."

"Okay, thanks."

Father Rick smiled as he opened the door, his Roman collar peeking from underneath a vintage Notre Dame sweatshirt. A cherub of a man, no taller than me, his rounded belly and soft, puffy features belied the toughness required of an urban pastor.

Looking down at the cuffs of his black trousers, I noticed he was wearing slippers. Obviously I'd interrupted an evening of relaxation. How many times had I done that to Dr. Padgett?

In his office the priest lit up a cigarette and offered me one, which I readily accepted.

I told him my story, the stress of the family gathering, the steady decline into the depths of depression, the fact that Dr. Padgett was on vacation and I was completely lost without him. They were the same things I'd written on the ledger pads over the past few days, the same things I would have told Dr. Padgett had he been accessible. But somehow, in this context, it didn't seem to be enough. Self-disclosure in the presence of a man with a Roman collar had a way of becoming a confession, complete with all the guilt.

"Fact is," I confessed, "I can't stand the sight of them. My own family. Right now I'd like to kill them. I hate their guts. Not exactly a Christian attitude, is it?"

"Perhaps not. But it doesn't sound like they were acting very Christian either. Or that they did when you were growing up."

"But aren't I supposed to love my enemies? Turn the other cheek? Forgive? The whole thing? Somehow I just can't do that."

"Maybe you just aren't ready for that yet. It sounds like you still have a lot to work out on your own."

Was this a priest saying these things? Surely my words deserved some punishment, some penance—ten rosaries, fifty Our Fathers—anything. I was confused, which obviously did not escape him.

"You know," he said, extinguishing one cigarette and promptly lighting another, "there's an interesting theory on original sin I'd like to share with you."

I nodded.

"Some theologians believe that the true original sin wasn't about Adam and Eve eating the forbidden apple but about child abuse."

"Child abuse?"

"Yes. Can you think of any other sin that passes its legacy down through generations? Child abuse spans generations. The abused children, hurt and damaged, become abusive parents—who in turn abuse their children, who become abusive parents themselves. So the abusive sins of a parent can have a ripple effect to descendants twenty or thirty generations removed."

"Interesting theory."

"With real-life implications. The message of Adam and Eve is that all of us, somehow, are interrelated—even amongst relative strangers. When we act in a hurtful way to another person, the hurt doesn't stop there. The pain is spread. Maybe someone gets told off by a customer or a boss in the workplace. And that person comes home angry and says or does something hurtful to his spouse. Who may, in turn, inflict the anger and hurt on the children. It goes on and on and on. A chain effect."

"Whatsoever you do to the least of my brothers . . ."

". . . that you do unto someone else," he finished for me.

"Scary thought. What ends the chain?"

"As Jesus said, love ends the chain. Acts of kindness end the chain. Had the boss or the customer given words of kind encouragement rather than cynical criticism, that same person probably would have come home and spread the kindness to his spouse, who would have spread it to the children."

It was astoundingly similar to Dr. Padgett's analysis of the power of love versus the power of hate—the tiny drops of love we give to the most casual of acquaintances that feed our souls and keep us going. Perhaps, despite his refusal to directly discuss his religious views or notion of God, Dr. Padgett was a more spiritual man than I had thought. As a priest, Father Rick was obviously going to be quite open in his references to Jesus and scriptures, yet the underlying themes were almost identical.

"It makes sense."

"I would guess that your own parents were abused, weren't they, Rachel?"

The truth was that I had been so consumed with coming to grips with the legacy of my own abuse and filled with anger toward my parents with every new discovery that I hadn't much given this question much thought.

But . . . yes. Dad's half-joking references to his own childhood, becoming the fastest kid on the block to dodge his father who had come home drunk once again. Mom's refusal to talk much about her childhood at all, the telltale signs of an awkward and cold relationship with her mother that persisted into adulthood. Both of them had told tales of rising from the roots of poverty, the same kind of family folklore that surrounded my own childhood, much of it, when I considered it, also abusive.

They were at a point now where I had been before I had come to face the truth in therapy, still recalling their childhoods through the rose-colored lenses that spared them from the pain of reality. But, like mine, it was a pain that could not ever be avoided, only submerged—with destructive results.

I had long since come to recognize myself as a victim. But now I could see them as victims too. They were the legacy of abusive parents who had been the legacy of abusive parents themselves. And on and on and on. Nancy, Sally, Bruce, and Joe—all of them were victims as well. I still hadn't reached a point where I could excuse my family's behavior, but at least I was beginning to find a basis to understand it. It was easy to accept Father Rick's theory of the ripple effects of child abuse.

A larger question filled my mind, however: *Where is hope? Not in the past, but the future?*

"So what ends this cycle of child abuse? It sounds like it just goes on forever and ever—a cancer of sorts with a terrible path of destruction. Pretty depressing, to tell you the truth."

"Miracles," he said, "stop the chain. Miracles turn it around. The miracle of love. The miracle of forgiveness. The miracle of a change of heart. No one can force these miracles on anyone else—not even God. It's called free will. We can choose to be open to these miracles, or we can choose to keep our hearts closed and run from them out of fear. It's an individual choice."

A miracle. Stopping the chain. I could not rewrite the past or change history. But I could change the future.

"So what you're saying then is that I can't stop what my parents did or their parents did, but I can stop it from happening to my own kids."

"Exactly," he smiled. "As painful as it is for you right now, you are part of a miracle. You are, at least in your little corner of life, stopping a legacy dead in its tracks. The legacy that may well have been passed down through dozens of generations. It takes a lot of courage."

"But how can that be happening?" I asked. "A miracle. That's quite a thing. I've got to be honest with you. Even though I go to church, even though I sing in the choir, I'm not at all convinced that God even exists."

"You might not be sure you believe in God, but God clearly believes in you. He has chosen you to end the cycle, and you have been open enough to take that journey."

I could feel a tremendous burden lifted from me, a respite from the depths of pain. As embarrassed as I had been sitting in that parking lot fearing the stigma of being the lady who "just couldn't pull herself up by her bootstraps and get over it," I now felt a sense of pride. A purpose to the pain. Once again Father Rick had come through in the clutch. I knew it wouldn't be easy. I knew I had a long way to go. But I felt a new surge of strength to forge ahead, to not give up.

"Thank you, Father Rick. This means the world to me. I may not believe in God, or Catholicism, or in any of it. But I'm really glad you chose to be a priest. Thank you."

He gave me a warm embrace.

"Someday, Rachel, you'll be able to forgive the person you need to forgive most—yourself. And you will realize what a special person you are."

As I started to open up the front door to leave, Father Rick called after me, a cellophane-covered plate of Christmas cookies in his hand.

"Here, take these with you. I get more of these than I could possibly eat." He patted his rounded belly. "I don't need them, but you could use a little more meat on your bones."

"Thanks," I said, taking the plate.

"Take care of yourself," he said in parting. "You're one of God's chosen people, you know."

Chapter 19

It was hard to believe the day had finally arrived when Dr. Padgett returned. The vacation countdown had been sheer anguish.

We spent most of January rehashing the Christmas break, exploring the dynamics of the family, speculating on the origins of my parents' dysfunction and the legacy of their own abusive childhoods.

We talked about Father Rick's concept of original sin and the notion of stopping the chain. It was becoming an increasingly intellectual and detached process as the focus steered away from my own childhood feelings and toward those of my parents and siblings. They were interesting sessions, but after a few weeks my anxiety and frustration grew, and the stubborn numbness crept in again.

I wondered if this lack of emotion were somehow a sign that I had taken therapy as far as it could go. But deepest within me I still felt a gnawing emptiness: a warning that I was avoiding something.

I had been going to therapy sessions for more than a year and a half now—long enough to detect some clear patterns. As much as I loathed pain, progress did not seem to come without it. I still had not reached a point where my deepest emotions could surface spontaneously without some catalyst. Usually that catalyst came in the form of some emotionally charged event or on the heels of a belligerent confrontation with Dr. Padgett. I had picked more fights with the man in nineteen months than I had with everyone I'd ever known over a lifetime.

While these one-sided battles often served to prod the feelings out of me, I was growing battle weary. No matter how much I tried, I could not simply snap my fingers and conjure emotional openness.

It reminded me of when I was a kid, nauseated from the flu or overindulgence in candy or dessert. I lay in bed, feeling horrible, my stomach rumbling, threatening to erupt. Yet I willed myself to avoid vomiting. Indeed, I could recall times when I'd literally prayed to God that I wouldn't throw up. As much as I knew that vomiting would bring relief, I feared and loathed the act of throwing up even more. I'd hold it back, totally miserable for hours.

It was the same way with getting to the root of emotions in therapy. I knew that in the end letting go would bring relief. And yet I was still resistant about going through the painful process it took to get there. Thus January was a period of relative calm in sessions but a miserable choke of repressed feelings.

The calm before the storm.

A longer than usual midwinter thaw had fooled February into an early spring. Already the trees and flowering bushes had begun to bud and bloom, boldly defying the likelihood that the winter's freeze would visit again. The city was energized by a collective bout of spring fever, hordes of children set free to ride their bicycles, the parks filled with joggers, cyclists, and in-line skaters. The smoky smells of barbecue grills wafted through the air.

Spring. The season of hope and renewal. There was an extra bounce in my own step as well as I had decided to arrive for session an hour early, strolling through the immaculately landscaped hospital grounds in a floral print blouse and white slacks, glad to be alive.

My stomach was rumbling a bit, which I attributed to a particularly heavy bacon-and-egg breakfast. About twenty minutes before my session, I stopped in the restroom.

The tiny red spot in my underwear threw a wet blanket on my high spirits. Resigned once again to the inevitability of nature, I reached into my purse. But I didn't have any tampons. Rolling my eyes, I dug a quarter out of my purse and went to the tampon machine. Out of order.

My disappointment was replaced with panic. I was wearing white slacks! And now I had less than fifteen minutes to make it to session. Stuffing my underwear with a wad of toilet paper, I walked awkwardly to the hospital pharmacy— which charged the outrageous markups of a monopoly.

The clock behind the pharmacy counter read 2:50. I had only ten minutes. I needed to hurry. Scanning the shelves, I found nothing, my panic beginning to rise. Finally, with seven minutes to go, I saw the familiar blue boxes stacked on a shelf behind the counter. I was going to have to ask for them. How humiliating! Filled with anger at the counter clerk, convinced that she was the one responsible for forcing me to shamefully request a box of tampons, I muttered my request to her.

"Excuse me?" she asked innocently.

"Tampax, damnit," I snapped, not daring to look up. "I said I need a box of Tampax! Are you deaf or what?"

A bit rattled, she retrieved a box from the shelf behind her. Three-fifty for an eight-pack! It figured.

By the time I had myself put together and rushed to Dr. Padgett's waiting room, it was already 3:05. Five minutes late. I knew what the rules were. If he were running late, it was okay. If I were running late, however, the time was docked from my session so as not to disrupt his schedule. His receptionist, noticing my arrival, had picked up the phone to notify the doctor. He came to greet me at 3:07. Seven precious minutes lost to "the curse," as if it weren't enough of a burden to begin with.

I was an emotional wreck, on the verge of tears, when I finally settled into my chair, not only disappointed at the lost time but also mortified at the prospect of having to explain the nature of my tardiness. This was infinitely worse than the bed-wetting incident.

My cheeks were flushed and burning as I began to feel the weightlessness of shame. The cramps had become more severe, exacerbated by my embarrassed awareness. How could I tell him?

Dr. Padgett was obviously aware that something was up. My awkward silence was not the product of a lack of things to say, but of something too painful to articulate. All the signs were there—the rocking, swiveling chair; the tapping feet; my head shaking as I grabbed fistfuls of my hair. The longer the silence lasted, the more painful it became, the deeper I sank into the pit of shame.

"What's going on?" he asked softly.

"Nothing!" I pouted.

You moody bitch! See what the hormones do to you?

"Nothing?"

"Nothing that's any of your goddamned business!" I snapped, the pain of my cramps rising to epic proportions.

You think he can't guess you're on the rag? Get a grip!

"Whatever it is, it's obviously upsetting you. We've been through this before, Rachel. You don't have to tell me anything you don't want to, but as we've seen in the past, sometimes the things that are hardest to talk about are the things you most need to talk about."

More painful silence.

"Like you don't already know?" I cried, surprised at the hysterical edge to my own voice. "Like it isn't fucking obvious?"

You hysterical hormone-crazed bitch! You're giving it away!

Dr. Padgett, showing no signs of impatience, said, "I can't read your mind. I honestly don't know unless you tell me."

"I . . . I . . . I can't," I stammered, shaking my head through my tears.

He sat there waiting. At times like this he rarely pushed me. Indeed, it wasn't necessary. My charged emotions would break through the surface driven by their own velocity. Anything he could say at a time like this would only serve to keep them submerged.

Finally I could no longer contain the burning secret.

"It's that time," I muttered softly.

Clearly he wasn't getting it, as evidenced by the confused expression on his face.

"I'm sorry," he said, "but I don't know what you're getting at."

"What do you want me to do?" I roared. "Write it on the walls? Send you a press release?"

"Rachel," he said kindly but firmly, "I'm not here to attack you. I'm here to help you. And you aren't helping yourself by holding this in—whatever it is."

I stared at him for a moment, then decided to tell him.

"That time," I said, forcing the words, "that time of the month."

"Oh," he replied. "You're menstruating."

The words cut at me like a sword, a fresh surge of shame shooting through every part of my body. There I was, bleeding in the middle of his office, and Dr. Padgett now knew it. A horrifying thought.

"You didn't have to say it!" I retorted angrily.

"Say what?" he asked innocuously. "That you're having your menstrual period?"

Another plunging stab. I was sobbing uncontrollably now, afraid to look at his face.

"Do you have to use those words? Why can't you just leave me alone? Why don't you mind your own business? Why are you humiliating me?"

As much as he tried to mask it, he still looked surprised at the vehemence of my reaction.

What the hell is wrong with this guy? He acts like it's nothing. I'm bleeding here, drowning the place in hormones. How much more disgusting can I be?

"There's nothing at all shameful about the menstrual cycle," he said delicately, as if walking on eggshells. "It's a natural process."

Those words again! I wasn't sure how much more of

this I could take, afraid the embarrassment would literally blow me apart, wishing in a way that it would, longing to crawl under a rock and hide.

"Nothing shameful?" I asked incredulously. "I'm sitting here bleeding, a raging bitch, disgusting and gross, and you don't think it's shameful? You liar!"

"No," he said in point-blank fashion. "I don't see anything shameful about it in the least. Clearly, however, you do. Which is something we need to work on."

"What do you know? Huh? What do you know about it? You're lucky; you're a man. You don't have to deal with this shit. You don't know the first goddamned thing about what it's like. You don't know how horrible it is. If you weren't disgusted with me before, I'll bet you are now. You probably can't wait until I get the hell out of here."

"Why would I be disgusted with you for being a woman?"

"Oh, you say that, but you don't mean it. It repulses you, but you just won't say it."

"It may repulse you. It may have repulsed your father. But that's a distorted viewpoint; it isn't mine—"

"It's disgusting!" I repeated, ignoring his comments.

"I realize," he said slowly and deliberately, "that menstrual periods can be messy, inconvenient, and uncomfortable. But it's purely physiological. There's no shame in menstruation."

A slew of blades piercing me.

"Quit using those words!" I demanded.

"Menstrual period?"

"Damnit! You're doing it again. Quit rubbing my nose in it, will you?"

"You can't say those words, can you?" His face filled

271

with sadness at this question to which he already knew the answer.

My parents had not been ones to discuss sexuality openly. My mother seemed to be as embarrassed about these things as I was, seldom discussing them. Despite the presence of three girls in the house, I didn't recall her ever mentioning a word about periods, cramps, or anything biologically feminine. My father had been more prone to mention the menstrual cycle, mostly as a means of discounting his daughters' emotions or logic. He never easily tolerated moods and emotions, but the onset of adolescence in his daughters had given him a new way to stop them cold.

"Are you having your period?"

"You aren't making any sense. Is it your period?"

"Quit crying. Is it that time of the month or something?"

For some reason it hadn't seemed to thwart the emotions of my sisters, who would often run out of the room crying—in my eyes simply proving him right. For me, however, it was all the more reason to keep my emotions in check, to handle things "like a man." I would have preferred being beaten, grounded, anything, than to have him level that accusation at me. No matter how many emotions were churning within me, I'd made certain to avoid this ultimate humiliation and would put on a brave, tough front.

Even in the confines of my own room, I'd feared that he would walk in and find me there and shame me by attributing my isolation to my period. Just as in the earlier years of childhood, I had not felt safe at home. In adolescence I felt even less so and had engaged in a nomadic life of outside activities even more than before.

Dr. Padgett was right. Over the years I had established an array of euphemisms to be used in times of absolute necessity. "That time." "The biological processes." Some-times just a pained look on my face until someone else could guess its origin. The mere mention of the words "menstrual period" could immediately send me into a flood of painful embarrassment.

"Never!" I exclaimed. "I never ever use those words, and you can't force me to use them!"

"I have no intentions of forcing you to say anything," he replied. "In fact it appears that you are trying to humiliate yourself, not me. Trying to drive yourself further into shame because a part of you takes pleasure in humiliation."

Not much remained hidden from this man.

"You are trying to humiliate me! Rub my nose in it! You are disgusted with me. You think I'm immature and revolting!"

"Rachel," he said firmly, "you're doing it to yourself again. I'm not going to be a party to your self-shaming. I don't find your womanhood disgusting. I don't find it revolting, and I haven't shown you a shred of evidence that I do. You know that. But this isn't about sharing your feelings in order to relieve them; this is your own game to exacerbate them. You are digging a hole for yourself, and in your own best interests I can't just sit back and let you continue it."

"You're censoring me?"

"I'm pointing out exactly what's transpiring here—and letting you know I'm not going to go along with it."

"Because you don't want to hear about it? You don't want to be a part of such a disgusting discussion?"

"Because, in your own way, you're trying to hurt yourself."

Once again he left me without a comeback. The truth of his words stung, and I resented the way he had taken control of the session's direction.

But the blanket of shame receded a little. I knew he was right, but I was too proud to say so. Instead I pouted, unwilling to admit it. As usual he didn't force such an acknowledgment.

"I know the shame doesn't come from you," he said gently, softening the blow. "It's sad to think that something so natural could be given such distorted connotations. You feel the shame because your parents were ashamed of your femaleness. Nature's sign of maturity became a curse you felt you had to hide. But that's not the way it's supposed to happen."

"Oh yeah?" I asked, wounded pride still stinging. "So I guess you threw a party when your own daughter started."

"No party," he said, ignoring my sarcasm. "But I was proud."

"For having her first period?" I asked, surprised to hear the word come so easily off my tongue.

"For being a woman. For growing up."

I contemplated the notion for a minute, then asked him, "If I'd have been your daughter, would you have been proud of me?"

"Of course," he replied gently, his tone soothing, bonding me to him. "A good and loving father is naturally pleased to see his daughter blossoming into womanhood. Proud to see his little girl growing up."

"Dr. Padgett, did you ever talk to your daughter when she wasn't a little girl anymore? You know, about feelings? Did she ever cry in front of you?"

"Sure," he smiled. "She cried; she laughed; she got angry at me sometimes. Some things she felt more comfortable discussing with her mother, but we talked about things too."

274

"So, if she came home upset and locked herself in her room, you talked to her about it?"

"If she wanted to talk, we talked."

"About everything?"

"About anything she wanted to talk about."

"And she wanted to talk to you?"

"Yes."

"She wasn't afraid?"

"Why would she be afraid?"

"Wow," I said, struck by the stark contrast with my own adolescence. "She was lucky, you know. To have you as a father."

"Thank you," he said, graciously accepting my sincere compliment. "You deserved the same kind of father. It's a shame he didn't realize how lucky he was. But at least now you have a place to get what you always needed, always deserved and never got. You have a safe place here."

My eyes were filled with tears, not of shame or anger, but of emotions so intense they could not be contained. I wanted to tell him how much I loved him at that moment, how grateful I was to have him in my life, but I couldn't find the words.

His warm smile told me he knew my feelings nonetheless. Some things just didn't need to be said.

"Well," he said softly, "that's about it for today."

∞

The early spring air once again rejuvenated me as I breathed in the scents of blooming nature. The burden of shame had been lifted, albeit not completely, but enough that I could at least consider a different way of looking at my womanhood—

as something not simply to be accepted with resignation, but something of which, perhaps, I could someday be proud.

Many more issues remained to be discussed, far more work had to be done in the area of my gender, but the wall of shame that had previously surrounded it had started to crumble. A seed had been planted within me that, with gentle tending, could someday bloom and flourish.

And my dreams, thoughts, and writings were filled with fantasies of how my life would have differed had Dr. Padgett been my real father.

Chapter 20

A few more arctic blasts came and went—Mother Nature's reminder that she still called the shots—until the hint of spring became spring in earnest.

Dr. Padgett and I spent several sessions addressing the gender issue without reaching any final resolution. I couldn't discuss it at all without exploding. At first I had expected some kind of instant benefit from my newfound openness on a topic that for so long had been taboo. My disappointment and frustration increased as change only inched along. I felt as if I had hit another wall of resistance, and I could go no further.

In just one more month it would be two years since I had first begun therapy. I was getting better at controlling my emotional reactions. When feelings overwhelmed me, I learned to thwart the burning temptation to act self-destructively and to sit with the feelings instead. By now I had accumulated hundreds and hundreds of yellow legal sheets of paper containing my emotions—written down so I wouldn't take them out on myself or anyone else.

At 118 pounds I was healthier and stronger, although I still had mixed reactions when I saw the increasing number on the scale. I could still be belligerent and combative in therapy sessions, but not as frequently. It had been months since I'd contemplated suicide, although mine was not so much a full acceptance of life as it was a wait-and-see attitude, having decided to defer these thoughts until I had let therapy run its course.

These were definitely signs of progress that even I could not deny. Still an unreachable emptiness ached deep within me. I wondered if I had gone as far as I could in therapy. It was enough to keep me from wanting to end my life but not enough to make life satisfying and enjoyable. I felt like a paraplegic who could learn to do things she never thought possible when the car accident first occurred—but still could never walk. Perhaps I had reached the limits of my own handicap: borderline personality disorder.

Maybe this was as good as it gets. Maybe it was time to take my father's advice and pull myself up by my bootstraps, accept the reality that life basically sucked, and grow up and give up on fantasies that it could somehow be better.

Chapter 21

Back in my college days I'd scoffed when several of my friends had enrolled in a three-credit course focusing entirely on dreams. I figured it was one of those classes designed to accommodate academically struggling scholarship athletes and those simply wishing to lighten their course load.

To me the conclusions of dream analysis had seemed as arbitrary and contrived as the kaleidoscope of written interpretations. A million different people with different attitudes and agendas could analyze the same dream in a million different ways. How could anyone say that they had meaning?

Two years of therapy had changed so many of my other strongly held convictions; the relevance of dreams was just one more. How could I doubt the existence of the subconscious mind when it pushed its way into my life nearly every single night and day?

No matter how resistant or obstinate I was within the

therapy sessions themselves, my subconscious had been awakened and was making its voice heard. At night. In my sleep. My dreams, my nightmares, had become the window to the inner reaches of my soul.

The dreams I'd had in the hospital and afterward were gut-wrenching, horrifyingly explicit affairs, jolting me awake in a fury of screams and a pool of sweat, leaving me shuddering in the wake of emotions for hours and sometimes days. Along with my conscious thoughts and feelings, I had gotten into the habit of recording the dreams as well, with their plots, characters, scenes, and emotions.

Eventually I no longer screamed and cried when awakened from a disturbing dream. I saw it as an opportunity for insight. I didn't reach for tissues at 2:00 A.M., but the pen and yellow legal pad, not wanting to let a single detail slip from my mind.

As my behavior and emotional reactions both in and out of session grew less erratic and more focused, so, too, did the content and context of my dreams. They were far more complex now, more symbolic than horrifying, but still leaving a clear and intense emotional effect in their aftermath. Dr. Padgett, Tim, and the kids, who had been relatively absent from the earliest dreams, now appeared in many of them. I was no longer the little wooden infantile figure but a cross between child and young adult, filled not as much with screams as with angst.

For weeks now my dreams were set in an urban landscape of decay and deterioration as unsettling as a ghetto war zone—my own declining neighborhood.

In reality our historic neighborhood was still thriving with a population determined to thwart the tide of decay, ready and willing to keep up the fight for years to come. In the dreams, however, the battle had been lost, and nearly everyone had vacated—except us. We were trapped. The only other signs of other human life were the occasional gunshots that pierced the silence.

My favorite building in the neighborhood had always been a three-story brownstone commercial building, an old department store converted to an antique mall. The rounded turrets were reminiscent of an ancient majestic castle, painstakingly carved gargoyles at the cornices surrounded by intricate wrought iron.

In one of my dreams this landmark was also teetering on the edge of collapse. The wrought iron was detached; a second-floor window railing hung grotesquely from the masonry, waiting for the last bolt to give way. The entire structure was leaning precariously, the brick sidewalks in front cracked, peaks and valleys of crumbled red brick unearthed by a rapidly slipping foundation and the sinking ground below.

The green tile roof was disintegrating as well. The wooden decking beneath, showing in places, leaked so badly I could see through the cracked and broken windows that the floor was sagging from the weight of rainwater.

As I stared at this decay in my dream, I could not believe that this had happened. Tim and I, among many others, had worked so hard to preserve this architectural jewel that now was a dangerous eyesore. I was stunned to hear the stirrings of people inside. Didn't they realize how dangerous it was? "Get out!" I cried to them. "You'll die in there!"

"No!" cried a voice just like my own. "We can't let this place die; we can't let it go." I heard a small child whimpering, and my heart raced in panic.

"You have to get out of there, don't you see?"

"No," the voice replied. "If this goes, it all goes."

Despite my better judgment, I went into the building to find them, to try and talk them out of there. Upon entering I was sickened by the sight of fallen plaster, the exposed and bowed walls of latticed laths covered with the spray-painted epithets of vandals. A second-story floorboard gave way as I leaped for safety. I could hear it tumble with a crash to the floor below. I heard a roof beam collapse above me with a sickening loud splinter. It penetrated the ceiling just inches from my head.

"Where are you?" I screamed desperately. The voice so like mine did not reply, although I could have sworn I heard soft footsteps. She was hiding. She and her entire family were in danger. But she did not want my aid, preferring to collapse with the structure.

Another roof beam collapsed, then another, piercing the ceiling until I could see patches of gray sky. Someone was frantically calling my name as I began to realize that I, too, could be destroyed. Suddenly an entire wall came crashing toward me, awakening me in a terrified sweat.

"Rachel! Rachel!"

Tim's face appeared above me, brows knotted in concern as he prodded me out of my dreamworld and into consciousness.

"What? What? It's caving in. We can't let it cave in!"

"Rachel, you're having another nightmare. It's me, Tim. You're okay; the kids are okay."

I was still breathing heavily, the panic having not yet subsided, semiconscious, a limbo state between the horror of the dream and reality.

I rambled on about the dream, still not completely convinced it hadn't really happened while Tim, still groggy, half listened and fought the urge to fall back asleep. Sleep, for him, was peaceful. I envied that. I couldn't remember the last time I'd slept an entire night. Often the emotional terror that besieged me in my sleep left me more exhausted than if I had not slept at all.

Once he was certain I was completely roused and had escaped the riveting nightmare, Tim settled back into slumber as I furiously scribbled out every detail.

By the time I was finished, the sun was rising, and it was time to wake the kids for school. Cursing my subconscious, I wondered if I would ever have a peaceful night's sleep again.

∞

With notes in hand to prompt me, still groggy from the lack of sleep, I told Dr. Padgett every detail of the dream in session.

"What does it mean?" I concluded.

"What do you think it might mean?"

The frustrating phenomenon of answering-a-question-with-a-question. What an infuriating habit. He always had his own views and perceptions. But he never shared them with me until mine were spoken first. It made me look stupid at times, as his perceptions were always more profound, made more sense, were better than mine. I sighed. It was another of those bizarre aspects of therapy, supposedly in my best interest, that still irritated me, but one I had come to accept.

"I'm not sure. That's why I asked you."

"Well, how did you feel about it?"

"It was disturbing, really disturbing. I felt like I was

trapped. There was no way out. It was really depressing—and so vivid. I had to drive by the place on my way over here just to make sure it was all a dream."

"Anything else?"

"I wanted to save the building. It made me sick to see it like that. To see it crumble and collapse. Kind of ambivalent, I guess. Part of me was scared to death, just wanted to get out of there so that I wouldn't get crushed. But part of me was like the other voice; I didn't care if it was collapsing. It's crazy. I mean, the place was about to cave in. Staying would be suicide. But part of me felt just like that voice. I couldn't imagine leaving the place, and I'd rather die than leave it."

"Who do you think the other voice was?"

"Me. Both of them were me."

"And what do you think the building represented?"

"I'm not sure. I've been racking my brain over that one. I thought maybe it was there because I've been putting in a lot of time on neighborhood stuff and it's beginning to get to me."

"That might be one meaning. Most dreams have several. I think there's a deeper one."

I sat silently for a few moments, thinking, like a contestant on *Jeopardy!* racking my brain as the little musical score played on. Still I was drawing a blank. Bzzzzzz. Time's up. I waited for him to give his own answer.

"No ideas?"

"An honest blank," I said. "I swear to you."

"The building is the way you think and feel, the old ways and coping mechanisms you've used to view and deal with life."

"Which is pretty shaky," I added.

"Yes. The building represents your way of dealing with things, of seeing things. This worked for you when it had to work for you. But now it doesn't. Now it can even be dangerous."

"But I don't want to leave it."

"Exactly."

"Even though it's dangerous for me, it isn't good for me."

"Right. Because you're attached to it. It's all you've ever known."

"Maybe."

"In ways you'd rather die than let it go. You'd rather die than change."

"Now *that* doesn't make any sense at all. Why would I want to stay in someplace that is definitely going to kill me, that's falling apart? And as far as the change goes, if I'd rather die than change, why have I been coming here for two years? Why do I keep coming?"

"Ambivalence. A part of you really wants to meet the goals of therapy. But another part, represented by the voice in the dream, would rather, as the old cigarette commercial goes, fight than switch."

"But the dream wasn't about fighting. Fighting is what spared the building in the first place. The dream was about dying."

"That too. A part of you would rather die than let go of the old ways of thinking."

"So what are you saying? That I'm not out of the woods yet? That I haven't made any progress?"

"You've made progress but only to a point. And you can't go much further until that part of you that would rather die finally lets go. In a way it's a trap—your own trap."

"It's that damned inner child again, isn't it? Why can't she just go away? Why can't I just overpower her and tell her to put up and shut up?"

"Because that inner child is you. You can't just banish her. Part of her problem is that she's been overpowered and told to shut up for all of her life. You've got to try and understand her, to listen to her."

"I'd still rather slap her," I sighed. "Besides, what on earth could she possibly have to say? She's completely unreasonable; she makes no sense."

"She's afraid. And as long as she is paralyzed by fear, she's not going to let go, and you will always be trapped."

"What could she be so afraid of? What could be worse than the whole building collapsing on her and crushing her?"

"Because as much as she might fear those things, she fears something else even more. If the building goes down, there will be nothing there to take its place. She fears nothingness most of all."

Nothingness. It brought back shades of the night terror from my earliest years when I hadn't feared death nearly as much as I'd feared the thought of what I was before I existed. I'd feared the decades, centuries, and millenniums of nothingness from the beginning of time—a paralyzing fear of the unknown. At my core I'd feared being nobody. Perhaps the notion of wanting to collapse with the building wasn't so strange after all.

∞

The dreams of urban decay continued to haunt me in my sleep. Dr. Padgett had helped me see a few pieces of the puzzle that were key to understanding them. I tried to listen to what these dreams were telling me, to hear the message beneath the terror. Until—finally—I could hear it.

The decaying buildings were, as Dr. Padgett suggested,

my old flawed way of thinking and distorted perceptions, summarized by the label "borderline personality disorder," but far more complex and deeply rooted in my being than even that. The familiar buildings represented all I had ever known.

The magnificent facades, the stunning turrets, and intricate wrought iron were the socially acceptable faces I put forth to those around me. The tough chick. The grinning joker. Streetwise, smart, and savvy. The "life of the party." In order to cope, every image had been carefully crafted to make it appear that everything was okay.

But the old means of coping, the flawed thinking and perceptions, were no longer serving the purpose—because, underneath the structure, the very foundation was flawed. The house, built on shifting sands, was crumbling before my eyes. Therapy had not done this. It had begun to happen long ago, almost the moment it was built. The plaster in the walls was cracking badly, the roof was leaking, the floor tiles cracking. The signs of deterioration and perhaps, someday, inevitable collapse.

For years I'd tinkered at the edges. Patchwork repairs. Stopgap measures. If the walls were cracking, I'd plastered the surface back to smoothness. If the floor tiles were crumbling, I'd replaced them. If the roof was leaking, I'd patched the leaks. I'd pretended that, because the "house" still *appeared* okay, all was okay. Nothing had changed; all had been fixed. Nothing else needed to change.

But as long as the house had been built on shifting ground and a faulty foundation, the cracks would unfailingly reappear, and the roof would start leaking again. No matter how many patchwork repairs I made, the house would continue to slide and settle badly. A home on a faulty foundation simply cannot last forever.

There was only one solution of any lasting permanence. No matter how much effort I had put into keeping it intact, the structure was going to have to come down. The walls, the beams, the roof, the facade—every bit of it. Right down to the bare earth. And *I* would have to be the one to tear it down alone until what once had been my only home would be a gaping hole in the dirt. Nothingness. A frightening task—but only half the job.

From that nothingness I would have to build a new house. A sturdy foundation would have to be poured. I would need to erect a new shell, new walls, new roof, new everything. Then, and only then, would my home be truly safe. I would be sturdy and secure.

I shared this interpretation of my dreams and the therapy process with Dr. Padgett, who agreed with it. It was satisfying, perhaps, to have developed such insight on my own. Obviously I was understanding myself and the process more. I was able to hear the message from within.

But it is one thing to understand what I needed to do and another to actually do it. For the first two years of therapy, all I had been doing was slowly tearing down my old ways of thinking. I'd been tinkering around the edges, hoping that there could be an easier solution, some way of changing without demolishing everything I had worked so hard to build and preserve. Surely there was a way to avoid the awful face of nothingness.

The borderline personality disorder books and descriptions had all mentioned the borderline's fear of having no identity. Up until this point it had been a nebulous concept at best. Now, reality confronted me. Even if I were able to let go and tear down the framework of my feelings and perceptions, what would take its place? If I could not rely on the familiar, what could I rely on? Certainly some things needed to go. But if I tore the whole thing down, what else might I lose forever? My sense of humor? My assertiveness? The fighter attitude that had kept me alive for so many years? Who would I be? What would I be like?

Then again, how could I continue to live in a framework that was on the verge of collapse?

I thought of the movie *A Clockwork Orange*. The central character had been a despicable rogue, boldly raping, robbing, pillaging, and committing crimes of violence with a sinister smile. Once he'd finally been apprehended and incarcerated, the corrections officials decided to conduct a rehabilitation experiment on him. Classical conditioning. For hour after hour they had forced him to watch scenes of violence, securing his eyelids open so he could not look away, using the method of negative reinforcement until the man could no longer bear to witness the slightest act of aggression.

But the man who emerged was a shell, incapable of surviving, unable to muster even the smallest acts of assertion or self-defense. By stripping him of his violence, they had stripped him of his humanity, his essence. By the end of the movie I'd wished that the despicable rogue I had so hated could have his life back.

Is this what would happen to me? If the borderline rage that had fueled me for so long was torn down and taken away, would there be anything left? Or would it take the life, the spirit, right out of me?

I was daunted by the prospect of letting go without a clear idea of what would emerge in the old framework's place. It would be demolition without the blueprints for reconstruction, with no guarantees. The only possible way I could do this was to place all of my trust in Dr. Padgett, to trust that the hole of nothingness would lead to something better. I was not sure that I could do this. But at this point I wasn't certain I had a choice anymore.

The framework was half torn down anyway. I was like a heart surgery patient lying on the table, my chest already cut open and exposed. I could not simply walk away at this point. The thing I knew I needed to let go of most was anger. I would have to take on faith that something else would come in its place.

Chapter 22

Spring passed into an exceptionally hot summer. City dwellers took refuge in their air-conditioned homes and offices. Emergency heat alerts and the sad plight of those who couldn't even afford fans dominated the newscasts. Spring fever turned to cabin fever. The sticky heat was so oppressive that by noon most people were indoors for the day. A combination of the weather and vacation season translated into a slow period for Tim's business. As it always seemed to be, business was slow for me as well.

After my morning ritual of watering the lawn and bushes, I headed indoors, already woozy from the heat. As if the confinement were not disconcerting enough, it was also the two-year anniversary of the day I'd started therapy with Dr. Padgett. Two anguishing years had passed, and yet here I was—bummed and broke. Would this be the story of the rest of my life?

My thoughts were interrupted by the footsteps of the

mail carrier on the porch as Jeffrey and Melissa bickered over who would get to the mailbox first. The arrival of the mail still signified hope for them; there might be a *Highlights* magazine or a postcard from Grandma and Grandpa.

I had long since abandoned a child's delight in receiving mail. The bills seemed to arrive daily. The credit card balances I had once paid in full each month now reached such astronomical levels that even meeting minimum payments was a struggle. The insurance company no longer covered the therapy bills of $360 a week. We'd kept up with them as long as we could, but lately they, too, had accumulated an outstanding balance. I could not stomach asking my parents for another handout. They believed the doctor's visits were a waste of money, which led to an unspoken agreement that none of us would mention the issue of therapy at all.

Melissa had won the day's battle over who got the mail and handed me a stack of envelopes. Junk mail and bills.

At the bottom of the stack was an ivory bond envelope addressed to me and bearing the insignia of my college alma mater. I opened it. It was an invitation to my ten-year class reunion.

My mind flashed back to the vows my friends and I made to each other on that tear-filled graduation day, in our caps and gowns, high on champagne. We knew that all of us would be going our own separate ways; the idyllic life of academia was over now.

We'd promised that no matter where our adult responsibilities brought us, we would never lose contact with each other and would meet at the university pub on the first day of our ten-year reunion. In the early years of weddings and birth announcements, we'd kept our promise of staying in touch. But now, a decade later, calls and letters had become increasingly less frequent. Since I'd gone in the hospital and started therapy, I'd not made contact with anyone. How could I possibly explain what was going on?

Quarterly issues of the alumni magazine were now the only way I kept up with any of them. Many of my fellow accounting majors were highly placed on the corporate ladder of Big Eight accounting firms; others were comptrollers and chief financial officers of large corporations. The "Class News" pages never failed to depress me, but I always read them anyway, just in case there was news of anyone I knew. Of course, with my barely part-time freelance business, I had not dared to write in. I'd wondered if my classmates were as universally successful as the news tidbits I read or if there were others like me, trapped in a dead end, who wouldn't dare to write in either. How could I possibly go to this reunion and expose myself as the failure I had become?

Digging through the literature and itinerary, I was stunned by the price. It was $250 for the weekend. This revelation buried me even deeper in miserable self-pity. Not only couldn't I face the thought of going to the ten-year reunion as promised, I couldn't even afford it. I gathered all the paperwork and promptly threw it in the trash.

My goddamned career consists of going to a shrink! Even that sonofabitch is successful, the rich bastard. And I have to scrape to pay the goddamned electric bill.

Once upon a time, before therapy, I'd been an achiever, with promise and potential. Now I was a nobody, who could barely make it from one session to the next without seeing Dr. Padgett. Pathetic.

Who was Dr. Padgett to tell me I needed to tear myself down just to build myself back up? Who was he to tell me what I needed and what I didn't? Granted, at one time I had been clearly distressed and had really needed him, but what about now? At $120 per fifty-minute hour, three days a week? Maybe if I were some kind of a rich bitch, I could afford the luxury of fine-tuned self-improvement. But the fact was that I wasn't. I was flat broke. It was about time I started making a bona fide financial contribution to my family.

It was time to leave the nest and grow up.

∞

I did not meet Dr. Padgett's greeting smile with one of my own. I had business to discuss. Despite the pain I'd endured in getting there, I'd come to peace with my decision. The best way to end this business was to end it quickly and cleanly.

"This is my last session," I announced.

The raised eyebrows again.

You don't believe me, do you? Well, you won't convince me this time. I've got a mind of my own. I'm doing what I need to do. This is an adult decision.

"The decision to continue therapy has always been yours, Rachel," he said. "But, as we've discussed before, the usual way to end therapy is to set a termination date a few months away so we can deal with your feelings about leaving."

"I don't have that kind of time, Dr. Padgett. And I don't have that kind of money."

"What made you reach this conclusion?"

I went on to outline my financial situation and the fact that the time involved in sessions and the time spent getting over the emotional effects of them was making it nearly impossible to pursue my career and to bring in some sorely needed income.

"I'm just not rich," I concluded. "I'm not even middle class right now. With the medical bills, we're in debt up to our eyeballs. You've been a great guy. You've helped me out a lot, and I appreciate it. But I've got responsibilities. It's time to move on."

"This isn't just about money, is it?"

"I knew you'd say that; $360 a week might be nothing to you, with your fancy car and your luxury home. But I don't have your silver spoon. Can't you get that?"

"Do you honestly feel you've met your goals?"

"Goals?" I scoffed. "What goals? All this psychobabble crap about letting go, getting in touch with my inner child— what kind of goals are those? I've got news for you, Dr. Padgett. There are all kinds of people dealing with much worse shit than I am who have never seen a psychiatrist and never will because there's no way in hell they could afford it. Just how in the hell do you think all of those people managed to survive before Sigmund Freud came along?"

"They felt a helluva lot of pain," he replied. "Mental illness has been around for all of time, way before people began to find ways to treat it. Those people just suffered."

"But they survived, didn't they?"

"Not always."

"Let me tell you something," I leaned forward with an air of authority. "I'm a businesswoman. I pay you; you are my employee, my advisor. I am your client. But part of what you advise me to do is to stick around here, that somehow I need you. You're basically advising me to keep paying you. Psychiatry may be a bunch of psychobabble crap as a science, but it's sure as hell a cash cow of an industry, making your repeat business dependent on you. What a fucking marketing coup!"

"You know the way that therapy is structured, and you know the reasons why it is. And deep down, you know that this issue runs deeper than money. It taps into fear."

"Fear? You think I'm afraid? You think I'm a chicken shit? Listen. I'm not afraid of anything! This is a financial decision, a practical decision. Period. You're the one who's afraid because there's 360 bucks a week sitting across from you about ready to walk out the door."

You're losing your cool. Get a grip on yourself, Rachel. This fear crap is just a ploy. He's trying to lure you in again. You made a decision. You've got to stick to it—even if it kills you. Who gives a damn if you're dead anyway?

Suicidal ideation. Was it back? I was flooded with second thoughts, my resolve weakening by the second.

"My concern for you is based on a lot more than my fees, and deep down, you know that. You can't buy compassion and love for any amount of money."

I broke into sobs, my cool business facade shattered.

Look at the mess you've gotten yourself into now, Rachel. You can't quit; you don't want to quit; you aren't ready to quit. You're wishing yourself dead now, aren't you? You've made an idiot of yourself.

"Whatever," I mumbled.

"Excuse me?"

"I said, whatever. I don't care anymore, okay? Stay here. Leave. Live. Die. I just don't give a damn."

"I sincerely doubt that leaving right now would be in your best interests, Rachel."

My eyes were filled with tears. "The money is killing us. I can't focus on things if I'm paranoid about money. I just can't afford this anymore, and that's the honest truth."

"I have a suggestion, a possible solution to ease the

financial pressures, which I agree can be distracting, and still let you get the help you need."

Could there be hope? My ears perked up.

"I think at the phase you're in, you could manage with two sessions a week instead of three. That should ease the financial burden a little bit and give you more time to devote to other things."

The tears swelled in hysterical panic.

"You're throwing me out, aren't you? Pushing me out the door. You want to get rid of me. I'd rather be dead!"

Twenty minutes ago you were ready to quit all together. Now you'd rather be dead than cut back a session. Grow up!

"You aren't ready to terminate today, are you, Rachel?" he asked gently.

I shook my head, unable to speak, stinging with shame at my outburst and wild contradictions. My eyes were cast downward, staring at my shoelaces.

"Cutting to two sessions a week is part of the solution. I'm also willing to slide my scale and cut my fee in half, to sixty dollars an hour."

I looked up.

"You'd really do that for me?"

"I told you, Rachel. You mean a lot more to me than the money. You aren't the only one committed to this therapy. I am too."

"There's something else too," I said meekly. "I'm already behind on my therapy bills. About two months behind actually."

"This has been bothering you for a while, hasn't it? Why haven't you told me sooner?"

"Well," I felt sheepish, "I was afraid if you knew, you might not see me anymore."

"I promised you from the very beginning that I wouldn't abandon you. We've been through a lot together. There's nothing that we can't work out somehow. I tell you what. You can pay me when you have the money to pay me. It's okay."

"But your invoices say 'due at session.' Things are really tight right now. Tim's in a slump, and I'm not bringing in any money. It might be awhile before I can catch up."

"That's all right. Pay when you can. As long as it takes."

"You're really serious, aren't you? I mean, I appreciate it, but you've got a business here. Why would you do this for me?"

"Because I care about you. And I trust you. You'll pay me when you can. You aren't the type to take advantage of me."

"No, I'm not. I promise. I'll pay you every dime as soon as I can pay it."

"I know," he smiled. "Well, time's about up for the day."

I started to reach for my purse and get up, then stopped.

"Dr. Padgett?

"Yes."

"Would it be okay if we eased into the reduced sessions too? Like a termination—not right away?"

"Sure. We can set a date for reducing sessions in the next session or so. That's a good idea. We can discuss your feelings about seeing me less often."

I started to get up and halted once again.

"Dr. Padgett?"

"Yes?"

"I really appreciate this. Sometimes I've said some

298

pretty raunchy things about you, your motives, and every-thing, but deep down, I've always known you really do care. You really are a wonderful man."

"I thank you for the compliment, Rachel. I know that's how you've felt. And, by the way, you're a pretty wonderful person yourself."

I left his office beaming, warm all over. For yet another time I felt the pleasant surprise and relief of having navigated safely through what I had sworn to be an inescapable trap—and was more confident than ever that, whatever might come up in the future, the two of us could manage it together.

∞

Days passed.

The afternoon sky had turned a gray midnight blue, torrential rains pelting against Dr. Padgett's office window like tiny daggers, vivid streaks of lightning flashing across the horizon, splitting the sky in pieces. Fear shook me with every boom of thunder that rattled the windows, leaving me almost breathless. The sky. The storm. The therapy office. Therapy. Waiting to be struck. Nowhere to hide. From the storm. From Dr. Padgett. From myself.

"I just don't know if I can do this," I said, voice quiver-ing on the edge of panic. "I've been thinking about it. I'm just not sure."

"Do this?" he asked calmly, as if unaffected by the storm or the intensity of the moment. "What do you mean by that?"

"This business of letting go. I'm not sure if I can. I'm not sure if I want to. And, quite frankly, I'm not sure if I even know how. I've told you everything I can possibly remember from my childhood. I've been more honest than I've ever been with anyone in my life. What more do you want from me?"

"You've been as open as you've been able to at this point," Dr. Padgett said, walking over to the windows to shut the blinds and block out the flashes of light, "but a part of you still holds back. You've taken down many of the walls that surround you, but there is still one at your core that you keep barricaded—a part of yourself you won't allow yourself to reveal."

"Say it in English, Dr. Padgett. You're being way too vague. You keep telling me what I ought to do, but you never tell me *how*."

"You can't get to the deepest issues, Rachel, unless you let go entirely. Take down all the walls. Until you are willing to trust me completely. But there's still a part of you that fears the vulnerability of doing that."

"Don't you think that fear makes sense?" I asked him. "Can nothing be mine and just mine? On the one hand you claim the ultimate goal of therapy is for me to become independent. On the other hand you want me to be totally vulnerable to you, to depend on you. It's a big contradiction. What the hell do you want from me?"

"Without one," he answered deliberately, "the other can't exist. You've never trusted anyone completely, which should be a normal phase of development for a child. You've never felt safe enough to do that. But if you don't go through that phase of total trust, of total vulnerability, you can never grow to independence. A large part of you does trust me, and I know that. But a part of you doesn't. And as long as it doesn't, it won't reveal itself, and fears and anger will stay buried."

"It isn't natural!" I cried. "Not natural at all. No one in their right mind would leave themselves open like that!"

"A child does. She has to. It's the only way she can learn how to trust."

"Well, there you have it then. I'm not a child. In case you didn't notice, I turned thirty-one years old a few weeks ago."

"The part that won't let go to trust *is* a child."

"You've got a lot of nerve, do you know that?" I shook my head in disgust. "You expect me to rip myself open and just sit here and bare my soul. Would you completely expose yourself and leave yourself wide open?"

Silence.

"You don't answer my question because both of us know what the answer is. You wouldn't because you don't have to. You don't have to do anything here. I'm supposed to tell you everything; you don't tell me a damned thing. What in the hell makes you so worthy of trust anyway?"

"That's something you have to determine on your own: whether or not you are completely safe here. From our very first sessions, Rachel, I've never asked you to blindly trust me. I've encouraged you to be as skeptical as you need to be, to question me at every turn. Ultimately you have to be the one who determines if I'm safe to trust. When you are ready to do that, you will. But there's nothing I will say to try and convince you. Trust is given, not coerced."

"Great," I quipped sarcastically. "'Trust me.' Famous last words. Walk to the end of the plank with a blindfold on and just hope that somehow everything's going to work out. Hope that I won't be shark bait. No guarantees, mind you. Just 'trust me!'"

"You're afraid."

"Of *course* I'm afraid, you fool! Who wouldn't be? Trusting completely is an invitation to be burned."

"In your past experiences, yes," he said, ignoring my insult. "Which is why you have to learn that trust doesn't universally lead to being burned. Sometimes it leads to feeling even more loved, safer, and more secure than before."

"But don't you see? It *hurts* to trust. It already hurts to need you, to trust you as much as I do."

"Why?"

"Because, once I open up, I can be burned at any time. I could let go, and you could decide to quit seeing me. Or go start a practice in a different city. Or maybe get in a car wreck, go nuts, even die! Do you have any idea how much that would fuck me up? Do you have any idea what you're asking me to do?"

"Yes, I do know what I'm asking you to do. That's why I'm saying that you shouldn't trust me because I tell you that you need to, but because you've looked at the history of this relationship and drawn your own conclusions. It's painful and it's hard, but it's necessary. If it weren't in your best interest, I wouldn't even bring it up."

The sharp crackle of a nearby lightning strike and a pounding, shaking jolt of thunder rumbled the room.

"I don't know. I'm going to have to think about this a helluva lot more."

"Take all the time you need. I'll be here for as long as it takes."

∞

Driving home in the storm, windshield wipers barely keeping up with the wall of rain, I found myself praying to God to take me right then if I were destined to be devastated anyway.

How am I supposed to trust this man, I asked the skies, *when I can't even trust You! Where were You the first time I trusted when I was a kid, when I was supposed to trust? You sat back and watched me get screwed! And didn't do a thing.*

Do me a favor, God. If I decide to trust Padgett, and I'm destined to get screwed again, strike me dead right now! Take me! Because if I do let go, and I get burned, I'm not going to take the pain of being burned twice. If that's my fate, You may as well strike me dead this minute, or I'll just do the job myself later.

Chapter 23

I'm sitting on the front porch of my childhood home, grown, but still living there with my parents. A sleeping bag and overnight case are parked next to me on the wicker chair as I wait for my ride to show up. I don't want to go, but Mom insisted. The man's rich and successful, and she says it's high time I learned how to be rich and successful. "You don't turn down an invitation to a mansion on the North Side," she said. So, despite my own reluctance, here I am, sitting alone, waiting.

A black stretch limo pulls up, complete with mirrored one-way windows and a mustached driver clad in uniform and cap. As he places my bags in the trunk, I can see my mother peeking through the living room window, happy to be rid of me once again.

She's right about one thing. Dr. Padgett's place is certainly a mansion. It's a replica of a European castle with a stone wall and gated entry, a long road leading to a circular driveway, and a plush, immaculately kept meadow of a lawn punctuated by colorful flowering gardens and gazebos. Dr. Padgett greets me with his customary welcoming smile. He's wearing a baby-blue Polo golf shirt and khaki shorts. He shakes my hand and then gives me a warm hug. The implications of the moment finally hit me.

I've been touched. I've been invited to his home, his private life, to be like his real daughter. A dream come true! Excitement and anticipation fill me as I realize I'm no longer limited to just the therapy hours. He'll be there for me all the time.

I follow him into the mansion to meet his family. A matronly woman with gray, thinning hair; thick, knotted hands; and a mossy-toothed smile emerges from the parlor.

"This is Anita, my wife," Dr. Padgett says.

At first I thought she was the maid, having expected the doctor's wife to be an aristocratic goddess. What she lacks in presence, however, she makes up for in warmth and sincerity, making me feel welcome.

Dr. Padgett invites me to drive tee shots out on the grounds with him, but I decline not being much of a golfer. I'm more interested in exploring this man's castle, his family, his lifestyle, the parts of his life I've never seen.

A husky teenage girl with frizzy, strawberry blonde hair and a sea of freckles invites me into the lower-level rec room. Husky, actually, is a generous term. The girl is fat and plain with the glassy eyes and pale complexion of a veteran party-goer. She's as friendly and warm to me as her mother, opening the refrigerator to pull out a few beers. She's probably not a day over fourteen, and it's not even noon yet. But I accept one anyway.

Turning on some acid rock music, she returns with a

small mirrored tray filled with lines of cocaine, politely offering me a shortened straw. I decline. I want to keep my wits about me as I observe the other side of Dr. Padgett. She's not offended by my refusal, instead cleanly snorting a few lines herself.

"So Dad brought you by for a visit, huh?"

"Yes, he wanted me to be like part of the family."

She rolls her bloodshot eyes.

"Typical," she says. "Good old Dr. Compassion, saving the world again."

Her voice drips with angry sarcasm.

"Does he do this a lot?"

"Oh yeah. He brings his patients here a lot. Watches them walk around in awe; these people worship him."

My heart sinks. Somehow I'd deluded myself that his invitation had set me apart, made me special.

"He is a great guy, don't you think?" I ask her.

She rolls her eyes again.

"So he's got you fooled too, eh?" she laughs, shaking her head. "God, what a prick. Come on, Rachel, I'll introduce you to my brother."

Dr. Padgett's son is sitting out on the huge screened-in porch with a panoramic view, leaning back on the padded wicker couch, eyes glued to MTV, not bothering to turn around at the sounds of our footsteps. He's a suburban parent's worst nightmare—hair shaved to the skin on one side, hanging down past his ears on the other, feathered earrings dangling from both ears, acne scarring his face, and a tattoo on his left arm. His eyes are glazed as the tiny burned end of a joint smolders in the ashtray.

At that moment Dr. Padgett comes in through the back door, face flushed from activity, wearing the same greeting

307

smile he had when I'd first arrived, the one from the beginnings of sessions.

"So you're meeting the family?" he smiles at me.

"Yes, they've been very nice."

He moves directly in front of the couch, deliberately obstructing his son's view of the television.

"Paul," he says, still smiling, "did you finish your overdue science project yet?"

Paul says nothing, just glares at his father.

"You're pushing your luck with the extension, you know," Dr. Padgett says, his smile now clearly forced from the strain of knowing he is being observed.

"You were gonna help me, remember?" Paul finally speaks in a voice saturated with resentment.

"Well, you know I've been busy with my patients," Dr. Padgett replies, the smile no longer concealing the anger in his eyes. It's a phony and none-too-convincing facade for my benefit.

"When aren't you, Dad? How come all of a sudden you give a shit today? Is it because you have one of your precious little psychos here?"

The sarcastic jabs bounce back and forth, raising the tension in the room to a crescendo. Dr. Padgett is restraining himself but is slowly and obviously losing control.

Finally the sharp crack of his hand slapping his son's face ends the argument.

"Damnit," he says underneath his breath and through clenched teeth, "you worthless little piece of shit. Act straight, will you?"

"Go ahead, Dad, beat the shit out of me! Why not? Why don't you let your little patient here see the real you?"

For some reason I feel I have to cut in and defend the

man who's shown me nothing but kindness for as long as I've known him.

"He's always been good to me."

"Yeah, you and all the others. Dr. Wonderful. King of the Lost Causes. You're just the next experiment, the next big challenge. Just wait. He'll give up on you too, leave you hanging. Just like he has with us, just like he has with all the others. He does pretty damned well on his fees, wouldn't you say?"

There's another slap—harder this time. And another. Then a fist blow to Paul's stomach, knocking him to the ground. Then kick after kick after kick to the stomach, the head, the groin, until Paul is silent, lying there bleeding.

I run out of the place, vomiting. My fantasy dream has turned into a nightmare. I can't stay there. I can't go home. I just keep running.

∞

Another rousing shake from Tim made me realize that it had only been a dream. Yet the anger I felt for Dr. Padgett did not fade, as if the whole scene had really happened. I chose not to mention this to Tim, who himself had tired of awakening to a wife embittered at him for something that had happened in a dream. The fine line between conscious and subconscious, already blurred, was obscured again.

Thinking rationally, I realized that my dreams were rarely the premonition variety of biblical fame but the embodiment of my deepest fears. A small part of me, however, wanted to cling to this dream as tangible evidence of the danger and folly of letting go of the last remaining walls and trusting Dr. Padgett. Granted, there was no proof whatsoever that even the most minute aspects of the dream could be true.

But, I reminded myself, there was also no proof that it was false. For as long as I had been seeing Dr. Padgett, there was very little that I knew about him outside of therapy. It was the most diabolical of conspiracy theories: all of the "history" of therapy, all his kindness and patience had been a deliberate act to set me up, to persuade me to let go and be vulnerable, and then to render a crushing blow. Why? Because he hated me. Which only made sense. There was plenty to hate. No one knew that better than me.

∞

My next session was like an FBI interrogation, a no-holds-barred inquisition in an attempt to unearth some sordid alter ego that lay hidden and dormant behind the blank screen, in the "other life" in which Dr. Padgett would not include me. In typical fashion he refused to confirm, deny, or directly respond to any of my inquiries. Not only would I be forced to judge for myself whether he was worthy of trust, I would have to judge for myself whether or not he was a murderer, rapist, child molester, or any of the many other accusatory labels I hurled his way. He was implacable as always.

It figured. Both Tim and Dr. Padgett had been put on trial before for the actions and contents of dreams. It had always unnerved Tim, but Dr. Padgett must have been a tested veteran since he showed not a shred of emotion.

True to his word, the therapist was not going to lobby for his cause or campaign for my trust. I would have to make this conclusion, like so many others, on my own.

Chapter 24

With fall came a renewal of annual traditions. Once again I sent Jeffrey and Melissa off to the first day of school. Jeffrey was in the first grade, already at an age where he was becoming reluctant to show the world that he had a mother. Little Melissa was no longer so little, the baby talk and baby fat fading as she diligently worked to learn her letters, colors, and numbers.

Fall meant the return of Saturday soccer games. Last year's little mob of five-year-old boys had developed into a coordinated team of six-year-olds. College football season had come once again. We watched the afternoon games and colorful marching bands on TV while devouring beer and pretzels. Now that we were able to afford a road trip to a game, we had too many commitments to get away.

Autumn also marked a new season for the church choir after the summer break. It meant a lot to me to be in this group, a curious assortment of strange bedfellows who were anything but pious yet were a close community. The strains of practices, the demands of weekly Masses, the Christmas and Easter seasons, and the concert performances often led to frayed nerves, short tempers, and frequent bickering by the season's end. Refreshed from a three-month hiatus, however, we were ready and eager to begin anew.

The choir had been like a family to me when my family of origin had turned its back. Its members had not gossiped when I'd endured the embarrassment of three psychiatric hospitalizations. Instead people pitched in to help. They had cooked meals for Tim and the kids when I'd been away and even for a while upon my return. They had visited me, bringing cards and flowers. Above all, they didn't think I was crazy or wretched. They didn't judge or condemn me but prayed for me. They had been there to listen, offering shoulders to cry on.

Like any group that worked together closely and intensely, the choir had its share of rivalries and occasional harsh words. But, in moments of crisis, we somehow managed to pull together in support of whoever needed it.

Often I couldn't help but wonder if my presence there wasn't a grand act of hypocrisy. Here I was, the agnostic soloist, sweetly singing words she could not bring herself to believe. The choir director had always known my feelings, as had the pastor, but neither seemed to have a problem with my obstinate agnosticism. People who are honest with themselves, they had both said, have doubts sometimes.

Faith, Father Rick had said, was like passion. Sometimes intense, sometimes seemingly nonexistent—it could never be forced. I had been torn between accepting their views and believing their acceptance might be rooted in their desperate need for a first soprano.

Despite my unease, I never seriously considered leaving the group. Music had a way of releasing my passion, of calming my soul. And, despite the battles I'd had in my worst moments with both the director and others in the group, I needed these people. They were like the family I'd never had, a lifeline as critical to me as therapy had become. Like my ambivalent, often turbulent relationship with Dr. Padgett, being a part of this group was something I could not give up, no matter how much it confused me at times.

The first Sunday Mass of the season was always a big event. We had practiced for a few weeks to get back to form, assembling a selection of our best hymns and musical pieces. A kickoff for a new year.

For some reason I was seldom nervous when soloing. Perhaps I felt that those who'd dare be critical when they were supposed to be praying were far more hypocritical than even I was. I had come to develop a performer's detachment, the calm confidence of a professional. I had managed to separate myself from my emotions even at the funerals I had sung for occasionally. I no longer worried about the effects of stage fright. But sometimes I wondered if, perhaps, I should be feeling *something*. Music, as in so many other realms of my life, was yet another case of all or nothing—drowning in emotions or total detachment, with little in between.

Entering this first service, I was unexpectedly seized by a feeling of unease, the butterflies of nervousness once banished by years of experience now back in force. I wasn't sure if it was because I was back with the group again after a long absence or because of the unpredictable emotions spurred by therapy. But I could feel the stinging in my eyes, the pit in my stomach, and the quiver in my voice as I stood with the soprano section for the opening song.

I felt a tinge of panic. What would happen when I sang the solo piece after the sermon? Would I fall apart? I found myself wishing that the piece, which I loved, had gone to another soloist.

After the scripture readings the choir and congregation were seated to listen to the homily. Our church was our new associate pastor's first assignment since ordination, and he was fumbling through his notes as he struggled through his sermon on pain and loss. The parishioners had already come to know him as long-winded and not particularly compelling. I noticed a few of them beginning to nod off, and I drifted off into my own world.

Pain and loss. My eyes wandered to the large, sculpted crucifix hanging over the altar. I had seen it countless times. Yet this time it captivated me. It was an exquisite work of art, the realistic sadness in the eyes of the crucified figure, the sagging, slumping body. Pain and loss. Suffering. Betrayal. Crucifixion.

I had known the story since childhood. The lesson had become dull and rote, devoid of any real meaning to me. The words of the Creed, recited every Mass in the congregational monotone: *he suffered, died, and was buried. And on the third day, he rose again.* And on and on and on. I had recited them so often I could virtually do it in my sleep.

He suffered. Oh yeah? Well, I've suffered too. I've suffered plenty. And I haven't risen, have I?

The sad eyes of the crucifix were staring back at me, as if they were truly watching me. I'd never noticed before just how much sadness lurked in these eyes, the unspeakable pain that went beyond the pain of crucifixion. The gut-wrenching pain of betrayal.

Jesus, too, had also felt the bitter pain and anger of

betrayal as the same throngs of followers who had cheered him with palms jeered him at his crucifixion, and even his closest friends denied and betrayed him.

Pain? Why didn't God spare you the cup, spare you the pain of betrayal? What kind of sick Father do you have anyway? You were supposed to be his Only Son—and just look at what he let happen to you! I feel for you, Jesus. I really do. Your Father screwed me over too. Left me hanging, an innocent little kid, to destroy me for the rest of my life. Some Father you have! I can relate.

The eyes were still burning into me, reflecting my pain and agony. I was beginning to squirm in the pew, wishing that the young priest would finish so Mass would continue and I could be distracted from the disturbing presence of the crucifix and my thoughts.

It was a homily prefaced with six major points, and the priest was just moving into the third one. We would be here awhile.

Leave me alone, will you? Get your pathetic eyes off of me! Your Father abandoned you, just like he did me. Why do you still have faith? And where the hell were you for that matter? You're supposed to be God too. Omniscient. Omnipotent. And yet little children get abused every day. Where the hell are you? Where the hell is your Father?

My body was beginning to shake as tears filled my eyes. One of the other sopranos put her hand on my shoulder, asking if I was okay. I nodded. I just wanted to be left alone.

Mine were not tears of sadness, but of all-consuming anger and hatred. Had it been possible, I would have run up to the altar, climbed up on it, grabbed that crucifix, and torn it down. All of it was hypocrisy, a charade suckering in billions of people to believe in a God who, despite his purported power, let pain and suffering go on without so much as lifting a finger to stop it. How could I possibly sing to a God I now knew to be a complete fraud?

I was tempted to run out of the place never to return, but, somehow, the eyes of the crucifix still had me under their spell. Transfixed, I couldn't move.

No wonder I can't trust anyone. If I can't trust God, who in the hell can I trust? The last refuge for the meek, the humble, the poor in spirit, the downtrodden. Does God make life any better? No wonder I don't have faith. It isn't because God doesn't exist or you don't exist; it's because both of you do! And both of you are cruel hypocrites!

Abusive scenes of childhood began to flash through my mind as I winced, my anger having turned to pain, sorrow, and desperation.

Where were you, Jesus? Where was your Father? Where are you now? All along you could see what was happening. But you never stopped it. All along you knew. But you kept letting me go on, believing it was somehow my fault, hating myself passionately, tortured in a living hell. Couldn't you at least let me have some peace? Let me know it wasn't my fault? How could you have let me go on for so many years believing that?

Out of nowhere the Footprints story came to mind, the poetic text of it hanging in my entry foyer, a carved plaque I had received for my First Communion many years ago.

One night a man dreamed he was walking along the beach with the Lord. As scenes of his life flashed before him, he noticed two sets of footprints in the sand. He also noticed that at the saddest, lowest times there was one set of footprints.

This bothered the man, and he asked the Lord, "Did you not promise that if I gave my heart to you that you'd be with me all the way? Then why is there only one set of footprints during my most troublesome times?"

The Lord replied, "My precious child, I love you and would never forsake you. During those times of trial and suffering when you see only one set of footprints, it was then that I carried you."

The single set of footprints. I knew them well. I had been alone and on my own, wandering in search of peace and comfort throughout my childhood and even now.

But I'm here now, aren't I? Sitting in the middle of a group of people who have shown me more love and acceptance than I ever could have believed possible. How did I end up here? I have two beautiful children, somehow emotionally healthy despite all that has gone on, loving me with no questions asked. Loving me because I am Mommy.

And Tim. Of all the self-destructive relationships I've been in, of all the risks I took, how did it happen that I became pregnant by a man who really cared about me? Who loves me, who has never left my side, never even considered leaving me when other men would have been long gone?

And where had I turned when I reached the bottom that June day, when I was ready to die? The church! The Catholic hotline. Father Rick. It had been Father Rick's day off, but he was there at the rectory, wasn't he? And he got me to go to the hospital.

It could have been any psychiatrist on call that day, but it wasn't. For some reason the medical director of psychiatry was on call, covering for somebody else. How is it that my crisis led me to a man like Dr. Padgett?

Too many people have come into my life at just the right time, too many things have ended up okay to just be coincidence. And the tiny drops of love, more powerful than hate, have been the ones that have kept me going. They are the

317

reason I sit here, a thirty-one-year-old woman, no longer emaciated, with two healthy children, a loving husband, surrounded by people who care, with my whole life ahead of me.

The single set of footprints. I looked again to the crucifix.

You carried me. All this time you carried me. Until, on a day like today, I would be ready to see that I've never really been alone. All those years when I thought you loved everybody else but me, you were carrying me, loving me, letting me get to this point.

I was certain then, for the first time in my life, that I believed in God. I had not needed to trust in him or believe in him. He had carried me nonetheless. So this was what having faith felt like; this was what has kept people attending churches and synagogues across the world for millennia. This was why, in a culture that tries to downplay and even mock the notion of God's existence, faith in God has never died.

My eyes were now streaked with tears. The woman next to me was hugging me as I shuddered in sobs. Now, however, they were tears of joy. At the age of thirty-one I finally knew what it felt like to have faith, to believe, to feel comfort in the notion that at least one being existed in whom I could trust. Someone who would never forsake me. Who, as promised, would always be there, even in the most troublesome times of trial and suffering.

Mercifully the young priest brought his wandering sermon to a conclusion. A few in the congregation watched me, curious and confused by how anyone could have been moved by a homily as long-winded and dull as the one that had just been given. Everyone stood to say the Creed; it would only be a few minutes before I was supposed to sing my solo. The director came over to me, putting a gentle hand on my shoulder.

"Are you okay, Rachel? Can you do this?"

I wasn't at all sure that, in my emotional state, I could manage to even get through the refrain without breaking down. I looked back at the crucifix, a prayer of sorts for the strength. "Yeah," I smiled through my tears, "I'll make it. Everything's going to be okay."

"Is something wrong?" he whispered.

"No. Actually, something is very right."

As I rose to go to the microphone, I felt a sudden burst of strength and calm.

The Lord is my shepherd;
I shall not want.
In verdant pastures he gives me repose;
Beside restful waters he leads me;
He refreshes my soul.
He guides me in right paths for his name's sake.
Even though I walk in the dark valley
I fear no evil
For you are at my side
With your rod and your staff
That give me courage.

You spread the table before me
In the sight of my foes;
You anoint my head with oil;
My cup overflows.

Only goodness and kindness follow me
All the days of my life;
And I shall dwell in the house of the Lord
For years to come. (Psalm 23:1–6)

It was a new beginning to me, a proclamation of new-found faith known only by God and me. I had found myself in that area between numb detachment and total breakdown called passion, a voice on the emotional edge of tears, just on the cusp of breaking down and wavering, filled with soul and belief.

When I was finished, I noticed tears on the face of the director, on the faces of a few of my friends in the choir, and on the faces of several people in the congregation. They had been touched, as I had been touched. Then I, too, cried—tears of joy and relief.

"That was absolutely beautiful," the director whispered as he hugged me, his eyes still watery. "You've never sung with so much passion before. It was inspiring."

"Thank you," I said. "It's the first time I actually believed the words I was singing."

Chapter 25

Thanksgiving dinners at Tim's parents' were as laid-back as Christmas dinners with the Marsten clan were arduous.

I remembered the first time I had met Tim's parents. I'd been sitting nervously in the observation car of the Amtrak train with Tim, both of us wondering how we were going to break the news. *Hi, Mom and Dad, this is Rachel; the one I told you about. I hope you like her. We're getting married in two months. Oh, and by the way, she's pregnant too.*

We'd planned a four-day visit, figuring that we'd take the first three days to let them get to know and hopefully approve of me and then spring the news. As it turned out, they'd been so open and easy to be around that we'd told them the very first day. Surprisingly they'd been delighted and had immediately welcomed me into the family without the slightest reservation.

Despite the distance, Tim's parents had visited me in the psychiatric ward more frequently than my own parents, who lived only twenty minutes from the hospital. They'd stayed to help with the kids. Just as they hadn't judged us for getting married, they hadn't judged me for being hospitalized three times for mental illness.

Tim's mom brought out the home-baked apple, pumpkin, and cherry pies. Everyone rose to get a slice or two. There were none of my father's disapproving looks and wagging fingers, his silent warnings about obesity that had made such festivities and overindulgence feel sinful.

There were none of my mother's and sisters' litanies of guilt: "Oh, I really shouldn't" or "I need this like I need a hole in the head." Pleasure without guilt—it was a foreign concept to me.

Without question I was the thinnest adult in the room. I didn't know if overweight people in the country outnumber those in suburbia or the city, but I did notice these people didn't seem to be as bothered by their weight, or even as conscious of it, as my family and neighbors back home.

Sunday came too quickly. None of us wanted to make the drive back. But urban reality beckoned. The kids had to go back to school. Tim and I had to work, and therapy had to resume.

∞

Monday morning, once Jeffrey and Melissa were off to school and Tim to the office, I slipped downstairs to the hidden scale in the basement. The moment of truth. I'd forgone breakfast and had stripped down to my underwear to tilt the scale in my favor. Grimacing, recalling the four-day feast of country cooking, I stepped on the scale. One hundred and twenty-seven pounds! It had to be a mistake. I tried again.

The red digital display was stubbornly unchanged.

Three more times, the same result. One hundred and twenty-seven pounds. Panic filled me, as well as all-consuming guilt and self-hatred. How could I have let myself go? I started beating myself up for every plate of seconds, every slice of pie, every butter-topped roll.

It was a conspiracy. Tim, his parents, his relatives, Dr. Padgett were trying to get me fat. And I had succumbed to the trap, losing all self-control.

What next? 130? 140? 150? 200? Would I continue to expand, to bloat, to become a slovenly sow? Not only crazy, but *fat* and crazy? I reached into the medicine cabinet for relief.

Ex-Lax. The box said a dosage was one or two of the small, scored pieces of what looked but didn't much taste like chocolate. I couldn't wait for gradual results and opted instead to take four of them, vowing to lose the excess weight as quickly as possible. To never let it happen again.

∞

Dr. Padgett and I had not discussed the anorexia issue in quite some time, in part because I was no longer in the dangerous range, in part because he insisted that the underlying issues and not the eating disorder itself needed to be addressed. The past few months had been fairly calm as I had felt freer to open up. The one-sided battles had been fewer, as my sense of connection and constancy in the relationship had become more secure.

That relative calm, I decided as I sat in the waiting room on Tuesday, was only because I had been oblivious to how fat I was becoming. Surely he must have noticed how big

I was getting. But he hadn't said a word about it. He'd tricked me! I was seething with anger at his subtle conspiracy.

I'd spent a frenzied hour at home, digging through my drawers and closets, trying on outfit combinations, then tossing them on the bed in disgust, searching for anything that would hide the awful fat.

Dr. Padgett came out, clad in one of his shrink outfits, a tweed jacket-over-turtleneck combination that made him look like an over-aged beatnik, part hippie professor and part nerd. In lighter moments I would sometimes joke with him that his wife must not have been around to dress him.

Today, however, I was struck by how thin and trim he was in comparison to my own budding obesity. Seething with jealousy, I became even angrier.

With my arms crossed and eyes focused on the ceiling tiles, it was the beginning of another cold war of silence.

Nearly ten minutes had passed before Dr. Padgett prompted me.

"What's on your mind?"

The spark to gasoline. I exploded.

"I'm fat, damnit! Fat as hell! You wanted this, you sonofabitch, didn't you? You wanted me to be a pig!"

"Rachel," he said patiently. "You're hiding behind weight again. There's more to this issue than a number on a scale."

"Don't give me that crap! Do you have any idea how much weight I've gained in the last two years? Twenty-five pounds! I'm a goddamned pig. I'm disgusting!"

"You aren't overweight, Rachel, and you know it," he said. "How much do you weigh?"

"You wanna humiliate me? Okay then, I'll tell you. One hundred and twenty-seven pounds. Are you happy?"

I was in hysterical tears by now.

"One hundred twenty-seven pounds at five-foot-six. That's normal. Probably the lower end of normal on the weight charts, actually."

"Well, it isn't normal for me. Those weight charts don't mean shit!"

I pinched the flesh of my thigh.

"See this, Dr. Padgett? It's fat. I hate it. I liked myself better before. I'd rather be dead than be this fat."

"In my opinion you look a lot more attractive now than when you were in the hospital. As a matter of fact, you looked best when I first met you."

"My God!" I cried in astonishment. "I was a complete pig back then. I weighed 135 pounds. It was because I'd tried to quit smoking. I'll never ever do that again. I'd rather drop dead of cancer than be that fat."

"Actually, 135 pounds was a good weight for you."

"I wish I still had the discipline," I lamented, ignoring him. "I wish I weighed what I did when I went in the hospital the third time. I never looked better than that."

"You looked like a ten-year-old then. A skinny ten-year-old."

"I looked like a *model*," I corrected him. "I made it all the way down to a size three. Now I'm going to have to start stuffing myself back into a size eight again. Then what? Size ten? Size twelve? Plus sizes?"

"First of all, you aren't wearing plus sizes," he sighed. "Second of all, most of the models you see are grossly underweight. Besides, what size you wear isn't what this is about. This is about fear."

"Fear of what?" I seethed, burning him with a hateful stare.

"Fear of extremes. Fear of black and white. Fear that unless you completely limit yourself, totally abstain from all pleasure, you'll immerse yourself in it and never be able to stop."

"What are you saying then?" I challenged him, the edge off my anger but still irritated. "That I'm afraid if I start eating, I'll never stop? I'll just keep stuffing my face until I weigh three hundred pounds?"

"On one level, yes," he replied. "You're afraid that if you begin to rediscover the pleasure of food, you'll lose all sense of control. You won't be able to enjoy it in moderation. But it isn't just food that makes you feel that way. It's *all* pleasure, *all* feeling."

"What other pleasure?" I asked him.

"One of the reasons you're reluctant to let go and trust me, to get in touch with the strength of your feelings about me, is that you're afraid if you do, you'll smother me, drown me in your needs. Love me too much."

"Maybe," I mumbled, too proud to openly agree with him.

"And your sexual feelings of pleasure," he continued. "They scare you too."

Not the sex thing. I don't want to deal with the sex thing. Who the hell do you think you are anyway, Padgett? What is this Freudian fixation with shrinks that they think everybody wants to fuck them?

"With Tim?" I asked hopefully, wanting to avoid the issue.

"Your sexual feelings toward me."

"I don't have any sexual feelings at all toward you," I said flatly.

"It's okay, Rachel. You might be afraid that somehow,

if you get in touch with them, you'll end up rejected or exploited. But there's a middle ground. It doesn't have to end up that way. Still you're afraid of how I'll handle these feelings, afraid to trust that there can be a satisfactory outcome without the nightmare scenarios you envision, the trap you see."

"I told you," I repeatedly firmly. "I don't have the slightest sexual interest in you."

"Not as an adult, but you do as a child."

We continued this circular argument for the remainder of the session, Dr. Padgett maintaining that I had sexual feelings toward him and that it was important that I get in touch with them. Me steadfastly insisting that he didn't know what he was talking about. Meanwhile I could feel the tingling sensation between my legs as I wondered if the sex issue was ever going to go away.

∞

It's springtime, and I'd gone to session in a cream cotton dress, long and flowing beneath my waist, clinging tightly to my well-developed breasts. I'd spent quite some time applying my makeup, assessing myself in the full-length mirror, for once feeling pleased with what I saw—not disgusted by fat, but proud of my curves.

We'd been discussing issues of my childhood, the sadness that I had never been able to enjoy my femininity. The melancholy was bittersweet, the recollections painful. But the sense of connection with Dr. Padgett was strong enough to make it bearable. The pain of memory was intertwined with the warmth of feeling loved and cared about.

"You look beautiful today," he says. "Very feminine."

"You really think so?" I ask him, beaming with pride.

"Yes, I really do."

"I'm glad I've gained the weight back. I've got curves now, breasts. Do you like them too?"

"They are beautiful."

I begin to feel aroused, a longing to be touched, a frustration in knowing that I can't be.

And then he rises from his chair and settles beside me on the couch.

"I know this has been a difficult session for you. Would you like to lay your head on my lap and relax?"

"Yes," I say, thrilled by the warmth of his body.

He begins stroking my hair, relaxing me so much, his calming touch a lullaby as I struggle to keep my eyes open.

"It's okay," he says. "You don't have to say anything. Just close your eyes. Relax. Enjoy."

Soon his hands wander to my thighs, caressing the curves of my hips, and then settle on my breasts. A gentle, soothing touch, not at all aggressive or clumsy.

"But Dr. Padgett," I begin to sit up, overwhelmed by the pleasure, afraid of where this might lead, "should we be doing this?"

"Relax," he says. "Just enjoy. Nothing bad will happen. Just sit back and feel the pleasure."

He continues stroking my breasts, his hands so gentle, the warmth of his soft fingertips touching my hard nipples through the cotton dress, the erotic pleasure seemingly infinite.

As the session ends, I explode into climax. Satisfied, content, I prepare to leave, already anxiously awaiting the next session.

"You are a beautiful woman," he says as I walk out the door. "Exquisitely feminine."

"Aren't you supposed to be meeting a client at nine?" I saw Tim standing above me, already dressed for work in a blue suit and tie.

I looked at the clock. Eight o'clock in the morning. How long had I been dreaming? I could feel the wetness between my legs, the vestiges of the dream. I was embarrassed and more than a little guilt-ridden that I had been dreaming about another man yet resentful that Tim had tried to wake me up. "It's been a bitch getting you up this morning," Tim said. "But you looked so content I didn't want to wake you up any earlier than I absolutely had to. It must have been a good dream."

I was usually very open with Tim about my dreams and about what happened in sessions. But I could not bring myself to tell him about this erotic dream with Dr. Padgett, especially when Tim had been so patient about my complete lack of sexual desire in our marriage.

I was relieved when he left. The arousal of the dream stubbornly lingered, so distracting that I masturbated myself to climax in the shower, guilty at having done so. Tim was the one who deserved the pleasure, not me.

∞

Reluctant as I was, I knew I was going to have to tell Dr. Padgett about this dream.

I regretted that I had agreed to reduce the number of weekly sessions. Financially it had been a good idea, and I had been able to devote more time to my business. But now it was hell having to wait an extra day to discuss what I knew I needed to discuss.

On Wednesday night I was gripped by the same dream, awakening to find Tim already gone to an early breakfast appointment. This time I chose not to masturbate. I walked into session frustrated, overwhelmed by my arousal, dreading having to tell Dr. Padgett that he had indeed been right about my sexual feelings toward him.

By the time I took my place in the chair, I could barely stand it as I burned with the desire to masturbate right then and there, my back slightly arched, my pulse racing, my breathing quick.

I'd often wondered during the past two years where the sexual desires that used to be unquenchable had gone. Had I turned irrevocably frigid? As embarrassed as I was to be feeling like this, a part of me was pleased that my ability to feel sexual pleasure was not dead.

"I had a dream last night," I started, and told Dr. Padgett the details. As the story went on, I realized I was embellishing it somewhat, savoring it, taking on the vernacular of airbrushed erotica, a woman's poetic version of a *Penthouse* story. My already burning desire was increasing as I noticed my hips subtly moving back and forth, my legs crossed and rubbing slightly, stimulating myself even further.

The guilt was gone. I didn't want to hold myself back. I didn't want it to stop. Dr. Padgett listened intently, interested, but not giving any visible reaction.

"I guess you were right," I concluded, a bit surprised at the sultry and seductive tone of my voice but still not wanting to stop it.

"What are your feelings about this?" he asked, cautiously objective.

"Oh God," I said, the subtle rock of my hips becoming increasingly less subtle. "I forgot just how incredible it feels to be this turned on. I'm not frigid anymore. I'm *really* not frigid!"

He listened silently with still no visible reaction. Then

again, he wasn't stopping me either. My back began to arch more; my head was slightly back; I could feel my eyelids droop a bit, forming the classic bedroom eyes of seduction.

My God, Rachel! You're playing with fire. You're not just sharing your feelings, you're trying to seduce the man.

"You wouldn't believe how badly I used to need sex," I continued, my voice even huskier, my breasts thrust out slightly. "All the time. I couldn't go a day without it. When I'd go to a party, it was all I could think about. It consumed me—like I feel right now. I could do anything right now, you know, anything. I need it right now. God, do I need sex right now!"

No comment from Dr. Padgett. Was he turned on and hiding it? Was he disgusted and hiding it? I couldn't tell from his facial expression. Discreetly I glanced at his crotch to see if he was aroused as well. I couldn't tell unless I stared, and I wasn't about to stare. Even sexually he was a blank screen.

"Dr. Padgett," I said a bit timidly, "I'm afraid I might have an orgasm."

"It's okay, Rachel. I won't judge you if you do or you don't."

"You know," I said. "I am really good in bed."

The text of the personality profile flashed in my mind. Seductive. Yes, I was seductive. A seductive borderline. Nymphomaniac by pathology.

A part of me knew this was getting out of hand, but I figured that since Dr. Padgett had been the one to bring up sex in the first place, he was getting what he asked for. After all I was a mental patient. What did he expect?

By now my body was in complete erotic motion. I'd crossed my arms over my chest, discreetly—but not invisibly—rubbing my left nipple with my right thumb.

"I was a slut, Dr. Padgett," I told him, the breathlessness of my voice more apparent, "a real nymphomaniac. I ached for it." I was just on the cusp of an orgasm when he interrupted.

"Rachel," he said, "you aren't feeling anymore. You're acting out. The adult isn't present anymore. It's the child co-opting the adult's body."

The climax didn't happen. I was irritated by his interruption, frustrated as my passion ebbed and my impending orgasm retreated.

A flashback from childhood overwhelmed me. I'd been six years old, sitting in Dad's chair, a blanket on my lap, a flashlight in between my legs, rubbing against it, getting lost in the pleasure. Dad had bellowed at me, shocking me out of my bliss.

What the hell are you doing? Shame on you!

A spanking had followed, the sting of his belt against my behind, the pain mixed with the tingling pleasure between my legs. I'd needed to pee but was afraid of what would happen if I did. Agony. Ecstasy.

Banished to my bedroom by my father later that evening, I'd replayed the entire scene in my mind, silently gasping as I rubbed myself to relief in the darkness, deeply ashamed but unable to stop.

"Rachel," Dr. Padgett said gently, "these are the child's feelings, not the adult's. You have to remember that. As a small child, your sexual feelings were as intense as an adult's, but you didn't know what sex was. There's no shame in that. It's important to remember that these aren't the feelings of the grown married woman but the little girl within."

I uncrossed my arms and dropped them to my side. Sheepishly I uncrossed my legs as well. Dr. Padgett had to have known what I was doing but found a way to stop me without scolding me. The intensity of the arousal faded, then dissipated.

"It's natural for a young girl to have sexual feelings for her father. It's nothing to be ashamed of. A good father can handle these feelings without shaming his daughter, without making her feel rejected, while still realizing that he is the adult, the one who has to be in control of himself and trustworthy. It's all a part of growing up, of a little girl's feelings of love for her father that grow into maturity as she does.

"Unfortunately you never had the opportunity to experience this naturally and safely, without shame."

He was right, and I knew it. The adult part of me knew the ramifications of having sex with a therapist. I was married. He was married. As he was a surrogate father of sorts, it would be like incest; it would shatter me. My intense arousal, my attempts at seduction, were those of the child within, a child residing in a body that was no longer hers to control.

I was still curious about what it would be like to make love to him but relieved that he hadn't exploited the situation.

In the crescendo of the moment, had he chosen to take advantage of the circumstances of my arousal, he easily could have done so. But he hadn't. Still there was a vague feeling of rejection.

"Dr. Padgett," I asked him. "I want you to be honest about one thing. Do you find me, the adult, attractive?"

"I'm a normal, healthy man," he answered carefully. "I see what everyone else sees. As you've already said, there have always been men who've been attracted to you. Why would I see anything differently than they do?"

It was an indirect answer, not quite the of-course-you're-attractive response I'd been looking for, yet an answer

333

nonetheless. And I knew why he had to answer the question as he had.

"Do you think I'm feminine?" I asked.

"Do you think you're feminine?" he asked in response.

I thought about it for a minute.

"Yes, I do."

"How do you feel about that?"

"I think that maybe, someday, I could come to like it," I answered sincerely.

He smiled at me, looking into my eyes as I beamed back. We sat like that for a few moments, neither of us saying a word. Neither of us had to. I had let down one of the last barriers, had let go, and trusted him.

And true to his promise, I had emerged feeling neither exploited nor rejected. My heart was filled with the same passionate intensity that had flooded my erogenous zones earlier in the session. So this was what letting go felt like.

"That's about time for today," he broke the silence.

On the way out the door, I stopped one last time to look in his eyes, to drink in the pleasure of feeling safe and connected.

∞

I had walked, blindfolded, off the plank of trust and landed safely.

We would devote more sessions to discussing sexuality, acceptance of my own feminine body image, the self-destructive legacy, and my regrets about the promiscuity of my past. But the door to sexual issues had been opened wide now, a great fear overcome.

The little girl was growing up.

Chapter 26

There'd been many a teenage boy in my high school days, many a steamy night inside a car on a dimly lit street. I remembered a teenage boy in the struggle of his desires against my own ambivalent resistance. *C'mon, you know you like it. I can't have sex before I'm married; it just isn't right. Then you shouldn't have led me on like that!*

We would abruptly release from heated embrace, he'd turn the key hastily in the ignition, and the car would fill with the smoldering silence of his anger and my guilt as we would drive home wordlessly.

Home alone afterward, I would feel ashamed, not because I had let a boy bring me past the heat of passion, but because the boy had been *right* to chastise me. I had led him on. I hadn't been fair. I had tortured him.

The truth was that longing wasn't sexual. I wanted to be the entire focus of any person I was obsessed with. My incessant hunger for attention had been a part of my life for as long as I could remember. The burning heartache of emptiness obsessed me even when my peers had been taken with Barbie dolls and coloring books. I knew even then that these constant feelings were not normal. I had been deeply ashamed of them, not daring to breathe them to another soul, particularly to the objects of my longing.

As the years passed, my longings had taken on a sexual component. Perhaps in the seventies era of free love and the *Cosmopolitan* woman, they'd been easier to accept. On a far deeper level, I thought my desire to be the center of attention, usually from an older man, was worse than sexual promiscuity.

When the object of my longing—the teacher, the coach, the boss—was present in a room, I geared everything to that person. I contrived every word, action, inflection, and facial expression for him. *Does he see me laughing? Does he see how funny everybody thinks I am?*

Now Dr. Padgett was, undoubtedly, the most compelling and long-lasting object of my fantasies in my entire lifetime. In many ways my relationship with him was a dream come true. For the fifty minutes I was with him in a given session, I was the center of attention with all others excluded. Everything focused on me. I did not have to wonder, as I had with the others, if he could see my every expression, could hear my every word, was paying attention. I knew without a doubt that he was. Indeed such intense focus on all aspects of my feelings and emotions were the means and purpose of therapy.

With Dr. Padgett, as with the others, I attempted to give the message that I didn't care what he thought and had tried every possible venue of rebellion. Yet he had refused to be driven away. He wished to probe even deeper, to know more about me than I wanted to reveal. In ways it had been easier to maintain my fantasies from a distance. The secret longing for attention was becoming harder to sustain.

Finally it became obvious to me what Dr. Padgett meant by "letting go." The sexual aspects were secondary. Window dressing. They were a distraction from the real dilemma that faced me—allowing him to know just how much I needed him, just how much he consumed my thoughts and fantasies.

To be open with my feelings, I would have to abandon the cloak of secrecy and to trust him with my vulnerability. I would have to have faith that he would not reject or ridicule my intense longing nor parallel it with a needy vulnerability of his own—one I could not handle.

Revealing my sexual feelings was easy in comparison.

∞

It took a few sessions and much internal debate before I could share my newfound revelations with him. The frustrations of withholding them outweighed my fear of vulnerability until I couldn't bear the emotional battle any longer.

It was a snowy day in mid-December, just one week before his scheduled vacation. My hands were shaking as I shared my painfully embarrassing secret, revealing the cowering little girl behind the I-don't-give-a-shit facade, my lifetime of fantasy objects who never knew of my obsessions.

"It's the same thing with you," I concluded. "Only worse. I've never felt it this intensely in my life before. I hate it."

"It's worse to feel love than hatred?" he asked, eyebrows raised.

"But this isn't love, Dr. Padgett. Can't you understand?" I pleaded. "This is obsession, plain and simple. It's more than infatuation. It's not normal. I've always known it's not normal. It's downright pathological!"

"And it bothers you because you don't think it's normal?"

"Of course it does. It always has. It's embarrassing, don't you see? It's sick. Normal kids never felt the way I felt. I know they never did. And normal adults *never* feel this way."

"They're *feelings*, Rachel. That's all. Just feelings. You may be ashamed of them, but I'm not."

"Well, then you should be! You should be very ashamed of them!"

"Why? Because you are? We've already uncovered a lot of your feelings that you've been ashamed of and shown you've had no reason to be ashamed of them. Because your parents would be ashamed of them? We've been down that road too. Those are distorted yardsticks. We can't rely on them."

"I don't care," I insisted. "Those have been about *other* feelings. Maybe I've been wrong about them, or maybe my parents were wrong. But this is different. Some things are still shameful. Some things are just plain wrong."

"And what is it that you see as so shameful and wrong?"

I breathed deeply and swallowed hard. True confessions once again.

"Wanting to be the center of attention. Underneath it all that's what all of this is about, being the center of attention."

There. I said it. The ball was in his court. How could he defend this one?

"So you think there's something inherently wrong,

inherently bad and shameful about wanting to be the center of attention?"

He might as well have asked me what was so wrong about being an ax murderer.

"Do I think there's something inherently wrong and bad about it? What kind of question is that? Of course there is! My God, Dr. Padgett, I've just confessed a mortal sin, and you're sitting there like I haven't said a thing."

"This isn't a confessional, Rachel," he sighed. "And, in any event, I just don't see the sin."

"The sin is being totally self-centered. The sin is thinking I'm the only person in the world."

"The sin, in your eyes," he said slowly, "is being like a child."

"In case you haven't noticed," I seethed, "I'm not a child. It's high time I grow up."

"Not exactly true," he replied. "You know that part of you is still a child. You believe the child exists. The problem is that you can't accept her. You never could. In a lot of ways neither could your parents."

"Don't you see?" I was exasperated at hearing the same old theories. "This isn't about love—a child's love or anyone else's. This is about clinging. About smothering. About a world centered around myself."

"Which is a perfectly natural state of childhood."

"I've read my damned Freud, okay? Spare me the id stuff, will you? It doesn't apply here."

"It really is sad that you've never been able to accept being a child."

"Doesn't the word 'selfish' mean anything to you? You think being self-centered is honorable or something? Would you tolerate it in your wife? Would you tolerate it in any other relationship? Hell no! And you shouldn't."

"This isn't like any other relationship for either of us. As a parent, as a wife, you can't be too self-centered. It would be very destructive. And you aren't too self-centered in those relationships. But it's safe here, safe to feel a child's feelings."

"Safe to be selfish?"

Dr. Padgett sat back for a moment. This track was going nowhere.

"You say you're familiar with Freud," he said calmly. "Then you know that the id phase is just that, a phase. The child becomes more secure with herself and begins to discover that a world exists beyond her. Then the ego develops, a child's realization that she lives in a world with other people. That she needs to coexist with them in order to meet her own needs. Then comes the superego phase, where the child is not only aware of the existence of others but has some concern for their feelings and needs beyond what directly benefits her."

"And I'm stuck in the id mode," I snapped, disgusted with myself. "Doesn't say much for a thirty-one-year-old mother of two, does it?"

"You can't skip a phase, Rachel. You can't go to the ego phase without first going through the id. There are no moral implications to it. A child needs to be self-centered long enough to feel secure before she can move on. Whether you go through it when you're three or thirty-three, it doesn't matter. You have to pass through that phase and feel secure enough to move on. And, most important, the phase can and will pass."

"How?" I pouted.

"Needs don't just go away on their own. They have to be satisfied. And if they aren't, they just fester beneath the surface and grow even more shameful and frightening. You have an inordinately strong need for attention because you feel, rightly, that you didn't get as much as you needed when you should have. You buried it in shame, which only served to make the need seem more intense until, finally, you became afraid to need because you figured it would overwhelm anyone you let it touch.

"But your need won't overwhelm me, Rachel. It won't drive me away. You don't have to hold it in anymore, and you don't have to be ashamed of it. When you let go—and *only* when you let go—and feel free to feel the need for attention in all its intensity, then it can be satisfied. Until it isn't so important to you anymore.

"Sure, even adults need and deserve some degree of attention. But once you reach this point, it isn't debilitating anymore. It doesn't obsess you."

"It's scary how much I need you," I admitted, the tears beginning to surface. "I need you so much it hurts."

"It isn't all need," he said softly. "A lot of it is love."

"Yes," I replied in a tiny voice. "It is love too. It's really hard for me to say this, Dr. Padgett, but in some ways I love you more than I've ever loved anyone. And the scariest part of that is that I feel this love intensely, and I know that someday I'm going to have to say good-bye. I can hardly bear the thought; it just seems so unfair."

"When you do say good-bye, which will only be when you decide the time has come, it will be because you've gotten what you needed from this relationship. As painful as it might be at the moment, you need to move on. The love doesn't have to end there. Once you have felt it, it can never be taken away. A part of me will always be with you for the rest of your life."

The notion was strangely comforting to me as I sat there soaking in his words, astounded that we had been able to approach the topic of termination without the hysterical fear of loss. With the cloak of secrecy shed, the pain of need was giving way to the warmth of love and the security of feeling connected.

I still didn't look forward to his two-week absence for Christmas vacation. Yet I felt a newfound confidence that, despite the pain of missing him, I could make it through the separation.

"Whenever I do decide to leave," I said, "I know it's going to hurt. I love you like a father. I really do. And I will never ever forget you."

"I'll never forget you either. The feelings are mutual."

The object of my love and fantasy had returned my feelings with warm feelings of his own, neither running from my intensity nor demanding his own needs be met in parallel fashion. It was an outcome I never could have anticipated even a year ago. My painfully hidden secret hopes and fantasies had intersected with reality.

The lifelong dream was indeed coming true. I loved him, I had let him know, and he hadn't run away in horror.

∞

The holiday passed quickly and relatively smoothly.

It wasn't until two days after Christmas that I found the time to escape to my room and pull out the pen and legal pad to write. I realized that nearly a week had gone by without writing my thoughts. I literally had to look at the calendar to calculate how many days remained until sessions resumed— a figure I had known during every waking moment of Dr. Padgett's previous vacations.

At times I still felt the angst of missing him, a melancholy feeling as I imagined what he might be doing with his family, wishing I could be there to enjoy it with him.

But, for the first time, I didn't resent his absence. Surely I preferred that I see him. But I no longer felt as abandoned. I knew he would be coming back, and I knew that the separation didn't sever our feelings.

Tim and I had hosted Christmas dinner once again. The simmering resentments, the absurd game of musical chairs, my father's outbursts, and my mother's alternating grandiosity and victim's pout had not changed. Nancy, as usual, didn't lift a finger. Sally still saw me as her waitress. Joe and Jackie fended off the direct and indirect attacks on their relationship, and Bruce played the middleman.

The script hadn't changed. The way I dealt with it, however, did.

With an emerging confidence, I calmly told Sally that what she saw on the table was what we were offering. If she felt her kids were being nutritionally deprived, she was more than welcome to bring her own food.

When Nancy called the next day, as she always did, to vent her caustic opinions about Jackie and Sally, I told her that I didn't see things quite the same way and preferred not to discuss the matter. And, for the first time that I could ever recall, when my father began to badger us, I openly disagreed with him.

In sum, I viewed the situation from the perspective of an adult and acted like one. While the members of my family were obviously stunned, there were no explosions. Armageddon did not come. It was the calmest family gathering I'd attended in years.

Afterward I noticed that nearly all of them were keeping a distance from me. The family roles had been set for so long

that the change in my attitude and behavior left them confused and not universally pleased. Only Joe and Jackie
seemed to be drawn closer to me. For years they'd interpreted
my silence during the attacks on them as passive agreement.
Now they knew differently. With all I had been through
myself, I couldn't fathom judging them for the strained and
often difficult course of their own relationship.

People could grow; people could change. If anyone
knew that, it was me.

∞

I was feeling good about myself and my ability to handle both
my family and my separation from Dr. Padgett on the eve of
1994's first therapy session. Tim and I had taken the kids out
sledding, and all of us glowed with satisfied exhaustion as we
sat in front of the fire when the phone rang.

It was Nancy.

"Rachel, there's something on my mind, and I have to
discuss it with you," she said with the authoritative air of the
oldest child.

"What's up?" I asked.

"You've been acting strangely lately. I'm pretty concerned about it."

Yeah, real concerned. I'll bet you are.

"How so?"

"You're so distant these days. Quite frankly I think
you're getting pretty rude and arrogant."

"Hmm . . ."

"I'm serious," she continued, clearly irritated that I had
not crumbled into a diplomatic litany of apologies. "You're
different."

"You're right. I've changed."

"Well, it's pretty disturbing to the rest of us. The way you treated Mom and Dad, the way you talked to Sally. You were very cold, you know. Very rude."

"So suddenly you care about how Mom and Dad feel? How Sally feels? *This* is news."

"See?" she exclaimed. "See what I mean? It's that kind of thing. That . . . that . . . I don't know. . . . That *attitude* you've got now!"

"What attitude?"

"You're so . . . so *flippant*. You really don't care what you say anymore; you don't care whose feelings you hurt."

"I say what I think is true," I replied calmly, noting that the calmer I was, the more emphatic she became, a fact not necessarily displeasing to me. "I have a right to my opinions, and you have a right to yours. Obviously there are some things we don't agree on."

The baby of the family had stepped out of the role of compliant peacemaker, and Nancy had no intention of accepting it.

"You know, I'm beginning to wonder about that therapist of yours. He's driving you away from your family. What kind of a therapist is he anyway?"

My family had driven me away years ago and had been turned against each other for as long as I could recall. The only difference was that now I was realizing that sad fact. But I couldn't let the comment about Dr. Padgett pass.

"Dr. Padgett is a damned good psychiatrist," I replied, trying to maintain my calm facade but feeling the anger rise within me. "He's helped me change in ways I've needed to change."

"I liked you better before."

"It isn't about what you like or you don't like, Nancy. It's about *me* liking *me*."

"What kind of bullshit is that?" she exclaimed. "You're part of a family. You knew all of us before you ever met him."

Hold your temper, Rachel. She's trying to get a rise out of you.

"I really don't like the direction this conversation is taking. What I do with my life is my own business."

"Well," she sniffed, "I don't like the direction *you're* taking. You're acting like you're better than anyone else in this family."

"I'm not acting like I'm better or worse than anyone else. I'm finally saying what's on my mind, and none of you are used to that. If you don't like that, well, you're entitled to your opinion. You don't have to like it."

"How selfish can you be? All of a sudden you don't give a damn about anybody but yourself. That therapist isn't helping you. He's screwing you up!"

"And you care? Is that why you blast Jackie and Joe every time you get a chance? Is that why you haven't said a civil word to Sally in years? Is that why you slam Mom and Dad every chance you get?"

"You're hateful. You know that? How dare you say those things!"

"Not hateful, Nancy. Just honest."

"You don't give a damn about any of us, do you? Families are supposed to love each other. Sisters are supposed to stick together."

"It's up to you," I sighed. "If you want to stick by me, then you're going to have to accept the person I've become. If you choose not to, well, that's you're business not mine."

"What about Mom and Dad then? They're your parents.

346

How can you act like that to them?"

This from the woman who, in her days of therapy and well beyond, had blamed them quite openly and belligerently for her every shortcoming.

"They're going to have to accept me too. If they really love me, they will. If they don't, well, then I guess we'll all just have to learn to live with it."

"God, you're so distant. Mom's always been right about you. You're selfish as hell. Don't you even love your own parents?"

"I'm not sure what I think anymore, Nancy," I said, unsettled by the realization that I wasn't sure of the answer to her question. "I'm sorting everything out. I'm not sure who I love. Sometimes I've wondered if I've ever really known what love is."

Why do you have to be so goddamned honest, Rachel? Nancy's not going to understand this. Just lie and say, "Sure, of course I love them." It might be true.

"This is downright scary, Rachel. Let me ask you another question then. I'm your sister; do you love me?"

At the moment it was the furthest thing from my mind.

"I told you, Nancy, I'm not sure how I feel about anything or anyone anymore. I need some time to sort things out."

"You really are crazy, aren't you? Maybe you'll get enough of a grip to understand the horrible things you've just said."

"Maybe I will," I said unsteadily, now as upset as Nancy, both of us in tears.

With that, Nancy hung up on me.

My newfound confidence had been severely tested, and I was not sure if it would hold. Angry that she had destroyed what had been a quiet and relaxing evening, I was at least grateful that, tomorrow, I would see Dr. Padgett again and perhaps make sense of it all.

Chapter 27

January 1994.

It had been two and a half years since I had first entered the hospital and begun the painful introspection of therapy. Now I was in a frightening black hole, an emotional purgatory. I was no longer convinced that slow suicide was the answer, yet I was unsure of what to do with my potentially long life.

I had stopped running. But in doing so I found myself in an unfamiliar place. Much of what I had come to believe in the past had been refuted. I could no longer rely on the past. I could no longer rely on anything.

With the decision to live came the much more difficult choice of *how*. As dysfunctional as it was, I still had a family of origin, as well as a family of my own. My decisions would not just affect me, but my children too.

If I were to simply turn my back on the Marstens, I'd also be depriving Jeffrey and Melissa of grandparents, aunts, uncles, and cousins. Here I was, teaching them lessons about family, about caring for each other. How could I explain it to them if I opted out of my own family?

I'd come to the realization that nothing was black and white, that I was neither perfectly good nor perfectly evil. The issues of responsibility in relationships were never clear-cut. I wondered how much I contributed to the dysfunction in my family.

How many times had I reveled in Nancy's slander of my siblings? How many times had I been secretly pleased to outdo one of them, to see one of them abused because it further enhanced my own standing?

It was an emotional maze that grew exponentially. The deeper I delved into these issues, the more elusive the answers seemed to be.

I couldn't trust my own emotions. Which emotional reactions were justified, if any? And which ones were tainted by the mental illness of borderline personality disorder? I found myself fiercely guarding and limiting my emotional reactions, chastising myself for possible distortions and motivations.

People who had known me years ago would barely recognize me now. I had become quiet and withdrawn in social settings, no longer the life of the party. After all, how could I know if my boisterous humor were spontaneous or just a borderline desire to be the center of attention?

I could no longer trust any of my heartfelt beliefs and opinions on politics, religion, or life. The debate queen had withered. I found myself looking at every single side of an issue unable to come to any conclusions for fear they might be tainted.

My lifelong ability to be assertive had turned into a constant state of passivity.

Anger was also a perplexing dilemma. Could such an emotion *ever* be justified, *ever* be rational? Upon sensing the slightest stirrings of anger within, I quickly doused them. Rage is one of the primary defining characteristics of borderline personality disorder. Any outburst could represent succumbing to my illness.

And yet I had a lingering fear that my story would follow the script of *A Clockwork Orange*. That, perhaps, deprived of anger as the rogue had been stripped of violent instinct, I would be denied the fuel of my life.

It was a painful state of near nonexistence, another trap. Perhaps I had finally reached my core, found my essence and identity. And nobody was there. Nothingness. I was an empty shell.

The words of my phone conversation with Nancy replayed themselves in my mind. If I was incapable of love, then what did I have with Tim? What did I have with Jeffrey and Melissa? It was a bleak time for me. I found it hard to even drag myself out of bed in the morning. Someone was getting up, going to sessions, and taking on the adult responsibilities of mothering, household, and career. But she was operating on automatic pilot without feeling or passion.

The house was cleaner than it had ever been. I was getting work done and providing the family with a flow of income. The unpredictable emotional outbursts and the arguments with Tim had all but disappeared.

Still Tim was disturbed by it all. He wanted his wife back, the passionate woman he had met years ago. I didn't know if she would ever come back or if her passion was forever lost. Tim continued to support me, to encourage my therapy, to say the words and show the signs of his love. But I knew his fear was much like mine. Maybe I had been better off as an untreated borderline than what I had become.

Sessions with Dr. Padgett lacked the explosions of earlier ones. Rarely, if ever, did I come up with conclusions of my own. When Dr. Padgett did, I simply acquiesced. Even when I felt he might be wrong, a flicker of disagreement rising within me, I quickly thwarted it.

Who was I, after all, to be able to trust my own judgment when it had proven to be distorted so many times? If Dr. Padgett was surprised by my sudden change in disposition, he did not express it. Instead he reassured me that there was a core within me, that I had an identity, and I would ultimately find it. In the interim he would be at my side, accepting me no matter who I was or how confused I might be.

The Stepford Wife. Was this destined to be a perpetual state?

∞

There wasn't a flicker of sunshine as the snow continued to pile on the ground as it had for nearly two days. Somehow Tim had been able to maneuver his car out of a freshly plowed mound of snow and make it to the office, but the streets were barely passable. Almost every school and many businesses had closed for the day.

At noon I had gotten a call from Dr. Padgett's service. He, too, had been unable to navigate through the snow and had to cancel my session. The kids were as housebound as I was, bickering over a game of Candy Land.

I tried writing, but I wasn't in the mood for it, my thoughts forced and meaningless. I settled in with a trashy romance novel I'd picked up for a dime from a yard sale, but its foolish glamour and inane dialogue left me irritated and unable to concentrate.

Around midafternoon the phone rang. It was my insurance company, disputing a claim from several months before. Most likely a result of anorexic behavior, my periods had become highly irregular. I'd missed one or two and then had one that lasted for an agonizing twenty days. Not wanting to take any chances, Dr. Padgett had referred me to both a gynecologist and an endocrinologist.

It didn't surprise me that the insurance company was calling. Denying the first submission of a claim was the norm for them. With all the medical bills we'd accumulated and the number of specialists I had seen in the past few years, I had grown adept at the workings of insurance. The woman on the other end of the line was particularly surly.

"We've seen your appeal," she said, "but we have to deny the claim on these visits. We'll pay for the first gynecologist's visit but not the other doctor."

"Why not?" I asked patiently. This woman was fortunate to have caught me in my era of passivity.

"You are only allowed to see one specialist in a field," she answered haughtily. *Is she the one with the attitude, or am I just perceiving it that way?* "Any second opinions have to be preauthorized, and you didn't get preauthorization."

"These specialists aren't in the same field," I replied calmly. "One was a gynecologist, and the other was a hormone specialist."

"That isn't what my records show," she sniffed. "My records show that you consulted two doctors for a first and second opinion on irregularities in your menstrual cycle."

I winced at the words. I'd grown more comfortable in discussing such things with Dr. Padgett, but this woman was a total stranger. *She's a bitch. Stop it, Rachel. You are being irrational. She's only doing her job.*

"There must be some kind of misunderstanding. Actually my psychiatrist referred these two different specialists to me. I've been anorexic, and I've also been on a number of medications. He was concerned that the problem might be more than just gynecological."

"Apparently, your *psychiatrist* didn't do any preliminary research on your policy coverage before he made the referrals," she snapped.

Is this woman stigmatizing me, or am I just overly sensitive?

"Mommy!" Melissa ran up to me shrieking, her eyes streaming with tears. "Jeffrey says I'm too stupid to play Candy Land!"

"Mommy's on the phone," I said, my hand over the receiver. "Tell Jeffrey you aren't too stupid to play."

"But Mommy!" she protested.

"I'm on the phone, okay?" I said, irritated, not wanting the insurance lady to hear me. Melissa stomped off, flashing me a dirty look.

"I'm sorry," I told the woman apologetically. "You know how kids can get when they're cooped up inside all day."

"I wouldn't know," she replied tersely. "I don't have children. All I do know is that I'm very busy right now."

This woman is cold. No, you're the one who's cold. Why should she care about your kids anyway?

"In any event," she continued, obviously annoyed by the interruption, "we cannot pay this claim. You've exhausted your appeals. Actually, if it is related to anorexia nervosa, *both* claims may fall under the scope of mental illness, in which case, your copayment is 50 percent instead of 10 percent."

"How much are we talking about here?" I asked. *What's wrong with you, Rachel? How can you just sit back and take this? Who is she to try and reverse a claim that has already been paid? You're getting angry, Rachel. Watch it!*

"The second opinion claim, which is totally your responsibility, comes to $125. The gynecologist's bill was $80. If we determine that it was mental illness–related, your copayment would change from $8 to $40."

"Mom!" this time it was Jeffrey tugging on my shoulder. "She scratched me! Look. I'm almost bleeding!"

"Well," I said, less patient this time as I covered the receiver with my hand, "she shouldn't have done that. But if you go around calling her stupid, what do you expect?"

My words were met with an instant look of innocence, that of a martyr unjustly accused.

"I didn't call her stupid!"

"We'll talk about it later, Jeffrey. I'm on the phone," I said tersely, then continued with the insurance rep. "Sorry about that. Where were we?"

"Ma'am, I'm very busy today," she said haughtily. "I called to inform you that your claim is denied. Period. I don't have the patience to sit here while you lose your mind with your children. Maybe you ought to call your psychiatrist."

No doubt remained in my mind about that comment. It was a definite slam against me. Whatever attitude I might have had, she was out of line with that one, and I knew it.

I heard one slap, then another, and then both kids were in tears, each trying to shriek louder than the other.

I'd had enough.

"Damnit!" I cried out, not bothering to cover the

receiver. "I'm on the phone! Both of you, stop it—now! Once I get off this phone, you are both really going to get it!"

Jeffrey and Melissa sobbed softly, stunned by their mother's outburst. It had been awhile since one had happened. *Careful, Rachel, you're losing it!*

"I don't have time to waste on you," the insurance woman said. "I suggest you get out your checkbook. Both of these bills must be past due by now."

The dam broke.

"Listen," I said tersely. "I've been very patient with you and your attitude. I'm the customer, and I'm entitled to be treated with respect. I also know what my rights are. Anybody who doesn't know what the difference is between a gynecologist and an endocrinologist doesn't know her ass from a hole in the ground. It will be a cold day in hell before I let you get off the hook on this one. I'm not done appealing. I've just begun to fight!"

"I don't have to listen to this," she retorted. "Obviously you have an attitude problem."

"You *will* listen to this because I am the customer, and I'm in the right. And you have an attitude, not me! You wanna know what *I'm* tired of wasting my time on? I'm tired of wasting it on people like you in some glorified clerical job taking out your frustrations on other people because you think you have some kind of power over them. I'm tired of people like you and your company that don't recognize mental illness as an illness, even though science has proven it to be a fact!

"But you know what? You're messing with the wrong lady. I guarantee you that your company will pay every single dime of these claims."

"My, aren't we overemotional," she snapped sarcastically. "You really are crazy, aren't you?"

"No. You're the crazy one to treat a customer the way you have because I intend to document every word of this conversation and your discriminatory attitude and take it directly to your supervisor. You have just made a big, big mistake."

"Are you finished?" she said, still with a superior air but a glimmer of worry in her voice that I might carry out my threat.

"Yes," I said. "I believe I am for now. But trust me, you'll be hearing about this."

She hung up the phone. I, too, slammed down the receiver. I refused to listen to another word of Jeffrey and Melissa's self-righteous protests and banished both of them to their rooms.

Still shaking and a bit stunned at the re-emergence of an anger that had been absent for well over a month, I grabbed a pen and a yellow legal pad and began to write furiously. Undoubtedly I'd lost my composure and had probably over-reacted to the circumstances. A part of me, however, felt strangely relieved. I wasn't sure what to make of it.

∞

The falling snow had abated, but the temperatures had dropped dramatically below the zero mark. The streets were cleared, although a few icy patches plagued the roads. I had been relieved when I'd called Dr. Padgett's office and heard he was able to make it in for the day. I'd spent a few days replaying the altercation with the insurance representative.

I tried documenting the course of the conversation in a letter to the supervisor of the customer service department but was having a difficult time deciding what to say. I wasn't sure if I was accurately recalling the conversation or if my recollections were tainted by irrational anger. Half-written, the letter remained on my bedroom dresser.

When I related the incident to Dr. Padgett, I was torn between remorse and righteous indignation, between all of my ambivalence about my rediscovered ability to feel and express anger and my fears that I had somehow been irrational or had blown everything wildly out of proportion.

Bless me, Father Padgett, for I have sinned. It's been a few months since I really lost my temper. She may have felt she was just trying to do her job. In addition I didn't sit and listen to both sides of my kids' stories and render real justice. I just sent them to their rooms. I lost my patience. I promise to try and never do it again.

"That's pretty much what happened, as best as I can remember it. I just don't know what to think. A few years ago I wouldn't have given any of it a second thought. Now I'm not so sure."

"She said all the things you're saying?" he asked, assessing the situation with the objectivity of a judge.

"Yes, she did say those things. It's just that I don't know whether I overreacted or not."

"Do you think you have justification for the insurance company to pay both claims?"

The legal issues were far more clear-cut for me.

"Definitely. I think if I call the endocrinologist and have him resubmit the claim, emphasizing exactly what he did differently than a gynecologist would have, I have a good chance. And I know that they can't try and get out of paying for physical conditions just because I have a mental illness."

"So you think you were right to protest the denied claim?"

"Yes."

"Then why do you feel you were somehow unjustified in the conversation?"

"Because I got really angry. I threatened to contact her supervisor."

"Do you think what she said is the proper way to talk to a customer?"

I had to think about that one.

"No, I guess I don't."

"So what are you worried about?"

"Maybe I had a right to be angry. But maybe I overdid it too."

"Welcome to the land of imperfection, Rachel," he said. "Nobody can completely control their anger all the time. And even if you did overreact a bit, who doesn't sometimes? Everyone is irrational sometimes."

"Even you?" I asked.

He smiled broadly then. "Even me."

∞

The onus had been lifted. I'd been given permission to get pissed off again, to exercise my right to be assertive, even if I wasn't always in the right or crossed the fine line into aggression. Not all anger, not all irrationality was borderline rage or distortion. Some of it was just a part of being human.

Most people inherently know this and might never have given it a second thought. In the intensity of my introspection, where everything I had once taken for granted was now in question, the normal emotions and actions of life had become an issue that paralyzed me for many weeks. I had, nonetheless, found an answer. I was more than "just a borderline." I was also wonderfully imperfect. Human.

Chapter 28

Once upon a time perfectionism was my noble aspiration. My perfectionism extended beyond academics or career. I also aspired to be the perfect mother, lover, and friend, always appropriate in all my emotional expressions.

Of course I never reached it. Worse, given my all-or-nothing thinking, I viewed myself as an abject failure when I, like every other human, inevitably failed to reach that goal. It was a wretched trap.

As February rolled into March, the topic of perfectionism and my irrational expectations dominated sessions. My attitudes were changing as I began to realize that, although I could never reach such a state, I could still be satisfied with myself. A tremendous burden lifted as the tide of my self-hatred slowly ebbed. Laughter now reappeared in my life; the moments of remorse and self-recrimination were fewer and farther between. For the first time I was getting a taste of how it felt to have peace of mind.

Realizing the absurd impossibility of perfection in myself also had an impact on how I viewed others. The borderline fixation on hero worship fluctuating with bitter disappointment blurred as I began to understand that my expectations of others had been dictated by the same faulty yardstick of perfection. Increasingly I could see the gray area, and I was finding it much easier to handle my relationships with other people. Everyone had flaws, even Dr. Padgett.

Now the issue turned to my parents. I'd been more comfortable with them lately, and they, in turn, had seemed more at ease with themselves. Although I wasn't sure how I felt about them, Jeffrey and Melissa loved them. My mom and dad were good to them, playing, paying attention, and listening.

Were these the same people who had raised me? Had my recollections been tainted or had my parents changed? Did they love me now? Had they always loved me? How could they have acted abusively if they had loved me? How could they act lovingly now if they didn't?

Initially I had been reluctant to discuss my parents in any negative terms. But Dr. Padgett had encouraged me to reach into the memories and feelings of my inner child, which had led me to thoroughly despise them. He'd encouraged me to share the depths of my rage at them, the pain of the injustice, my childhood marred and, in many ways, stolen.

Indeed, much of my acceptance of the need to change was rooted in the perceived transgressions of my parents and the depths of my repressed resentment toward them. With these feelings roaring to the surface with the momentum of a speeding freight train, it was inordinately difficult to reverse course. But it was happening nonetheless.

I discussed these concerns with Dr. Padgett and

described my confusion about how I could loathe them so much and still feel pangs of guilt for judging them too harshly. His answer surprised me.

"You feel that way because, despite it all, you still love them. They always loved you too. It was an imperfect love, perhaps, but love was there. It's part of what helped you get by."

I was unnerved at first by his apparent audacity. Here was the man who had prodded me into seeing my childhood for the travesty that it was, and now he was telling me that I still loved them. Even more, that they loved me and always had.

It didn't make sense. If they loved me, then why had I spent these years in therapy? Why had I been hospitalized three times? Why had so much of my life been consumed by dreams of dying?

I felt a tinge of betrayal. Was he siding with *them*?

"A lot of awful things happened in your childhood," he explained. "You were abused, and it affected you. But not every act of theirs was abusive. You've felt the hatred that you buried for so long. Now it's time to feel the love."

Sure, Dr. Padgett. Let me just snap my fingers and feel the love. Let's just forget everything we've been saying for the past two and a half years and just call them lovable.

Was I screwed over, or wasn't I? If I was, then how do you expect me to just forget about it? If I wasn't, then what in the hell have we been talking about in here for all these hundreds of sessions? These thoughts just made me angrier. At my parents. And at Dr. Padgett. Why was I the one who had to feel all the pain and do all the work?

"It's up to you," he told me. "Whatever happened, happened in the past. You were helpless then. A vulnerable child.

But you aren't helpless now. They can't hurt you in the ways that they did back then. It's up to you to decide what kind of relationship you want to have with them now. Adult to adult."

"Sometimes," I replied, "I wish I could just go up to them and tell them about all of this. But I know they wouldn't accept it. I've dreamed sometimes of telling them off. I've even dreamed of . . . of . . . killing them—even though I'd never do it."

"Fantasies never hurt a soul," he said, "unless you act on them. It's natural to be angry with all that you've discovered. But at this point holding on to the anger doesn't do you much good. Someday you've got to let it go."

"Let it go?" I shook my head in disgust. "Everything is always 'let it go.' I always have to do everything! What about *them*? What are *they* supposed to do? Maybe they deserve to be hated."

"You can't control them. The only person you can change is yourself. Holding on to the anger and hatred hurts you a lot more than it hurts them. It consumes you; it distracts you."

"They deserve revenge," I snapped.

"The best revenge is living well," he finished.

I'd heard the old saying before but had never really given it much thought. Was that wisdom or merely a consolation prize where justice is absent?

I pondered it for a moment in silence.

"Let me tell you a story," he said, "about the politics of envy, of revenge. Maybe it might have some meaning here.

"There was an American farmer and a Russian farmer, both living in their respective countries. The American was out plowing his field when he saw his neighbor driving past in a brand-new Cadillac. The American farmer looked at his rusty, old pickup, then at his neighbor's shiny, new car, and vowed, 'Someday I'm going to have a shiny, new car just like his.'

"Meanwhile the Russian farmer was plowing his field and saw his neighbor driving by in the fancy luxury car. He looked at his rusty, old pickup, then at his neighbor's Cadillac, and vowed, 'Someday he's going to have a rusty, old pickup just like mine.'"

"Hmm. Interesting philosophies."

"Any thoughts on what it might mean in the context of what we're discussing?"

"That you're a capitalist?" I asked facetiously.

He smiled. "And?"

"The Russian farmer isn't going to be any better off himself just because his neighbor loses his nice car."

"Exactly," he said. "The instinct for revenge is strong. But in the end it doesn't do a person much good."

Intellectually the philosophy made sense. Reaching that point emotionally, however, was an entirely different story.

∞

With the March winds sandwiched between the few remaining snowfalls of the season also came the season of Lent, a time of introspection and preparation for Easter. In church we sang melancholy songs about ashes and repentance, and the altar was stripped of plants and other decorations to represent the starkness of fasting.

As a child, Lent had had simple meanings to me: fish sticks and macaroni in the school cafeteria on Fridays, shuffling into weekly stations-of-the-cross ceremonies to reflect on the story of the suffering Christ, and giving up chocolate. As I re-evaluated the whole notion of God and religion, however, so, too, had Lent taken on a deeper meaning. I couldn't listen to these readings about sin and repentance every Sunday without feeling the challenge within myself.

My pastor, the choir director, and my fellow parishioners had accepted me despite my professed agnosticism and mental illness. Tim had stayed by my side despite the turbulence in our household, the burdens he endured, the unpredictable emotions, and the huge expenses that derailed our dreams. Undoubtedly I had been the beneficiary of forgiveness and compassion.

God protects the fools and the children, and he had protected me when I was both, even when I pondered my atheism.

Now, feeling stronger than I ever had in my life, I wondered if it were my time to return the love and unconditional acceptance I'd been given by granting a little forgiveness of my own. The issue of how to come to peace with my parents, knowing full well they would never be able to admit or accept what had happened, loomed larger than ever. It became harder to sit in church hearing the exhortations of challenge while still very much at odds with my parents and family. My conscience would not stop nagging me.

Finally, on a blustery Saturday afternoon in late March, I decided to take the whole issue into the confessional.

The sacrament of confession—now called reconciliation—had changed dramatically since my days in Catholic elementary school. While the darkened little cubicles with the small grilled windows still existed for those preferring the traditional method, one could also see the priest in a face-to-face setting in the same small room. I opted for the latter approach.

Father Rick smiled and stood up to greet me when I opened the door to his small confessional office. Windowless, with a few religious poems thumbtacked to the corkboard walls and dated vinyl chairs of the vintage seventies, it was a far cry from Dr. Padgett's tasteful decor. Still it lacked the stark sackcloth-and-ashes theme I recalled from my youth.

Perhaps this wasn't where I should be. After all I wasn't at all sure that I was willing to do what my conscience was telling me I should. Fortunately Father Rick, who knew the broad details of my childhood and therapy, wasn't the kind of priest to condemn. He was an excellent listener.

"Bless me, Father, for I have sinned," I started. It was the one piece of the ritual I still remembered. Like many Catholics, I'd been avoiding the confessional for years. "I confess I forget what I'm supposed to do now. It's been awhile, Father Rick."

"The first thing to do is relax," he assured me, "and tell me what's on your mind."

I told him of my moral dilemma. I had recently discovered much of what had happened in the past, and I was still angry at my parents. I knew I should forgive them, but I wasn't sure what that entailed. Nor was I sure that forgiving them was something I wanted or was ready to do. Still it was eating at my conscience.

"Not much of a confession if I'm not even sure I want to take the penance, is it?" I smiled sheepishly. "I guess it's not very Christian to be that angry at my own parents, is it?"

"Whoever said Jesus didn't get angry?" he replied.

Father Rick went on to recall some of the stories of Jesus. Jesus had indeed gotten so angry that he'd kicked over tables and hurled goods to the ground when he saw the

367

money changers again hawking their wares on the temple steps.

"Do you think Jesus just calmly sat back and accepted his fate?" Father Rick asked me. "He spent hours agonizing in the Garden of Gethsemane, literally begging God to 'take the cup away' from him and spare him the ugliness of his inevitable betrayal and death. Ultimately he did his Father's will—but not without experiencing the same reluctance, bitterness, and hurt as the rest of us.

"Having human emotions isn't the sin, Rachel; it's what you do with them," said Father Rick. *Thoughts and fantasies never hurt anyone. It's the way someone chooses to act on them.* For a man who steadfastly refused to reveal the slightest bit about his religious beliefs or nonbeliefs, Dr. Padgett's words were strangely similar to Father Rick's.

"But you're missing something here, Father Rick," I said, my conscience still unappeased. "Jesus did go up on that cross. He did forgive them. 'Forgive them, Father; they know not what they do.' Pretty amazing words. I don't know if I can do that with my parents. I just don't know. So much has happened. I'm thirty-three years old, and I'm still bearing the brunt of it. I don't know if I can let go of it all like that."

"Notice that you didn't hear him say 'forget,'" Father Rick replied. "Jesus never said, 'Father, forgive them; forget about what they did.' He didn't say they hadn't done what they'd done to him. He didn't say they hadn't betrayed or hurt him. He forgave, but he didn't forget.

"*They know not what they do.* He wasn't calling them *innocent*; he was calling them *ignorant*. And there's a world of distinction between those two words."

Father Rick was telling me I didn't have to forget everything that had happened. I didn't have to deny the past. I didn't have to pretend that everything was rosy. Forgiveness didn't mean I had to forget.

Indeed, he told me, I *shouldn't* forget. To forget the past was to leave it wide open to be repeated. There was nothing wrong with being vigilant for an oncoming truck of destruction and to get the hell out of the way when I saw it coming. Because it very well could.

There was nothing wrong with protecting myself. But I could still forgive, not only because it was the right thing to do, but because to do so would benefit *me* as well.

"Forgiveness," Father Rick told me, "isn't just healing for the trespasser. It can set you free to move on and live your life."

Clearly the physical setting was not the only change in the years since I'd taken the sacrament of confession. I was struck by the change in its emphasis as well. It was on healing rather than punishment. For many years I'd viewed Jesus's challenges to forgive and to love one's enemy as a call to sacrifice the instincts and pleasures of this life in order to be rewarded by a life hereafter. Perhaps, however, his instructions were a means to make this life better as well. Maybe, if all people actually did all the things Jesus called them to do, we wouldn't have to wait for heaven. It would be right here on earth.

I looked at my watch. Father Rick and I had been in there for well over thirty minutes—most of his one-hour block of time allotted for confessions. Anyone else waiting to see him must have gone to the other priest. I felt a tinge of guilt for monopolizing his time, but Father Rick didn't appear to mind.

"Well," I concluded, "you've made some excellent points. I'm still not sure if I can forgive my parents right away. But at least I'm willing to consider it. I guess I need a penance then. Fifty Hail Marys maybe?"

The priest smiled, "No, your penance is to take care of yourself, to forgive yourself first, and to spend some time every day in prayer thinking about what we've discussed here."

"That's it?" I smiled back. "You're pretty easy, Father Rick. No wonder the line to see you is always so long."

We stood as he laid his hands on my shoulders and said the ritual words of absolution. "In the name of the Father and of the Son and of the Holy Spirit, I absolve you from your sins."

Afterward he gave me a warm hug.

"I hope you're realizing that you're really a special person, Rachel," he said as I walked out of the confessional.

"I'm beginning to," I answered sincerely. "I've got a ways to go, but I'm beginning to."

∞

As was my penance, I spent a lot of time over the next few weeks thinking about all that Father Rick had said, trying to decide what forgiveness entailed. After all, how could a person say "I forgive you" to people who had never asked for forgiveness, had never apologized, most likely never would, and who failed to see or admit any wrongdoing at all?

It would have to be a one-sided forgiveness, something within me that would in all likelihood never be recognized or appreciated. Any change of heart was going to have to be mine and mine alone.

The more I thought about forgiving them, however, the more it made sense to me. Dr. Padgett was right. The hatred

I had felt, while all-consuming, had not encompassed the full scope of my feelings. Despite it all, I *did* feel love for my parents. And in their own flawed way, they, too, had felt it for me. I could not remain in a distorted world of black and white. Sentencing myself to a powerful anger and desire for revenge would only hold me back.

Forgiveness was not an overnight phenomenon. It happened slowly over time. I was less bitter toward them and more open. Still aware that they had not changed, I did not leave myself vulnerable to the kind of pain they were still capable of inflicting. But, as I let go of the anger, I could also see some of what was good about them, what had been right in my childhood.

And even though the forgiveness remained unspoken, they must have sensed my change of heart. They, too, became more open, gentler, and seemed to be more loving.

They would never be the first people I called in times of emotional crisis. Many parts of my life would remain unknown to them, including the raging anger I had felt at the revelations of what the past had really been. Visiting them, however, was no longer such a painful obligation, and in many ways I came to enjoy their company as adults.

∞

The spring of 1994 was a peaceful time for me. I was not nearly so harsh on myself, nor was I that way with others. For the first time in my life I realized I had few enemies; many people, despite their individual imperfections, were truly my friends.

I had come to define an adult relationship with my parents, and I was comfortable with that, knowing what I could expect, knowing what I could never expect, and accepting the relationship for what it was.

I was more relaxed with Tim and the kids, and the passion had slowly crept back into our sex life. Business was growing. I was handling more clients than ever, yet I was able to leave my work behind me at the end of the day.

Sessions were increasingly less focused on events of the past as Dr. Padgett and I began to discuss my plans for the future. Sometimes we just shot the bull, enjoying each other's company, adult-to-adult. Like friends.

Still I wasn't ready to think about leaving therapy yet. I was enjoying the time we had together. Dr. Padgett had assured me that the warm feelings of companionship, therapy as pleasure, were also part of the process.

I'd succeeded in letting go of much of my anger, in defining my relationships, in accepting my femininity, in looking at the world in a completely new way, and in feeling a calm security I'd never dreamed of feeling. But a few matters still needed work. Foremost among them was the issue of termination, no longer just a far-off, "someday" prospect but an imminent reality.

Although sexual desire had reappeared in our marriage, there was still a long way to go. And even though I was no longer emaciated, I couldn't quite look in the mirror and accept what I saw. The morning trips to the hidden scale had not stopped. Nor had the routine doses of multiple Ex-Lax to assuage my guilty feelings about having gained back the anorexic weight. I hadn't found a way to tell Dr. Padgett about that yet. Things were going so well I didn't want to disrupt them.

Besides, a woman had to have a few secrets, didn't she?

Chapter 29

In many ways April and May had been the best months of my life.

No major events or surprises came my way. I was content, enjoying the fresh delight of looking at the world in a way I never had before.

I felt comfortable with myself. Things that used to worry me didn't concern me anymore. Like a blind person granted the gift of sight, I was astounded by the goodness in people despite their flaws. My reactions to circumstances were as different as they ever had been. My new ability to see the gray areas in life had opened my horizons and fueled my optimism.

In short I was realizing that, incremental and painful as the process had been, I was a fundamentally different person than I had been when I first entered therapy. For all the doubts and second thoughts I'd had, it was clear to me that the time and money spent, the delays in reaching my primary goals, were worth the pain.

Sometimes in the midst of discussing an issue with Dr. Padgett, I stopped midsentence, stunned by the stark difference in my reaction.

"This is definitely where I would have picked a fight, isn't it?" I'd ask him. "But somehow I don't find myself needing to fight the way I used to."

Dr. Padgett would smile back at me. I could tell he was proud of me and my progress. I was too.

So it was with surprise and dismay that I felt the tides of change roll in as I approached the three-year anniversary of my therapy. It was a subtle but steady shift as the sunny horizon began to fill with clouds; both my days and nights darkened.

The fight instinct was gone. The new lessons were not lost, perhaps, but I could feel myself slipping back into the depths of depression.

I knew the familiar symptoms. A decreased appetite. My newly emerging flickers of sexual passion dimmed. I was lifeless, listless, lacking in energy. Getting out of bed in the morning was a chore; making the bed was almost impossible. I was finding excuses to get out of social events, crafting alibis to get out of dinner invitations, and canceling client appointments.

I was retreating into my shell without any apparent clue as to why this was happening. Thoughts of suicide began to reappear and dominate my thoughts, the inner drumbeat of self-destruction softly tapping, growing to greater intensity, until it was a pounding roar and I could hear little else.

Why was this happening? I racked my brain to find an issue that had remained undisclosed, a subconscious origin, a buried secret begging to be revealed. But I could find none.

Knowing how pleased Tim and Dr. Padgett were with my progress, I didn't want to worry or disappoint them by revealing my feelings. Someday, I knew, I would have to handle these types of emotions on my own. Perhaps this was as good a time as any to try.

Both in session and out of it, my life was on automatic pilot as I put on a facade of togetherness. I faked optimism and inner happiness that didn't exist. It was a pretty convincing act. If Dr. Padgett or Tim had any doubts about my state of mind, they didn't express them.

In the privacy of my journal and my thoughts, however, I was thoroughly frustrated. What if my recovery had been simply an illusion, a brief respite in a life that was destined to be hell on earth? Once a borderline, always a borderline. Who was I to believe I could ever fundamentally change?

Pessimism overshadowed me as I slipped back into the mode of all or nothing. My life was shrouded in darkness.

The kids were in the backyard dousing each other with Super Soakers, but I couldn't find the energy to watch them or join in their antics. With the shades drawn and the air conditioner running, sealing myself inside, I flipped through the pages of a back issue of *Time* magazine. Kurt Cobain, the rock-and-roll icon, had killed himself, and suicide was a hot public issue. Was it a tragedy or a heroic exit? Speculation supporting both opinions filled the magazine.

Maybe Cobain, whose music I had never heard, simply understood life better than most people. Maybe he had looked deeply enough into the mysteries of life to reveal The Truth: optimism was just a fairy tale people desperately clung to because reality was simply too hard to bear.

Perhaps he had discovered the same answer I was

beginning to realize about the meaning of life: there is none. Life was a cruel hoax, and he had opted out. An act of ultimate wisdom. The heroism of facing The Truth.

As I sat in shaded darkness, the window unit still humming in the background, I began to ponder if death might not be the answer for me as well. Why raise my hopes just so they could be dashed again? Why not allow Tim and the kids to move on with their lives?

I started to speculate on how I could end my life in a way that would leave Tim and the kids none the wiser. A disguised suicide that could just as easily be an accident. A car wreck? A carefully staged fall? A car wreck seemed the best option, driving off the road in a way that would not injure anyone else but myself.

I hadn't yet settled on all the logistics but was feeling a strange sense of calm at making a major decision when Jeffrey came running inside the house.

"Mom, you've got to come out here," he cried breathlessly. "There's a lobster in the yard!"

Melissa followed.

"Yeah, Mommy, a lobster! Come and see it!" she said as she tugged on my shirtsleeve.

I had to admit a lobster in our yard would be a strange sight. I followed them to appease my curiosity, vowing that I wouldn't be distracted from my plans to die.

As it turns out, the "lobster" was a crawdad, most likely escaped from the neighbor's fishing boat parked on the driveway next door. I was amazed at how much the little creature resembled a lobster. A few of the other neighborhood kids had already assembled, circling around the newest addition to the block. Jeffrey and Melissa were beaming with pride. "Can you get us something for it?" Jeffrey asked. "It needs water or something. Otherwise it's gonna die."

"Can it be our pet, Mommy?" Melissa begged.

Thousands of dollars spent at Toys "R" Us, yet none of those toys were as fascinating as a slimy, shelled creature with snapping claws. I had to smile. Had life ever been that simple for me?

I retrieved a rectangular casserole dish from the kitchen and a big cup of water. With Jeffrey in charge, the cadre of kids set about making a comfortable environment for their new friend—a pile of mud for it to crawl on, surrounded by a moat to keep it cool and moist. Melissa came over and hugged me, beaming with joy and admiration. "Thanks for helping us make a house for our pet, Mommy," she said. "You're the best mommy in the whole world!"

My plans for suicide were quickly unraveling. Dr. Padgett was right. Suicide, in whatever form, would completely destroy these kids. There had to be another answer.

∽

When Tim came home from work, I confessed.

"The suicidal thoughts are back," I told him bluntly.

He paused for a moment, obviously surprised.

"How long have you been feeling this way?" he asked, a quiver of worry in his voice.

"I don't know. A few weeks."

"Have you told Dr. Padgett?"

"No."

"Why not?"

"I didn't want to bother him with it. I didn't want to bother you either. You've all been so good to me that I didn't want to let you down."

377

"Like killing yourself wouldn't let us down?" he exclaimed, then quickly resumed a calm demeanor, not wanting to upset me. "Rachel, that's what he's there for. That's what I'm here for. You've worked through so much. Don't you think you ought to try and work through this too?"

"What if I'm like this for the rest of my life?" I asked him, tears in my eyes. "What then? I'm really sorry you had to marry somebody like me, Tim. I really am. You deserve better than this."

"You have an illness, Rachel," he said emphatically. "An *illness*. I wouldn't leave you if you had cancer or diabetes, and I'm certainly not going to leave you because you have an illness of the mind and not the body. If I wanted to be with someone else, I would be. But I don't. I want to be with you. And if I had it to do all over again, knowing all of this, I would still marry you. In sickness and health. We can get through this. We really can."

Sobbing, I fell into his arms. One thing was certain. If I had to do it all over again, I would have married Tim too. Maybe he was right. Maybe we could make it through this.

∞

Dr. Padgett, although clearly concerned, did not appear to be thrown off stride by my admission of how I'd been feeling.

"What do you think it could be?" I asked him. "I've been racking my brain, but I can't find an issue. I'm really scared. I came so close, and now all that peace and serenity have gone away."

"What medications are you on right now?"

I had expected him to ask the routine question: "What do *you* think?" Instead he was acting like a medical doctor rather than a therapist. I was surprised.

"Desyrel. Three hundred milligrams."

He got up and reached into his desk drawer, pulled out a prescription pad, and scrawled the trademark chicken scratch of the physician. He handed it to me. I couldn't decipher a word. How did pharmacies manage?

"What's this?" I asked.

"I'd like you to try a new medication. It's called Effexor. It's relatively new on the market, but the clinical tests have shown it has minimal side effects."

"Do you really think drugs are the answer here? Maybe there's some issue we need to explore."

"Sometimes if you take an antidepressant for a long time, it begins to lose its effectiveness. A new one might help."

"You mean you think this is all because the Desyrel has stopped working?"

"I think it's a strong possibility."

For some reason I began to cry. "Am I going to be on drugs for the rest of my life? Don't you think that's a cop-out? I mean, other people seem to manage their whole lives without these drugs. Am I going to be a borderline for life? I don't know if I want these drugs. I don't want to be an emotional cripple."

"Rachel," he said firmly. "You're thinking black and white again. This is a temporary setback. And, in this case, I think it's purely chemical. The progress we've made hasn't been undone. And, no, I don't think that you'll need to be on medications for the rest of your life. But for right now this might help you get through a tough time."

"What does that say about my self-discipline?" I lamented. "What does that say about my ability to handle

379

things on my own? I don't want crutches."

"There's nothing to be ashamed of," he said gently. "You haven't failed. Let's go ahead and try these and see what happens."

When session was over, I shoved the prescription slip in my purse. I contemplated swerving off the interstate but dutifully drove to the drugstore to have the prescription filled.

∞

My body was shaking a bit, but I felt good. The phone rang a few times before Tim answered.

"Just thought I'd call and say hi," I chirped exuberantly.

"Hi," he answered, surprised at my newfound cheerfulness. "What's up?"

"This stuff is amazing," I rambled. "I could run ten miles right now. I could clean the whole house in an hour. It's just incredible! Kind of like the first blast of cocaine, except it lasts and lasts. And it's legal. Do you believe it?"

Tim chuckled at the other end of the line. "Maybe you've found a new discovery. It's great to hear you so happy—glad you're enjoying it. I'd love to talk, but I've got a prospect coming in five minutes, and I have to put a few papers together. I'll see you at five."

"I'll see you too!"

While Dr. Padgett smiled at my account of my Effexor buzz and expressed concern about my inability to sleep, he assured me that this burst of energy and hyperawareness was a temporary side effect. Despite the frustration of not being able to sleep, I was a little disappointed that the fun and giddy aspects were destined to fade. Common sense reminded me, however, that Effexor was not a recreational drug, but an antidepressant.

With a mild sleeping aid Dr. Padgett prescribed, soon the initial manic effect of the drug wore off. Within three weeks, I resumed a state of equilibrium. The darkness and the suicidal thoughts were gone, and I began to settle into the state of contentment I'd felt in April and May.

I wasn't sure how this chemical combination worked. But I was glad it existed. It reinforced that mental illness, depression, was indeed an illness with a physiological basis. It wasn't a sign of failure. I wasn't a failure.

I wondered why mental illness was surrounded by such hopelessness, shame, and stigma when treatments— sometimes as simple as a prescription—worked so effectively and could transform a person's life.

Long ago I had been taught my father's solution to emotional problems: pull yourself up by your bootstraps and move on. Psychiatry, he'd insisted, was nonsense. Believing this myth, I had resisted seeking help, had been driven away from it by my shame, until I, too, had been on the brink of becoming yet another tragedy. Another Kurt Cobain.

Mercifully my will to survive had superceded my misguided pride and distorted shame. The right people had come into my life at the right time, and I was spared long enough to learn the lesson of hope. As long as a person was still alive, help and hope were there if the individual dared seek it.

I vowed that whatever happened in my life after therapy, however full my life might become, I would never forget where I had been and the lessons I had learned. To make sure I could always appreciate the new light of day, I vowed to never forget the pain of the depths of darkness.

For some reason, God—or fate, or destiny, or whatever one might call the controlling forces of the universe—had decided that I would be given the gift of hope. I knew then that as bleak as life could become, I would never again seriously consider suicide.

Somehow, someday, I would share this message of hope. Maybe someone, feeling the pain of hopeless desolation, could take heart, see that anything could be possible, and choose to live.

Whatever I might do to spread this message, if it could spare even one life, kindle the flames of just one second chance, it would be worth it. After all, many, many people had joined forces to do the same for me.

Chapter 30

The summer of 1994 was hectic enough that my twice-weekly sessions with Dr. Padgett became more like the icing on the cake than the main course. Tim and I were both busy with our businesses. He was putting in night and weekend work, and I was now devoting about twenty-five hours a week to my accounting practice. Both Jeffrey and Melissa were playing T-ball. Tim and I were in a coed softball league. During the busy summer, therapy became a place I could relax and unwind from it all, with less focus on introspection about the past and more discussion on my present and future. Sometimes we just shot the breeze.

The first day of June was a landmark date in our lives as I walked to the mailbox to ceremoniously deliver the bill payments. I was now caught up with Dr. Padgett's invoices. We'd paid the last installment of the hospital bills we'd financed, and our credit cards, once looming in the $10,000 range, now all carried a zero balance. Since both of our cars were paid for, the only debt Tim and I had now was the mortgage on our home. As a bonus, there was still money left in our savings account.

We went out to dinner to celebrate our newfound solvency. Given the financial strain therapy and hospital bills had placed on us, becoming virtually debt free was as much of a success to us as if we'd been outright wealthy.

∞

Summer passed into early fall, and the church choir resumed its schedule. I loved being back with the group, and I felt emotionally strong, physically healthy, and closer to these people than I had ever been.

It was now my turn to cook for the meals chain, my turn to offer a shoulder to cry on, my turn to be the support person others could lean on as our intertwined lives marched on. I relished the role. For all the generosity these people had so selflessly given to me, I liked being able to return it in kind.

Each Sunday those of us in the choir had an excellent view of the congregation. During the course of a long-winded sermon, many of us covertly entertained ourselves by baby watching, occasionally flashing a silly face to bring a smile from a little one. Most of us were still of childbearing age but already had kids. Some women had children approaching high school and college; others had children enrolled in the parish school. A few younger women had babies or toddlers.

At one time or another over the years, it seemed, one of us could be found juggling a squirming infant our husbands could no longer placate as we held our music and sang. And, more than a few times, when a particularly cute cherub had delighted us in church, afterward we'd discuss our "baby cravings."

One day during Mass I watched a young mother rock her child, a tow-headed infant. I wistfully recalled when Melissa had been that young. As my entire life had changed over the course of therapy, she, too, had steadily grown and changed.

When I'd first entered the hospital, she'd been barely two years old, still in diapers, speaking in baby talk. Now she was in kindergarten, the baby fat all but gone, still calling me Mommy but once in a while shortening it to the more mature "Mom."

Although Jeffrey's birth was more a result of fate than planning, once he was born Tim and I had decided that we wanted three children spaced two years apart. Melissa came right on our planned schedule.

With the emotional and financial burdens of my illness, however, we never did try for the third one. Undoubtedly Tim would have been willing to have a third child in a heartbeat but respected my feelings that the timing just wasn't right. Was it too late? I was thirty-two years old, well within the low-risk range of pregnancy. The worst phases of my mental illness had passed, and I was feeling good both emotionally and physically. I was healthy enough to have a child, I thought. With the debts paid off and Tim's business in particular becoming more firmly established, we were in a good financial position.

As I sat there, the cravings became an obsession as I remembered what it was like to be pregnant, to hold a newborn in my arms for the first time, to have it accompany me everywhere snoozing soundly in a pouch.

By the time Mass was over, I had decided. I was going to have a baby.

Tim's eyes lit up at the news of my decision. We even discussed turning the attic into a bedroom for Jeffrey and using his current room as a nursery.

The joy of new life. The promise of the future. Everything seemed to fit in a perfect scenario. I couldn't wait to tell Dr. Padgett.

∞

"I'm going to have a baby," I announced proudly at our next session.

"You're pregnant?" he asked, eyes open wide, obviously surprised.

"No, no," I said. "I realize I have to quit the medications first. But we decided that we're going to try and have another baby."

"I really have to advise against it," he said bluntly.

His words stunned me. As a surrogate father, I thought he'd greet the news with the same joy as a surrogate grandfather. Here was a man who was so loathe to give direct advice he would barely tell me what time it was, and yet, on this matter, he was suddenly vested with a strong opinion. Things were not working out as planned.

"Maybe it's none of your business!" I snapped back, irritated that he'd burst my bubble.

"I'm speaking in your best interests, Rachel. I don't ever recommend that a patient of mine try to get pregnant during the course of therapy."

"So what are you saying?" I demanded. "That just because I've been mentally ill I can never have another baby? What gives you the right to butt into my personal decisions?"

"First of all, I didn't say you could *never* have a baby—

just that being in the middle of therapy is not a good time to do it."

"I'm almost done. And I've decided to get off the medications."

"It isn't just the medications. That's a separate issue. It has to do with emotions, unresolved issues."

"I've managed to be a good mother to my first two, haven't I?" I retorted angrily, disliking his implication that I was not emotionally stable enough to have another child.

"And it's been hard as hell, hasn't it? If you choose to have another child, it should be at a time when you are emotionally ready to do it, when you're doing it for the right reasons."

"I love the two I have. I loved them as infants. Isn't that reason enough? Why else do people have babies? It's natural. This isn't a therapy issue."

"I recommend that you wait until a year after terminating therapy to have a child."

"A year? A *year* before I can have a child?"

"A year before you try to conceive one," he clarified, which was even worse than I'd thought.

"How long could that be? I don't want to have a baby when I'm forty. I don't want my kids to be ten years apart. I can't believe you're saying these things!"

"You need the time for *you* right now. You need to resolve the final issues and put some closure on therapy."

"Issues like what?" I retorted in frustration. "I've been through every detail of my childhood with a fine-tooth comb. I'm feeling better now. I'm okay."

"For starters," he said in the same firm tone I had given him, "we need to explore why you suddenly feel this need to conceive."

"Because I'm in my thirties now. My kids aren't getting any younger, and neither am I."

"Any other reasons?"

"It's none of your damned business why I want to have a baby!" I exploded in tears. "Tim is my husband; you're my therapist. This is Tim's domain, not yours. I don't have to discuss my reasons with you."

"Pretty major life decision to not want to explore it, wouldn't you say?" he said as he raised his eyebrows.

I hated that look.

"Okay, Dr. Know-It-All," I quipped sarcastically, my arms folded across my chest. "What do *you* think my reasons are?"

"For starters, I think this baby could be a way of running away."

"From what?" I narrowed my eyes.

"The pain of terminating therapy."

"It always comes down to this, doesn't it? Everything is supposed to center around you. You're pretty self-impressed, you know that?"

Brushing aside the insult, he continued.

"The closeness a mother experiences with an infant could be a substitute for the closeness you feel here, a way to avoid the pain of separation.

"You've said that the time when your kids were infants was the most peaceful, secure time you'd ever felt. Things began to fall apart when they started to grow a little older, to become independent and separate. Another baby would inevitably grow up too, and you'd still be faced with dealing with separation without having worked it out here."

His words stung me. I felt as if he was reminding me of when I'd abused Jeffrey. The mere thought of the incident filled me with remorse. *How dare he!* I felt attacked.

"I know what this is. It's a trick to shove me out the door. I can't have a baby until I leave therapy, so you force me out of therapy."

I realized immediately that I had just underscored his point. His silence implied that he realized it too. I quickly changed my approach. I wasn't willing to give up so easily.

"We're talking about a baby here," I replied in as sincere a tone as I could muster. "A human life. That's God's decision, not mine or Tim's and certainly not yours."

I never had bought into the artificial birth control ban as expressed by more conservative Catholics and had always figured that the day the church hierarchy had the right to tell me I couldn't prevent birth was the day they were willing to cover all the expenses of child rearing. Nonetheless, the conservative Catholic view of birth control suited my purposes here, and I didn't hesitate to use it.

"We're not talking about therapy issues here," I concluded. "We're talking about religious conviction."

It was obvious that Dr. Padgett knew I was completely full of crap. He chose to ignore my recitations of religious dogma.

"Some people in this world are really ready to have another child. Some people aren't. I don't think this is something you should jump into recklessly without really sorting out the issues. Otherwise it might not only be detrimental to you, but to the child you bring into the world."

A crushing blow. In moments of desperation I could dismiss whether or not something was beneficial or detrimental to me. But my kids were a different story—my Achilles' heel—and he knew it. I wasn't sure whether he was using this approach as a strategy or was merely being painfully candid.

It was an acrimonious session, the first such battle in months. I was angry and disappointed in Dr. Padgett. What made me angriest of all was the logic in his words, the kernel of truth I couldn't dismiss. Still I felt enough stubborn pride to hurl a parting shot, the last word, as I walked out of his office.

"This isn't any of your business," I snapped. "I shouldn't have said a word. And if I walk out of here and Tim disagrees with you, I'm going to side with him and not you. He's my husband. I might get pregnant tonight, just to spite you!"

∞

Tim was as surprised and disappointed as I was by Dr. Padgett's reaction to the idea of my having another baby. After years of waiting and almost becoming resigned to the fact we would have only two children, his hopes had been high once again.

"It's none of his damned business!" he exclaimed. "Who the hell is he to plan our family?"

Tim disagreeing so vehemently with Dr. Padgett was a rare event. As a matter of fact, I couldn't recall if he had ever done so before. Having a third child, however, clearly meant a lot to him. I wasn't used to feeling thrust between two men I loved and respected. I was even more surprised when I found myself making some of Dr. Padgett's points, the same ones I had bitterly disputed just hours earlier.

"Maybe he's right," I said. "Maybe I'm just not ready yet. I did reach the decision pretty quickly."

"It was *our* decision," Tim said, still visibly upset, "not just yours. And Padgett shouldn't have a thing to do with it."

Despite Tim's persistence in the intense discussion

that followed, we both came to see that the third baby was not going to happen, at least for now. Tim spoke of "our" decision, but he would be ready when I was. Thus the true weight of the decision rested on me. Ultimately, as irritated as he was by Dr. Padgett's uncharacteristic intervention, Tim would not press the issue if I had reservations for any reason.

Had it been early on in the therapy process, I might have followed through on my threat, told Tim to forget the condom, and conceived just to spite Dr. Padgett. But I'd known the man for over three years now. He wouldn't venture into the realm of direct advice unless he had strong convictions. Right or wrong, I had come to realize that he had been sincere in saying his sole motivation was my own best interests. He also had an uncanny knack for being right, even when I fervently wished he wasn't.

Our plans for conception were tabled indefinitely as I sought to tame the insistent baby cravings and focus more on the underlying issues, particularly that of termination.

The time had come to seriously consider life without Dr. Padgett. In addition both Tim and I needed to accept the fact that the two children we had might well be the only children we were destined to have. We also needed to accept that they wouldn't be little forever and that someday our home would be an empty nest.

Even aside from conception worries, I decided it was time I was weaned from the Effexor. It had been more than three years since I'd coped without the aid of medications. As daunting as the prospect was, the choice was a tangible sign of my progress, one of the final stops on the route to termination.

Gradually tapering the medication, I was drug free by the end of September.

Much to my surprise, I still felt emotionally stable. The depression and suicidal thoughts had not reappeared as I had feared. We hadn't set a termination date, but I was much more comfortable discussing the possibilities. Instinctively I sensed that in a year's time, I would no longer be in therapy with Dr. Padgett, a situation that didn't disturb me nearly as much as I'd expected.

But, for now, I was intent upon savoring every session.

Chapter 31

Neither Tim nor I were of truly urban origin—he a small-town native, I a born suburbanite. However, we had developed a strong loyalty to the city and to its preservation.

The subtle changes in our own neighborhood—a slow but steady increase in crime, a growing number of absentee landlords who didn't seem to care about the condition of their properties—had begun to make residents nervous. More and more were trading their city homes for the haven of suburbia.

Jeffrey and Melissa were forbidden to ride their bikes on the sidewalk without us or to walk down the block to a friend's unaccompanied. Even when they played in our own backyard, we were vigilant, constantly checking to make sure they were safe, concerned about the street people who wandered the alleys in search of cans and other discards.

∞

I'd been running late all day. At seven o'clock the skies were already dark, and I was hustling to put away the bag of groceries I'd just bought at the store down the street. I still had hope that dinner might be on the table by 7:30.

"Mom!" Jeffrey ran into the kitchen, breathless with excitement. "I can hear a police radio and see flashing lights outside!"

I dropped a box of Apple Jacks on the counter and rushed to the front door. True to Jeffrey's account, two police cars were parked directly in front of our neighbor's house. I ran outside to see four uniformed officers in our neighbor Norma's backyard surrounding the elderly woman. She trembled, still in shock, as she described the encounter amid stunned tears.

"Two of them. They came up behind me. 'Where's your purse? Give me your purse!' Something sharp shoved in my back. I didn't want to turn around. They shoved it into my back even harder. One of them says, *'Get on the ground, bitch!'*"

The police were listening intently and taking notes. Norma continued to repeat the last phrase over and over again: "Get on the ground, bitch!" She was a kindly lady, much slowed by advanced years and arthritis. There wasn't a soul in the neighborhood who didn't like her. I doubted that anyone had spoken to her in such fashion before.

"Ma'am," an officer said, "I'd suggest you get your son to change your locks. Maybe you can stay with him tonight."

"I'm not leaving my house!" Norma cried. "It's *my* house!"

"You need to be safe," the officer continued. "Locks on the doors and windows. And from now on, you really should get your grocery shopping done in the daytime and stay indoors at night. For your own protection."

I gasped. The grocery store. Norma must have been followed from the grocery store. I felt a pit open in my stomach. I'd left the same place with Jeffrey and Melissa just a half hour before. And the armed robbery had occurred only twenty feet from the Little Tikes play set we'd just assembled for our kids.

"It's sad," said the youngest officer, the first time I'd heard him speak. "I live in the city too. I grew up here. But it's going to hell, and it's hard to keep up. It just isn't like it used to be."

I was surprised at his candor, but I had to agree. Unless there were police officers stationed on every corner, this kind of thing was destined to go on.

Norma's son showed up, and I went back to the house to fix dinner. Tim had come home and had tried, futilely, to usher Jeffrey and Melissa back inside. It was next to impossible, however, to keep the naturally curious kids away from such excitement.

We managed to get both youngsters into bed at nine o'clock. But before Tim and I had a chance to discuss the evening's crisis, Jeffrey appeared at the bottom of the steps. At first he began to complain about all kinds of minor things that had happened at school that day. But it soon became obvious that he was trying to stay up with us. We listened for a while and let him watch a sitcom rerun with us. At half past ten we attempted to put him back to bed.

I tucked him in and turned off the lights. I was about to leave the room when he asked in a small voice if I could stand by his second-story window and watch for a while.

"You're afraid, aren't you, Jeffrey?" I asked gently, sitting next to him on the bed. "It's okay. What happened tonight is scary. But Daddy and I will keep you safe."

"What if they come back?" he asked, his eyes wide in fear.

"They got what they wanted," I assured him. "They got Norma's purse. They have no reason to come back. We've got locks on the doors and the windows. We'll be okay."

"They had guns, didn't they, Mom?"

"Norma said they had something, but she didn't turn around to look."

"Were they guns?" he persisted.

"I don't know," I admitted. "They could have been."

"Don't go downstairs!" he cried in a panic. "Please, *please* stay here!"

It was painful to see his paralyzing fear. As placating and calm as I tried to be, the incident had disturbed me too.

"Jeffrey," I said, pulling him close in my arms, "Daddy and I will protect you, no matter what. We're your parents; we will keep you safe. You know those books you read about the jungle, how the mother tigers will fight to protect their young? Well, that's what Daddy and I will do too. There is nothing we wouldn't do to protect you."

"What if they came up to you with a gun and wanted your purse?"

"I'd give it to them. To protect you, Jeffrey, I'd not only give them my purse, I'd give them my car keys and give them everything I had. You kids are the most precious things in the world to us. We'd give up anything to keep you safe."

"Anything?" The thought was beginning to appease him.

"If it would keep you safe, Jeffrey, we'd give them the deed and the keys to our house. I guarantee you we would do absolutely anything to make sure no one even so much as touched a hair on your head."

Jeffrey smiled sleepily and snuggled into the covers. I'd succeeded in comforting him. Tim and I, on the other hand, had a very late night.

∞

In my afternoon session I immediately told Dr. Padgett all that had happened and everything that Tim and I had spent most of the evening and early hours of the morning discussing.

"How do you feel about it?" he asked me.

"Angry, very angry. And scared. Pissed off that a couple of punks do this stuff and get away with it. Disgusted that the cops can't do a thing about it. It seems that unless someone gets killed, it's just another routine report. Armed robberies are nothing in the city anymore."

"Do you see it getting any better?"

"God, I don't know. We've fought so hard. So hard. The politicians have had meetings with us. They talk big, but nothing seems to get better. Things just keep getting worse. The cops? Well, I guess you can't blame them. They have their hands full already. But it's really obvious to me that we can't count on them to protect us anymore."

"So what do you intend to do?"

"I don't know," I said. "If we leave, where do we go? Neither of us likes the suburbs. There's a few we like, but there's no way on earth we could afford them. We're trapped, Dr. Padgett. There isn't much we can do."

"You're trapped if you want to be trapped," he said. "You have to make a decision. Either you stay in a place where you don't feel safe and live with the chances that

397

something might happen, or you move somewhere else. It's up to you."

"I can't think of a place in the world I'd want to go, unless it was a small town. A long time ago we talked about a small town."

A small town. The thought hadn't occurred to us last night.

"There is this one place that we've visited before. It's absolutely beautiful, lots of historic stuff, straight out of a Norman Rockwell painting. It's about an hour's drive into the city, but some people do commute. Whenever we visit, we leave thinking that if we ever had to leave the city, we'd move to Nottingham."

"So you aren't trapped. You can choose to stay in the city. But if you don't, there is someplace to go."

∽

As obstinate and stubborn as I could be about a cause, as adamant as I was about being right, I realized some things in life were more important. By the time Tim came home from the office, I'd made up my mind.

"Tim, I think we ought to move to Nottingham."

Tim, as avidly as he, too, had fought the city battle, had always longed for the lifestyle he'd had growing up in a small town. He readily accepted the idea. He had been prepared to wait it out if I had really wanted to, but he was relieved that I wanted to move now.

We immediately set about preparing the house for sale, scouting out the real estate in Nottingham, and deciding how to break the news to the kids.

Tim and I, meanwhile, stumbled on our dream home

earlier than we had anticipated. Our city house wasn't ready to go on the market, but we knew that this house was perfect and we needed to act immediately.

By mid-November we had the house under contract with no contingency clause for selling our present home, a tremendous risk that could mean the temporary burden of two mortgages. But our kids' safety was worth the risk.

We worked diligently readying the house for market, investing some of our savings to make sure that it was absolutely perfect. In a tough city real estate market, we had to be competitive. In January we accepted a contract on the city house.

By a truly remarkable coincidence, both the Nottingham and the city houses closed on the same day. Our faith had paid off.

∞

Although Nottingham was definitely not suburbia, the commute was short enough for me to continue seeing Dr. Padgett if I chose. I had already been considering termination but decided, amid the hectic pace of home improvements, packing, and moving, to delay it until we were settled in our new home. We had a leaseback provision in our sale contract that enabled us to stay in the city house until the end of May so the kids could finish out school.

I didn't want to leave therapy in the middle of such a major upheaval in our family's life. But I realized that, given my newfound emotional strength and the practical considerations of time and distance, I could not continue therapy indefinitely.

So Dr. Padgett and I agreed that we'd take the first step

toward termination: we'd reduce our sessions to once a week beginning in January 1995. We also agreed that I'd set a termination date by the end of the summer.

Chapter 32

The early part of 1995 passed quickly as we arranged the financing and the closing. Both went smoothly. On February 28, 1995, the city home was no longer ours, although we still lived in it because of the leaseback arrangement.

We spent most weekends in our new home in Nottingham, painting, stripping woodwork, and preparing it for our move-in date. In between we shuttled the kids to ball games and Cub Scout and Daisy meetings, said good-byes, and squeezed in time to enjoy our last months in the neighborhood.

Meanwhile, in our now once-a-week appointments, Dr. Padgett and I prepared to end our sessions. Once therapy had been the central focus of my life. Now it almost felt foreign to go to his office. My life—my future—was swirling around me, and often I walked into his office with my mind elsewhere.

I still felt close to Dr. Padgett. His warm greeting smiles and soothing voice were still comforting. But I no longer burned with the need to be with him. Still I wasn't looking forward to actually setting a termination date.

We talked about the future. I showed him photographs of the new old house and discussed my career plans. He was still like a father to me, but now our relationship was adult to adult rather than father figure to child.

Occasionally I felt guilty, wondering what introspective work I was avoiding. But he assured me that sharing good news as well as bad was a step toward independence. Amid my wildly hectic pace, therapy was a haven where I relaxed and unwound.

As spring began to emerge, the move only a month or so away, we delved more into the specifics of termination. Dr. Padgett's policy was that termination initiated an agreed-upon, one-year no-contact period. The prospect made me uneasy.

"Why?" I asked him. "I've come to understand your other rules. But this one seems needlessly cruel. How do I know what might happen during the next year? What if I need you? What will I do?"

"Termination doesn't end the process," he told me. "Old issues will still come up, along with new ones you hadn't anticipated. It isn't the end; it's just the beginning of a new chapter in your life—one where you handle things on your own."

"What if I can't handle it on my own? What then?" I asked, beginning to panic, to regret the commitment I'd made to set a termination date in summer, just a few months away.

"Do you think you can?"

"I don't know. What if I can't?"

"I think you'll find yourself more capable of it than you might believe right now. But, if something became so burdensome you couldn't handle it on your own, I could refer you to another good psychiatrist."

"I don't want another psychiatrist!" I insisted. "I don't want to have to explain my whole life story to someone else. You understand me; we have a history."

"We do have a history, and that doesn't change. Our bond didn't end when I took vacations. Our bond won't end just because you've terminated.

"Don't you see?" he said. "You've changed, Rachel. In fundamental ways. You aren't the same person you used to be. You couldn't return to be that if you wanted to. Our history is a part of you now. No one and nothing can take that away from you."

"It sounds like death or something," I lamented. "Like this is forever. Except that, unlike a death, you'll still be here holding sessions, maybe with someone else who was where I was a few years ago. It's like mourning someone who's still alive. Why do I have to?"

"I didn't say forever," he reminded me. "I said a one-year no-contact period. After that time passes, you are free to come back again if you need it on a limited basis or an open-ended basis."

"Why a year? Why not four months? Six months? Forever? Why any limit at all? Don't you trust me? Are you afraid I'll cling to you for life?"

"The subconscious mind is always at work," he explained. "When you terminate, a part of you will feel pride, independence, and joy that you've moved on. But another part of you will still be ambivalent. You could subconsciously create a crisis just to avoid the separation."

"Like an emotional hypochondriac?"

"I don't know if that's exactly how I'd put it. But, after you leave here, there are going to be some hard times. They could be based on unresolved issues. But they could also be based on a subconscious desire to run from perceived abandonment. If you know that there is a defined length of time when you can't see me, you'll be more inclined to work through these temporary moments on your own and see them as challenges not failures.

"If, after a year, you still feel you have unfinished business to work on, you are welcome to come back. By having the limit, both of us can be assured that if you do opt to resume therapy, it will be for the right reasons, not just to avoid the pain of saying good-bye."

I considered this for a moment. I had to admit it made sense. As much as I wished the rule didn't exist, I had grown over time to understand that his rules and limits were there for my best interest.

"You know," I said sadly, my eyes filling with tears, "I'm probably going to cry like a baby when I have to say good-bye. You're one of the best things that's ever happened to me. I'm going to miss you."

"Believe me," he said, his own eyes glistening. "The feeling is mutual."

As wistful as I was at the prospect of saying good-bye, I did believe him. He would miss me too. Both of us had committed ourselves to therapy, and we had developed closeness and mutual understanding. Termination, while inevitable and necessary, wasn't going to be easy—for me or for Dr. Padgett. But, like the parent who puts on a brave face to his anxious kindergartner as she goes off to her first day of school, he wasn't going to let his emotional ambivalence exacerbate my own.

∞

Moving day went fairly smoothly. The friendly movers managed to move eight years of accumulated furniture and belongings out of our city house before noon. I felt a touch of remorse and fear as I looked around the now empty home. The walls were barren. Outlines still shadowed the bedroom carpets where the ghosts of bed frames and other furniture remained.

The previous week I had gathered nearly a thousand scattered yellow ledger pages, a series of emotional snapshots of my therapy process. I didn't want the movers touching these. I'd packed all of them away into a big, black filing box that sat in the corner bedroom as I vacuumed and swept, erasing our presence for a new family.

Once I finished the final cleanup, I snapped pictures of every corner of the house. I never wanted to forget this house and the years we'd spent there, the good times and the bad. The joy of bringing Jeffrey and Melissa home as newborns. The beautiful oak staircase we painstakingly restored.

After lingering in the house for a half hour or so, shooting pictures, letting the waves of melancholy wash over me, I had to leave. Mourning was a part of letting go and moving on to the future. I locked the door for the final time, took a few last photos of the house and yard, and drove through the neighborhood streets on my last day as a resident. Slowly I passed the houses of my friends, the neighbors with whom I'd worked side-by-side fighting the city battle. My role would be passed along to someone else.

I went by the homes of the choir members who had been there for me in my worst times, who had come to be the close and supportive family I had never known. I was tempted to stop at every one of them for a final hug and yet another round of tears. But my family was awaiting me in Nottingham. I'd had six months to say my good-byes. It was time to move on.

As I drove alone down the interstate, my car stuffed with cleaning supplies and the precious black box of writings, I realized that as sad as it was to leave, this time I wasn't running way from anything. This time I was going on to something better. The friendships I had in the city, like my relationship with Dr. Padgett, were a part of me now, and I vowed to keep in touch with them. The most important people in my life, Tim, Jeffrey, and Melissa, would be with me. By the time I reached the Nottingham exit, I was no longer looking behind but ahead to the life that awaited me there.

∞

With all the transitions in my life, I was glad that I still had Dr. Padgett. It was a one-hour drive each way to his office, which gave me time to collect my thoughts and reflect on the way home.

In late June, a few weeks after the move, I set a termination date for therapy. September 12, 1995. I circled the date in red in my appointment book. Twelve more sessions, marked discreetly in my planner by the code "Dr. P.," the final one with an extra line: "Termination."

Setting the date had been easier than I'd expected. I'd made so many changes in my life, and right now this seemed like just one more.

Now that I knew the end was near, I was determined not to waste the precious time we had left together. The good-bye, I realized, was not going to be limited to the final session but would last for three months.

During our sessions I told him just how much he had meant to me, just how much of a difference he had made in my life—in all of our lives. Because of him, Tim and the kids

406

would enjoy a healthy wife and mother who planned to live to a ripe old age and spoil her grandchildren. A man they had only met once spared them a potential tragedy. Someday, when they were ready, I would tell them about this man who had helped give their mother a second chance.

It was also a time of reminiscence. The changes had been so subtle and incremental they were impossible to see on a day-to-day basis. But over the course of four years, I had been completely transformed. I had fit every one of the terms in the psychological profile. "Manipulative." "Self-destructive." "Seductive." "Attention-seeking." "Histrionic." The fact that I could look upon those labels in the realm of the past gave me hope that I really had changed, that they would not be a part of my future.

"How did you put up with me?" I asked him. "I said some pretty vile things. I deliberately threatened you, manipulated you, and pushed you to the hilt."

"Because," he smiled, "I always knew that underneath the layers of caked-on dirt you had a diamond core. I knew it from the very first day."

"Did you ever dream that I'd make it to where I am now?"

"If I didn't, Rachel, I would never have taken you on as a patient. No one can read what the future holds. But I always knew the strong possibility was there."

"You never gave up on me, did you? You know, you should be really proud of what you've accomplished here."

"I just helped you," he reminded me. "You did the work. You're the one who never gave up on yourself. The real accomplishment, the real pride, should be yours."

It wasn't just false modesty. I knew he was right. Both of us were proud.

"One more question?" I asked, as that session was drawing near to an end. "Once upon a time you diagnosed me as a borderline. A lot of the stuff I've read says it can't ever really be cured. Am I a borderline now? Will I always be a borderline?"

"What do you think? Do you believe you're borderline?"

"You're the doctor," I said, wishing just this once he wouldn't answer my question with one of his own. "I'm not the expert in the field. You are."

"Right now," he said, "I'd say you have as thorough and intuitive understanding of what it means to be borderline as a lot of the psychiatrists who write about it and treat it. You are equipped to answer your own question."

"But that's something I can't find in the books," I persisted. "Everybody talks about what it is and its effects. But I can't find any that say it can be cured. Or, if it could be cured, what would constitute a cure. Cancer is more clear-cut: The tumor's malignant, or it's not. The chemotherapy works, or it doesn't.

"But with borderline personality disorder, who can tell? A few of the researchers seem to think that once a borderline, always a borderline. That you can't cure it—you can only control it. That a lot of people are destined to live their lives in and out of institutions, that there isn't much hope.

"I'd hate to think I've made all this progress but that there's some little vestige of BPD inside me, like a cancer cell, just lurking in the background, waiting to grow like a cancer and take me over again."

"I've told you before," he said, "that the BPD diagnosis is an incomplete definition—a rough guideline that's useful in some ways but very broad, encompassing all kinds of different people who manifest the illness in many different ways.

"In a lot of cases the writers you talk about are right. Some borderlines are destined to spend the rest of their lives in and out of psychiatric wards and prisons. But I've never looked at you as a borderline or used some cookie-cutter approach for treating borderlines. You're an individual."

"You still haven't answered my question," I sighed.

"I think the changes within you are significant and real. The agony you felt made you act as you once did. But at your core I've always seen you for the exceptional person you really are. Together we revealed that person and let her sparkle like a diamond.

"You're a strong person. One of the strongest I've ever met. And your future holds a lot of promise. The potential you've always had now has a chance to be realized."

After he finished I reflected. Some answers could not be found in a textbook or handed to me by a specialist. I had to discover them within. As it should be.

All I knew is that I now viewed both life and myself in a way I never would have dreamed possible. And the man now sitting a few feet away from me had stayed with me every step of the way to guide me and had seen my potential long before I'd been able to see it myself. Even in my darkest moments, Dr. Padgett had never given up hope. He believed in me until the day I could finally believe in myself.

Dr. Padgett was human and imperfect but one of the most remarkable, compassionate, and generous people I could expect to meet in a lifetime.

Saying my final good-bye to this man would be agonizing.

∞

As July moved into August, the prospect of termination became more real. I was already beginning to mourn my imminent loss as the number of remaining sessions dwindled into single digits. Seven more visits before the final good-bye. While Tim understood how difficult this was for me, I found myself wishing I could be among my friends in the city who knew my history.

The people of Nottingham were friendly, but I didn't feel comfortable sharing my feelings at this time. To reveal the history of my mental illness could risk attaching a label to myself in a town that had not yet fully defined me. My friendships were just beginning to develop; the whole BPD and therapy scene might be too much to share.

Had I been mourning the loss of a friend, a family member, or a debilitating disease, I wouldn't have been as reluctant to share my pain in this community. But even my friends in the city who did know me well would find it hard to understand just how emotionally gripping the entire therapy experience had been and just how difficult it was to say good-bye. Even Tim, supportive as he was, couldn't fully grasp it.

With the bulk of settling in completed and most of my client base too far away to keep, I was home with Jeffrey and Melissa a lot. Emptiness and boredom descended upon me. I was tired and had too much time on my hands to be filled with second thoughts about the wisdom of the move. I began to retreat within myself. Had I been in the city, my old friends would have noticed this and asked what was wrong. Here, however, no one knew me well enough to notice or even care.

I'd considered picking up the phone and calling one of my old friends a few times but chose not to. I hadn't been

410

keeping in touch as much as I thought I would and hated for the first words out of my mouth to be that I was down again. They'd supported me enough, I decided. I had to handle this on my own.

Was depression happening again? Had my chemical balance gone askew? Was this what Dr. Padgett had meant when he spoke of the subconscious motivation to keep therapy going on forever? Or were the experts right: once a borderline, always a borderline? Was I destined to be an emotional mess for the rest of my life?

I was slipping quickly.

Why don't you just call him? You can't keep running back to him, Rachel. What are you going to do when he's gone? He won't be there anymore. He'd want me to call if I were feeling this way. You've got to get used to handling things on your own, to flying solo. These feelings scare me. I need him! I just need to hear his voice. It's the subconscious thing, Rachel. The little girl's "last stand," a way to manipulate your way out of terminating when you said you would. I can't help it. I need him. I can't be the first patient he's ever had to go through this. He'll know what to do.

The internal battle settled, I picked up the phone and dialed Dr. Padgett's service, now a long-distance call. A part of me felt ashamed of what I saw as failure. But a stronger part of me desperately needed a solution.

The phone rang a few minutes later. Hurriedly I picked it up.

"Hello?" I said anxiously.

"This is Dr. Padgett," he said in the same calm tone he'd used to greet me with every emergency call. It was strange, though, to realize that his voice was coming from a different city. It had been months since I'd made a crisis call to him, and

411

I was beginning to regret this one. But I went on nonetheless.

"It's coming back, Dr. Padgett," I told him, my voice beginning to shake. "The depression. Horrible feelings. Can't eat, hard to sleep, hard to get out of bed. I've tried to deal with them, tried to put all of this into perspective. To handle it on my own. But it just keeps getting worse. I haven't done anything destructive, but I'm afraid I might if this keeps up. I'm so scared, Dr. Padgett. That's why I called. I'm sorry to bother you at night like this."

"You did the right thing," he assured me gently.

His words calmed me considerably. Obviously he wasn't taking my call as a sign of manipulation or failure.

"I don't know what to think," I continued. "I'm almost sure this has something to do with anxiety about termination. That's why I hesitated in calling you. I didn't want to keep clinging or anything. I figured I should get used to solving things on my own. I've tried. I really have. I've been writing like crazy, sitting here racking my brain to find a way out of this. But it isn't working. It's getting worse. Is this normal right before someone terminates therapy?"

As the words came out of my mouth, I realized just how neurotic I sounded.

"It's a normal reaction, and it's temporary," he said patiently.

"But I'm still afraid," I went on, in tears, unloading the burden now that I knew I had him with me. "What about all the progress I've made? Is it gone now?"

He paused for a moment.

"Have you ever seen a fire burn in a fireplace?" he asked, his voice soothing, almost a lullaby. "Can you remember that point when it really gets going, burning so hot that the logs are glowing red?"

412

"Uh-huh," I said, sniffling back the tears so I could hear him.

"At that point the logs still have the same shape they did when they were first lit. Only now they glow in heat, almost daunting, so hot, so burning. But it doesn't last. The logs look like the same ones you put in the fireplace, but they aren't. They aren't solid the way they used to be. They are just a temporary illusion. Pretty soon the glowing embers fall to the fireplace floor. Just ash. The fire has changed them. They look solid for a time, but they aren't anymore. The fiery hot vision of the log turns quickly to harmless ashes."

"Uh-huh," I repeated, listening intently, unsure of the point of his analogy.

"The feelings you used to have, hopelessness, despair, real depression, were like the logs before they were lit in the fireplace. They were solid, entrenched. But they've changed forever. For a short time it looks as if they are exactly the same, just as the glowing log looks the same. In a way they seem even more intense than they were before, shimmering red-hot as they are.

"But there's no real substance to them anymore. And soon they'll break apart and fall to the floor as harmless ashes.

"It doesn't feel that way right now, perhaps, but it's temporary. When you feel these momentary feelings of intensity, this temporary anxiety, you can know that they won't last. The things that used to solidify and fuel them aren't there anymore."

Now it made sense. Already the angst had begun to fade into relief.

"Thank you, Dr. Padgett," I told him, no longer crying. "Thanks for being so patient and for taking my call so late. I

413

understand what you're saying. It really does help."

"I'm glad you called me, and I'm glad I could help."

"You really are a wonderful man," I said wistfully. "I can't imagine how I'm ever going to get through that last session."

"You'll get through it," he assured me. "We can talk about it more next session."

"Okay," I said, for once not trying to prolong the conversation. "Take care of yourself."

"You too. See you Tuesday."

As always his words had made me think in a new pattern. Without making me feel foolish or as if the call had been unnecessary, he had found a way to reassure me that my disturbing feelings were short-lived, that my progress had not been lost.

I thought of how I could step out of my shell—call my old friends, develop a new support network somehow in my new community. Bolstered by our conversation, I began to think of solutions, the first sign of re-emerging hope. All was not lost.

∞

I had just completed the final touches on a cover letter when the phone rang in late August.

"Hi, this is Joe Blackburn from Enterprises, Incorporated."

He represented the company I had applied to a week before. Apparently my interview had gone well, or Joe would not have called.

"We've discussed it and decided we'd be pleased to have you as our new controller."

My heart leapt with joy.

"Great! When do you want me to start?"

We set a date and said our good-byes. Finally I was going somewhere. My career wasn't therapy anymore. Now I had a real one. I already felt as if I belonged in the working world.

∞

At the close of the next-to-the-last session, I could tell Dr. Padgett was also saddened that, at the same time next week, our four-year therapy relationship would come to an end. Driving home, I cried so hard I could barely see the road.

At least I knew that I had expressed every feeling of love, warmth, and appreciation for him in the previous months of sessions. He knew how I felt, and I knew how he felt.

One more session. All that was left was to tie a ribbon on the most painful, arduous, uplifting, and cathartic experience of my life.

Chapter 33

The last week of August I made sure that the household and our finances were completely organized before I took on the hectic schedule of a full-time career mom. But, in spite of having the logistical details under control, my enthusiastic anticipation of my new job had been fully eclipsed by termination, which consumed me.

Of all the books I had read on psychotherapy, only one dealt with the termination process to any significant degree. Leaving therapy was as emotionally raw as any issue I had faced in the four-year process, and I longed for a road map.

I read that some patients did not pay their final therapy bills, delaying payment for months. Some couldn't face the pain of opening correspondence from the therapist who had been so critical in their lives—and who they would no longer see. For others the nonpayment was a strategy to keep contact alive as therapists were forced to make follow-up calls to collect.

Determined to make a clean exit, I had called Dr. Padgett's receptionist the day after my second-to-last session to obtain my invoice balance. Adding a prepayment for the final session fee, I'd immediately mailed a check for the balance in full. I wanted to walk into my last session as an equal to Dr. Padgett, owing him nothing.

From there I spent a lot of time holed up in my home office in tearful reflection about the past four years of my life and what was left to come. Jeffrey and Melissa were confused, trying anything to cheer me up. They'd be rewarded with a flash of a smile from me before the tears resumed. Tim tried to explain that Mommy was just going through a rough time; she missed people, but she would be okay. It was best to leave her alone. Disappointed and still confused, they nonetheless complied.

Over the course of four years, I had faced many countdowns. Every vacation, every weekend had its dwindling "magic number" until I knew I could see Dr. Padgett again. This final countdown was bittersweet. For as much as I longed to see Dr. Padgett, I knew that when the magic number had reached zero, the countdowns were over. At least now I was still his patient. But on Tuesday, September 12, at 4:00 P.M., I would no longer be. Dr. Padgett's life, of course, would continue to go on. Another patient desperately seeking a second chance would soon be using my time slot. In a career that had spanned nearly three decades, he had obviously been through termination many times. For me, however, it was a first. I wondered how my own life would go on. On Sunday I decided to find him a parting gift, something that would always remind him of me. I had noticed in my very first days of therapy that the bookshelves and walls of his office were filled with small ceramic collectibles and little wooden sculptures.

Now I wondered about their origins. What patients did they represent? Who had given him the carved wooden elephant, the gold-etched coaster set, the porcelain bluebird that sat next to the clock? What pain had they shared? What were they doing with their lives right now? As much as I had resented his other patients, I wished that I could reach one of them now and ask how to say good-bye. Was there life after Dr. Padgett?

Tim had a golf outing with a prospective client that day, so I'd been forced to bring Jeffrey and Melissa along as I sought the perfect gift, a nearly impossible challenge. We strolled in and out of stores, scrutinizing every small item on the shelves.

"Why don't you just buy something, Mommy?" Melissa asked me.

The pained look I gave her stifled the question. I saw Jeffrey nudge his sister on the shoulder and heard him whisper, "Chill out, Melissa. Mommy's going through a rough time."

Even at the tender age of eight, having lived with a mother like me for as long as he had, Jeffrey had developed a sensitivity far beyond his years. His admonishment reminded me that as much as I was mourning termination, I was still an adult, still a parent. Even if for only that one reason, I was going to have to move on. My kids deserved to be kids. I should be comforting them, not the other way around.

"Don't worry," I said, forcing a smile that I didn't feel. "We'll find something in here."

The shelves of Bull's China Shop were cluttered with small collectibles. Angels. Babies. Puppies. Teddy bears. In the far corner was a collection named "Teddy Angels," small ceramic figures just the right size for Dr. Padgett's bookshelf.

Marked down to twenty-five dollars, I could afford them. A full-grown brown bear and a young tan one, both with angel's wings, were posed in a number of different settings, none of which seemed just right.

Then I saw one, nearly hidden behind the others, with the adult bear tucking the little one in to sleep using a blanket of stars. The inscription on the bottom read: "There Is Magic In The Simplest Things We Do"—*Casey Tucking Honey In*.

I knew I'd found my gift.

The statue, with its traditional parenting scene, symbolized the father-daughter relationship we'd had. Both figures had angel's wings to show the goodness inherent in both of us and the generosity of his goodness enabling me to find my own goodness within. The peacefully sleeping little bear was being gingerly covered in the blanket of stars, as Dr. Padgett had helped me to find my peace. It was goodnight not good-bye, a symbol that even though I would not see him anymore, he would still be standing by my side, comforting me, the blanket of stars the legacy he had left with me.

After much deliberation I selected a blank card with a photograph of a happily beaming little girl on the front. I had the sculpture professionally gift wrapped and walked home to write my own message inside the card. On the way home Jeffrey asked me whom the special gift was for.

"A good friend back in the city," I answered, eyes welling with tears.

"Is it her birthday?" Melissa asked.

"No. He's just a very special person. The gift is to let him know just how much he means to me."

Someday I would tell both of them just who that friend was and why he was so special. For now I retreated once again to my office, trying to find the words to summarize the most intense and healing relationship of my life.

Where once there was darkness
Now there is beauty.
Together we have taken the coal
And uncovered the diamond.
New life has begun,
A second springtime filled with wonder,
One that will never fade. . . .

Whenever I am happy,
I will think of you.
Whenever life has got me down,
I'll think of you and make it through.
Whenever I see beauty,
I will see your smiling eyes
And never forget the man who came—
The answer to my prayers and cries.
Time won't fade my love for you,
Thus I hope you'll always know,
My love, best wishes, and my prayers
Will be with you wherev'r you go. . . .

Your daughter in spirit,
Rachel

A teardrop landed on the card, and I carefully blotted it away. I sealed the envelope and set the neatly wrapped gift and card high up on the bedroom dresser, realizing that in fewer than forty-eight hours the little sculpture would be the only part of me to remain physically with him.

The alarm buzzed, and the morning sun burned through the window as I awakened from a dreamless sleep. For a moment I was energized by the sunshine. Then realization struck.

This was "The Day." Not wanting to take a chance on traffic or any conceivable delay, I left Nottingham a few hours earlier than usual and spent the extra time walking the hospital grounds. A group of psychiatric patients, recognizable by their plain clothes and hospital bracelets, sat on the grass just outside the psychiatric unit, squeezing a cigarette break into a heavily scheduled day.

Some were boldly outgoing, some quietly in retreat—laughter and conversation of camaraderie belying the emotional angst that had brought them there. I saw pain in their eyes. Most of them, no doubt, were feeling the hopelessness I had once felt. Another wave of broken hearts and lost souls searching for a second chance, finding it impossible to believe in the existence of any light at the end of the tunnel.

A part of me wanted to walk over to them and tell them that life could get better, that people could change, hearts could be healed, and souls could be lifted. But I knew that, in their state, they could not yet understand that concept, just as I wouldn't have. The only way to see the light at the end of the tunnel was to crawl through the mud in darkness.

Another part of me wanted to join them, be one of them again. To start the journey all over, with all its pain, so that the four years with Dr. Padgett would be ahead of me rather than behind me. Finally, with the colorfully wrapped and carefully ribboned package nestled on my lap, I sat in Dr. Padgett's waiting room for what would be the last time. I didn't bother picking up a magazine to skim as I waited. I drank in the surroundings, etching them in my memory.

At three o'clock sharp Dr. Padgett appeared with the same warm smile that had preceded every single session over the years, as if this one were just one more.

"I don't know what to say," I told him. "There aren't enough words, aren't enough ways to put them together to tell you how I feel right now, how much you mean to me. I just hope that you know. I hope, over the last few months, I've let you know."

"You have," he said.

I then handed him the gift, which he meticulously unwrapped as if the paper itself were also a part of me. As he looked at it and read the card, his eyes filled with tears. The blank screen was not hiding his personal emotions today. Soon both of us were in tears. We cried together for a few minutes, sharing the moment, grieving together, until he reached for a tissue and dabbed his eyes. I did the same.

"You know," I said, voice choked, "the irony is that all this therapy has brought us so close only to have to say good-bye. I realize why I can't see you anymore, at least for a long time. Sometimes I wish it didn't have to be that way, but I know that it does. I want you to know, though, that I consider you to be a lot more than a therapist. I consider you a father, a friend. If circumstances were different, I would never let a person like you slip out of my life."

He nodded, for a moment unable to speak. Then he said, "I feel the same way about you, Rachel. You're an exceptional person, and it's been an honor to know you and have you as part of my life. I'll miss you too."

"Sometimes," I said, reaching for another tissue, "I feel like I've taken so much more than I've given in this relationship. I wish there were something I could give you back."

"What makes you think you haven't given me anything? What greater satisfaction is there for a parent than watching his lessons be learned, watching his little girl grow up to be a beautiful woman, someone who makes him beam with pride?"

My tears flowed again.

"But if you were my real father, we'd be entering the next phase of life. I'd return the love by supporting you as you grow older. Visiting you. Bringing the grandchildren. Taking care of you when you get really old. You know, Dr. Padgett, I would do anything for you, anything in the world. If you ever called on me, I'd be there in a heartbeat."

"I know you would. And just knowing that you feel that way, knowing that you would, is a gift in itself. You've returned the love by meeting the challenge, by facing the changes, by never giving up. You return it by sharing it with your husband, your children, the people you know, and the people you'll meet.

"Believe me, Rachel, in many ways I've gained as much from this relationship as you have. You've learned from me, but I've learned from you too."

"I don't know what I possibly could have given, what I could have taught you, but if you feel that way, I'm glad that you do," I said.

"I honestly feel that way."

I glanced at the Teddy Angel sculpture resting on the end table next to the clock. Precious few minutes remained in the session.

"I know there's a difference between idealizing and overidealizing someone," I said. "But I want you to know that, human and imperfect as you are, you are one of the most exceptional, generous, compassionate people I've met.

424

The world is a better place because of you."

"Thank you," he replied, obviously touched by the compliment. "The beauty of it, though, is that I'm not that exceptional. When you open up your eyes to see them, compassion and generosity—kindness—are everywhere. And the world is a better place because of you too."

We sat there for a moment, eyes fixed upon each other's, savoring the moment, the strength of emotions that words couldn't summarize, neither of us trying, instead just feeling.

I wished the moment could last forever.

"Well, that's about all for today," he said.

The same words that had ended so many sessions. This time they were final.

I rose unsteadily into an awkward moment when both of us stood there. I took a chance and reached out to embrace him. He stepped toward me, and, to my surprise, hugged me tightly. It was the first and only time we ever had physical contact. The warmth of his body, the slightness of his stature suddenly made him all the more human. The mighty Wizard of Oz was revealed to be nothing more than just another human being, only this one far kinder than most.

"Rachel," he said from within the embrace, "it has truly been an honor and a privilege to have known you and worked with you."

"It's been an honor and privilege to know you too," I said, trying to hold back the tears, bracing myself for the final exit.

At the door I turned toward him.

"I hope that the rest of your life is blessed with happiness. And I'll never ever forget you."

"I wish you the same," he replied, "and I'll never forget you either."

With that I left his office, walking past the familiar sights as I returned to my car.

The tears were gone. A surreal feeling, akin to shock, filled me. I couldn't believe I hadn't become hysterical, clung to him, or begged to delay the termination. Instead I had calmly accepted the moment.

Outside the sun was shining, the linen delivery truck parked in front of the entrance as it always was at that time. A cadre of nurses came and went, the changing of the guard. Cars buzzed up and down the street; people went in and out of surrounding shops and businesses. Life was going on. I was just another driver in just another car as those passing me were going about their own lives oblivious of how much mine had just changed.

As I drove down the interstate, I was barely conscious of the exits and landmarks I was passing. No tears. No hysterics. Just an inexplicable feeling of emptiness mingled with hope. The warmth of Dr. Padgett's hug still touched me, sustaining me all the way home.

∞

Tim, prepared for The Day, had already returned home when I arrived. The kids were playing out in the yard.

"How are you?" he asked, reaching out to hug me.

"Numb," I replied. "Just numb."

He had, no doubt, expected more emotions, more tears, and had cleared his schedule to make sure he was there for me when I needed him.

"Want to go out to dinner?" he asked. "There's no reason to cook tonight. Name your place; I'll get the kids ready."

"Not hungry," I mumbled. "Not sure if I'll ever be hungry again."

Tim stood there with the helpless look of one who wants to erase the burden, make it all better, but has learned that sometimes he simply cannot. I went into the office, closed the door behind me, and began to type away at my PC.

∞

"We need to go eat," Tim said from the doorway a few hours later. "You need to eat too. It's getting pretty late."

"Why don't you just go ahead without me?" I responded, weary of writing down my feelings but not wanting to move.

"Please, Rachel," he insisted. "You really should have some dinner. Have you eaten anything today?"

"No," I answered, realizing that I hadn't. "Maybe I'll grab something later. Why don't you and the kids go ahead without me?"

"The kids are worried," he said. "Can't you just come with us?"

"No," I pouted. "I'm not hungry. I'm not coming. Go ahead, will you?"

With a sigh Tim went out to get the kids. From outside the window, I could hear them.

"Why isn't Mommy coming?" Melissa asked, her voice on the quivering edge of tears.

"She's sad," he answered. "She's not very hungry. She needs to be alone."

"But I miss her," she insisted. "I want to see her! We can make her happy again. I know we can!"

"She's going to be okay. I promise."

"Dad?" Jeffrey asked. "Is Mommy on a diet again? Is she going to go to the hospital?"

"No," Tim said in a worried voice that meant he wasn't so sure. "She's going to be okay."

"I'm not going without her!" Melissa insisted.

"Me neither!" Jeffrey echoed.

Tim's patience had worn thin, stretched by having to explain his wife's confusing behavior yet another time to his children, having to act as mediator between my pain and theirs, having to play the strong one, hiding his own pain and fear.

"Just get in the car *now*," he yelled. "We're going."

I could hear the kids crying as he pulled out of the driveway. I wished he hadn't been so harsh but understood that everyone had a limit. He, too, had emotions. The kids hadn't deserved his outburst, but I couldn't really blame Tim either.

My termination from therapy had been a graduation of sorts—a sign that I was an adult emotionally as well as chronologically. Now it was time to act like one. I had been pouting, forgetting that I wasn't the only one who could be hurt and confused.

I turned off the computer, found my keys, and snatched my purse.

When I entered the restaurant, I didn't see them at first.

Then I saw Jeffrey and Melissa, still pouting silently, toying with their straws. Tim looked grim.

"I decided to come after all," I said, smiling down at them in the booth. "I forgot for a moment that I belonged here, with all my family."

The kids squealed in delight, and relief flooded into Tim's face. The Homecoming. Jeffrey and Melissa both scooted in the booth to sit next to me, giggling and smiling, telling me about their day.

"Let me order you something," Tim said.

"No. I'm still not really hungry," I started. Then, seeing the pain in his eyes, the confused expressions of the kids, I relented.

"Okay, why don't you get me a cheeseburger and fries. Maybe I am hungry after all."

You return the love by sharing it with your husband, your children, the people you know, and the people you'll meet.

Saying good-bye to Dr. Padgett had left a void in my life, but it could be filled. This smiling family had been with me, loving and supporting me, long before I ever met the therapist and would be there long after I had stopped seeing him. I would still have painful and wistful moments of wishing Dr. Padgett were there. But the legacy, the blanket of stars, remained.

Now able to feel love—to give and receive it—I was no longer abandoned. I had my family. I had my friends. I had my church. I had my God. Now I could reach out and capture those many drops of kindness and love.

I would get by. And thrive.

Epilogue

It is now January 2004. It's been eight and a half years since I said good-bye to Dr. Padgett for the last time. It's hard to believe that I've now been out of therapy for a much longer time than I was in it.

Of course eight and a half years in the course of anyone's life is bound to bring all sorts of challenges and opportunities, victories and defeats, celebrations and tragedies. My own life has been no different.

Dr. Padgett once said that my journey to wholeness wouldn't end at termination but would take a new path. He believed that I was capable of withstanding all the good and bad that life has to offer. And, as usual, he was right.

My life since that fateful September day in 1995 has been hectic. I gave birth to our third child, Julie. I quit my job to become a writer. We buried Tim's mom and, a few years later, buried my own. I have been through all the turmoil and joy that comes with motherhood, marriage, and career.

While mine hasn't been a life of end-to-end happiness—as no one's is—I can honestly say that it has been one of emotional stability and lasting peace of mind that has weathered life's challenges.

For a little more than four years, I clung to Dr. Padgett, more akin to the child I'd never ceased to be than the adult mother of children I actually was. In that sense termination was a graduation of sorts: time for me to stand on my own as a wife, mother, and adult.

One aspect of psychoanalytic therapy is that it raised my awareness of just how much the events of childhood form a person's perspective and just how important the act of parenting is. Thus did I realize that while I was going through my roughest times, so were my kids. It was time for me to grow up and turn my attention to them. Now that I was healed, they needed their mother to help them heal too.

Once I'd healed from my own wounds enough to look beyond myself, I began to see what had become of Jeffrey and Melissa. Jeffrey, although very bright and sensitive, was also timid and self-conscious. It was as if he feared that anything he might do could provoke an explosion; the stability of his world was subject to change without notice. Melissa, beneath a sweet and somewhat shy demeanor, harbored an inner anger, a toughness born of necessity.

In the course of my therapy, Dr. Padgett spent many hours listening to me, gently calming me, being there for me. In our new home in Nottingham, I did the same for Jeffrey and Melissa. I was home for them when they came home from school. We went on long walks with no particular destination. Most important, I listened. I immersed myself in their world as Dr. Padgett had done in mine. Slowly, but not painlessly, they, too, began to heal. Like wisdom passed down through the ages, I have shared with them much of what Dr. Padgett once said to me. His words and thoughts have comforted them and helped them gain emotional strength.

Jeffrey and Melissa are in high school now. Both are very book smart, but more than that, they are life smart, the kind of insight and sensitivity that comes from having been through great trials and emerging even stronger. We couldn't be prouder of the people they have emerged to be, nor could we be more blessed. Teenagers though they may be, they feel quite comfortable spending some time at home and being around us.

Julie is in first grade. She is the one that Tim and I have been able to raise with the benefit of all we learned through my own therapy experience, without the burden of uncertainty that marked the toddler years of her older siblings. Teachers and others comment about Julie's irrepressible smile and happy demeanor, the product, I think, of being surrounded by a functional, though not perfect, family rich in communication and love.

The first time Tim tried to read this manuscript—the first draft of it written in 1997—he could not bring himself to finish it. It conjured too many frightening memories that were still too fresh in his mind. He is as strong and loving and loyal now as he was then. The difference is that now he has an equal partner. He admits that, at times, he wondered if there would ever be light at the end of the tunnel and if he could withstand anymore than what he had already faced. But he is now thankful that he stayed by my side as I went through therapy and learned to become whole again. I know that such is not always the case, nor should it be, for everyone. I'm just glad that it was in mine.

Perhaps the most healing experience for me through-out the course of my journey was my ability to forgive those who would never apologize. In time my relationship with my parents flourished as my understanding grew of just how much they did care, did try.

My mother died in 2003 after an eighteen-month battle with cancer. Despite her arduous suffering, her exit was a graceful swan song as, bolstered by the miracle of faith, she displayed more courage, strength, and insight than any of us had witnessed in her seventy-plus years of life.

During this time the two of us talked more openly than we ever had before. I didn't share the entirety of my story. I didn't need to. She told me she knew that she'd made a lot of mistakes in her life and knew that my therapy had had something to do with them. At the time it had frightened her, which is why she couldn't bring herself to visit in the hospital. She was afraid I wouldn't want to see her. But seeing how therapy had transformed me, she thanked God that I had been through it. I told her quite sincerely that I had long since forgiven her, that I knew she'd done the best she could under tough circumstances.

Most of all, I told her I knew that she'd loved me all along, and it was that foundation of love that ultimately helped me to land on my feet. The day before she died I held her frail body close to mine and whispered to her that I loved her, that I'd forgiven her and Dad too. I told her I would look out for Dad for her. Her eyes, which had been transfixed in a semicatatonic state for hours, flashed with life as she smiled and hoarsely whispered back the words "I know." I cried openly at the funeral, but they were the healthy tears of clo-sure not the bitter ones of remorse.

I have Dr. Padgett to thank for that too. And, of course,

God, whose presence runs through every chapter of this story and every one of my life.

Back in September of 1995, I wasn't sure if I could last a month without Padgett, much less twelve of them. Some people who have read my story have wondered why he was so insistent that we maintain such a strict no-contact period. I now fully understand. Knowing that he was inaccessible to me, I had to rely on myself to handle the challenges of day-to-day living. By the time a year had passed, I knew I could handle things on my own. And I have. Not perfectly every time. Not without some tears and times of doubt. But I've handled them.

I still send Dr. Padgett a newsy Christmas card every year, and he always writes back with a brief anecdote about his life as a grandfather. He has read this book, has given copies of it to his patients, and is glad that I've written it. While I may not have seen or spoken to the man for many years, the memories of the time I spent with him remain with me and sustain me in the most challenging of times.

This book will undoubtedly resonate with those who have faced mental illness in themselves or in a loved one, but this is just one woman's story. I am unique, as are my circumstances, family, and psychiatrist. Tempting as it may be to draw one conclusion or another from my story and universalize it to apply to another's experience, it is not my intention for my book to be seen as some sort of cookie-cutter approach and explanation of mental illness. It is not an advocacy of any particular form of therapy over another. Nor is it meant to take sides in the legitimate and necessary debate within the mental health profession of which treatments are most effective for this or any other mental illness.

What it is, I hope, is a way for readers to get a true feel

for what it's like to be in the grips of mental illness and what it's like to strive for recovery.

Most important, the reason I wrote this book is to serve as proof that miracles do happen, that love can and does heal wounds, that there is hope for those with the courage and fortitude to seek healing.

Borderline Personality
Disorder Resources

After reading Rachel's story, you may want to learn more about borderline personality disorder (BPD). But before you browse through your local bookstore or plug "borderline personality disorder" into your favorite Web search engine, read the following section. It will help you find information that addresses your particular needs and specific situation.

The American Psychiatric Association formalized the definition of BPD in 1980, when the phrase was placed in its profession's guiding book: the *Diagnostic and Statistical Manual of Mental Disorders*. Yet more than two decades later, most people have neither heard of it nor read about it. And among the clinical community, it's still controversial, stigmatized, and poorly understood. Until recently, even public and private organizations that address mental health issues have largely ignored BPD.

Fortunately, BPD has become much more visible in the past few years, as advocates, researchers, people with BPD, and family members have moved forward and developed their own online resources, self-help books, and educational opportunities. The resources listed in this section are a good starting point for those wanting to learn more.

One important caveat: While some of these resources fall into the category of "general information," many of them focus on either people with BPD or their family members—many of whom feel emotionally abused by traits such as rage, criticism, and blame. So at the outset, people who think they may have BPD traits are advised to stick with information directed specifically for them. Family member resources can come off as very stigmatizing and negative. While the negative effects of BPD behavior—especially on children—are very real, the information can be too much to handle for someone with BPD.

It's crucial for people with BPD and those who love them to keep in mind that the behavior of people with BPD varies enormously. If one source doesn't seem to describe your situation, try another.

Online Resources

www.borderlinepersonality.ca
This site "looks to provide an insightful understanding about Borderline Personality Disorder (from the inside out) and the accompanying behaviour and difficult challenges for both the person diagnosed with BPD and those around him/her." It contains a section of frequently asked questions, an article archive, links, book reviews, and a message board. This site provides information for people with BPD and their family members.

www.borderlinepersonalitydisorder.com
This is the Web site of the National Education Alliance for Borderline Personality Disorder (NEABPD), an organization devoted to providing scientific and clinical information about BPD.

www.bpdcentral.com
This site is maintained by Randi Kreger, one of the authors of *Stop Walking on Eggshells* (see the "Books and Workbooks" section). BPD Central is one of the oldest, largest, and most popular sites about BPD on the Web. Directed primarily to family members, BPD Central offers a variety of specific educational materials you won't find in bookstores, including information for

- parents of someone with BPD *(Hope for Parents)*
- partners of those with BPD seeking to understand romantic relationships *(Love and Loathing)*
- partners divorcing someone with BPD *(Splitting* and a three-CD set about custody)

The site also contains an online media kit, a large message board for family members, information on more than a dozen specialized e-mail support groups for family members, a place to subscribe to a free online newsletter about BPD, and much more.

www.bpdrecovery.com
This site focuses on recovering from BPD. It is dedicated to being "a safe arena for those with mental illnesses and disorders (specifically BPD) to share concerns, voice opinions, seek like-minded individuals, work toward recovery, discuss med-

ications and therapy approaches, explore the impact of [*sic*] their illness(es) have had on their life and the lives of their loved ones." The site contains information, a discussion board, an e-mail support group, and a section for personal stories.

www.bpdresources.com

This is the site of Helen's World of BPD Resources, a "do-it-yourself compilation of thousands of annotated Internet links, focusing on sites that contain significant amounts of information." It contains a good page entitled "Helen's Quick Top 40," an excellent section of links to information regarding frequently asked questions about BPD. It also contains sections on support and community, relationships, treatment, studies, research, books, and miscellaneous issues.

www.laurapaxton.com

This is the site of Laura Paxton, author of *Borderline and Beyond* and *Beyond Suffering*. It contains some overview information about BPD, links to books, and other Web links. This site offers a creative, effective, and innovative approach to the treatment of BPD. It also offers a message board, a chat room, a research room (on diagnosis- and treatment-related topics), discussion groups, and much more.

www.mhsanctuary.com/borderline

This site is dedicated to helping "stop the pain for those that suffer so incredibly due to mental health disorders." It contains a large collection of BPD-related information, which includes an "Ask the Therapist" section, a chat room, bulletin boards, forums, many BPD-related articles, and book reviews.

www.pdan.org
This is the Web site of the Personality Disorders Awareness Network (PDAN), which provides information for family members.

www.toddlertime.com
This is the site of Kathi's Mental Health Review. It offers information about BPD, narcissistic personality disorder, and other mental disorders from the point of view of someone who has struggled with these issues. The information is for people with BPD as well as their family members. The site includes personal reflections, essays, and articles for helping professionals. It contains links to an e-mail BPD support group and other helpful resources.

Books and Workbooks

Kraus, Caroline. *Borderlines: A Memoir*. New York: Broadway Books, 2004. This book is not yet available for review. But according to the promotional material, the book is a memoir much like *Get Me Out of Here*. The critical difference is that it comes from the point of view of the partner of a person with BPD. Kraus becomes obsessed by a borderline woman (Jane) who "becomes her friend, temporary lover, constant companion and, ultimately, 'worst enemy.'" The friendship soon becomes all-consuming and more entangled than the good-natured Caroline anticipated. Jane begins to eat away at Caroline's savings and mental well-being and pulls her into the undertow of a "frightening journey into the abyss."

Kreger, Randi, and James Paul Shirley. *The Stop Walking on Eggshells Workbook: Practical Strategies for Living with Someone Who Has Borderline Personality Disorder.* Oakland, Calif.: New Harbinger Publications, Inc., 2002. This book is by one of the authors of the best-seller *Stop Walking on Eggshells.* This book helps family members understand their own reactions to borderline behavior and how they, in turn, affect the relationship. Step-by-step suggestions—many from users of the author's comprehensive Web site (www.bpdcentral.com)—help readers set and enforce personal limits, communicate clearly, cope with put-downs and rage, develop a safety plan, and make realistic decisions. Includes worksheets, checklists, and exercises that build on one another and enable readers to apply the suggestions to their lives.

Kreisman, Jerold J., and Hal Straus. *I Hate You, Don't Leave Me: Understanding the Borderline Personality.* New York: Avon, 1989. This is the first consumer-oriented book published on BPD. It offers professional advice, which helps victims and their families to understand and cope with BPD.

———. *Sometimes I Act Crazy: Living with Borderline Personality Disorder.* Hoboken, N.J.: John Wiley & Sons, 2004. This book is not yet available for review. Promotional material states that the book delivers the latest information on the borderline personality disorder. Rich with dramatic case studies of Kreisman's patients, the book describes and offers advice on today's most promising treatments along with practical coping strategies for the loved ones of BPD sufferers.

Lawson, Christine Ann. *Understanding the Borderline Mother: Helping Her Children Transcend the Intense, Unpredictable, and Volatile Relationship.* New York: Jason Aronson Publications, 2002. Lawson vividly describes how mothers who suffer from BPD produce children who may flounder in life even as adults. These children futilely struggle to reach the safety of a parental harbor, unable to recognize that their borderline parent lacks a pier or even a discernible shore. Four character profiles describe different symptom clusters that include the waif mother, the hermit mother, the queen mother, and the witch mother. This book is not for people with BPD unless they have a borderline mother. Adult children may also want to join an e-mail support group just for them. See www.bpdcentral.com for more information. This site also provides e-mail support groups for those who are coparenting with someone with BPD traits. Resources for younger children can be found at the Personality Disorders Awareness Network (www.pdan.org).

Mason, Paul T., and Randi Kreger. *Stop Walking on Eggshells: Taking Your Life Back When Someone You Care about Has Borderline Personality Disorder.* Oakland, Calif.: New Harbinger Publications, Inc., 1998. Often considered the bible on borderline personality disorder, this book has sold more than 150,000 copies and has been translated into seven different languages. It is a self-help guide that explains interaction patterns between people with BPD traits and those who care about them. Then it explains in detail what family members can do to get off the emotional roller coaster—even if the person in their life does not want to change. This book focuses mainly on understanding and coping with "acting out" borderline behaviors such as false accusations, raging, blaming, and other traits that greatly affect family members.

Moskovitz, Richard. *Lost in the Mirror: An Inside Look at Borderline Personality Disorder*. 2d ed. Dallas: Taylor Publishing Company, 2001. The author writes "*Lost in the Mirror* explores the origins of Borderline Personality Disorder and offers its sufferers a framework for beginning to heal." The book elaborates on the kinds of psychotherapy that are practiced today. It describes mainstream approaches, such as psychoanalytic psychotherapy, cognitive therapy, and behavior therapy, as well as innovative treatments, such as Eye Movement Desensitization and Reprocessing (EMDR) and Dialectical Behavior Therapy (DBT). This is a gentle book for people who have just learned they may have BPD.

Roth, Kimberlee, and Freda B. Friedman. *Surviving a Borderline Parent: How to Heal Your Childhood Wounds and Build Trust, Boundaries, and Self-Esteem*. Oakland, Calif.: New Harbinger Publications, Inc., 2003. This book, written specifically for adult children of borderline parents, offers step-by-step guidance to understanding and overcoming the lasting effects of being raised by a person suffering from BPD. Readers learn what psychological criteria are necessary for a BPD diagnosis and identify the specific characteristics in their parent. It includes specific coping strategies for dealing with issues common to children of borderline parents: low self-esteem, lack of trust, guilt, and hypersensitivity. It discusses the major decision whether to confront your parent about his or her condition. Adult children may also want to join an e-mail support group just for them. See www.bpdcentral.com for more information. This site also provides e-mail support groups for those who are coparenting with someone with BPD traits. Resources for younger children can be found at the Personality Disorders Awareness Network (www.pdan.org).

Smith, Sally Bedell. *Diana in Search of Herself: Portrait of a Troubled Princess*. New York: Signet, 1999. This biography of Princess Diana offers a description of BPD behavior on every page. It concludes with the author's and a clinician's assessment that Diana most likely suffered from BPD. The author fully acknowledges Diana's positive traits: her compassion, her devotion to her children, and her warmth and generosity. This book provides a portrait of a multifaceted, emotionally complicated woman struggling with BPD under the scrutiny of the world.

Winkler, Kathy, and Randi Kreger. *Hope for Parents: Helping Your Borderline Son or Daughter without Sacrificing Your Family or Yourself.* Milwaukee, Wis.: Eggshells Press, 2003. This booklet is not in bookstores and is only available by calling 1-888-35-SHELL. Drawing on the experiences of 250 parents whose children were diagnosed with BPD, the fifty-four-page booklet helps parents of both adult and minor children who have BPD. The booklet offers suggestions for finding treatment, working with care providers, countering false accusations of abuse, handling crises, fostering independence, handling finances, protecting siblings, and maintaining hope. It is the only resource specifically for parents of a borderline child of any age. Parents may also want to join an e-mail support group just for them. See www.bpdcentral.com for more information. They can find additional support groups and sites for parents by searching the Web.

About the Author

Rachel Reiland is a wife, mother of three, accountant, and writer living in the Midwest. Through a combination of psychotherapy and spirituality, she has managed to overcome anorexia and borderline personality disorder, a shadowy and often misunderstood form of mental illness. Rachel Reiland is a pseudonym.

About Hazelden Publishing

As part of the Hazelden Betty Ford Foundation, Hazelden Publishing offers both cutting-edge educational resources and inspirational books. Our print and digital works help guide individuals in treatment and recovery, and their loved ones. Professionals who work to prevent and treat addiction also turn to Hazelden Publishing for evidence-based curricula, digital content solutions, and videos for use in schools, treatment programs, correctional programs, and electronic health records systems. We also offer training for implementation of our curricula.

Through published and digital works, Hazelden Publishing extends the reach of healing and hope to individuals, families, and communities affected by addiction and related issues.

For more information about Hazelden publications,
please call **800-328-9000**
or visit us online at **hazelden.org/bookstore.**